Advanced Rev

"*To Live Woke* provoked emotions in me of joy, deep sadness, blistering anger, and hope. The truly brilliant accomplishment of this book is its ability to evoke such powerful, polarizing emotions, while simultaneously taking the confusion behind them, and delineating in psychological terms how to untangle and handle them appropriately."

> — Anna Taylor, North Carolina State University Class of 2017

"For most of his life, Rupert Nacoste has been a leader in addressing the conflicts that are tearing the country apart–first as a young black sailor trying to quell race riots on the ships of the U.S. Navy and today as a social psychologist and one of the most admired teachers at North Carolina State University. His latest book, *To Live Woke*, conveys a message of hope and a great deal of important advice for mending the tattered fabric of our society.

> — Christopher Finan, Executive Director, National Coalition Against Censorship and author of *From the Palmer Raids to the Patriot Act: A history of the fight for free speech in America* (2007).

"*To Live Woke*, a book that I would recommend to people that I know regardless of race or age. As a black woman, I believe that there are issues discussed in this book that can be beneficial to anyone that reads it. The fact that this book emphasizes that there are no innocent is very important."

> — Kinesha Harris, North Carolina State University Class of 2017

"Here is the first authoritative dialogue written by a true expert in the field who optimistically shows how improving our individual daily encounters— ones fraught with more racial anxiety and social tension than many have felt since the late 1960s— can significantly redraw our inherited boundaries and turn the lines that seem to divide us into dashes. Based on career-defining experiences with the first integrated naval ships, a distinguished career spent pioneering university courses on interpersonal relations, and careful analysis of the shifting racial dynamics as they alter from the 911 era to the backlash of the Obama years, this is a profoundly moving book delivered at exactly a time when we need it most. With the belief that we can indeed fulfill Dr. King's dream and still save the soul of America, readers will find themselves sharply woke from their metaphorical sleep to act on the remarkably effective interpersonal strategies outlined in a book that can best be defined as essential— in every meaning of the word."

> — Dr. W. Jason Miller, Professor of English and author of
> *Origins of the Dream: Hughes's Poetry and King's Rhetoric
> (2015), Langston Hughes: Critical Lives* (Feb. 2020), &
> *Langston Hughes and American Lynching Culture* (2011)

To Live Woke

Thoughts to Carry in Our Struggle to
Save the Soul of America

Rupert W. Nacoste, Ph.D.
Alumni Distinguished
Undergraduate Professor

Apprentice
House Press
Loyola University Maryland

First Edition

Printed in the United States of America

Hardcover ISBN: 978-1-62720-268-8
Paperback ISBN: 978-1-62720-269-5
E-book ISBN: 978-1-62720-270-1

Editorial development by Kelly Lyons
Cover design by Chelsea McGuckin
Marketing plan by Paola Casillas

Published by Apprentice House

Apprentice House
Loyola University Maryland
4501 N. Charles Street
Baltimore, MD 21210
410.617.5265
www.apprenticehouse.com
info@apprenticehouse.com

Contents

Dedication

To my father, Mr. August (O-geese) Nacoste (1918-1998). A black man who at the grassroots level worked tirelessly for the voting rights of African-Americans; who put himself in harm's way by running for public office in 1966 in the still rigid and violent segregated deep-South bayou town of Opelousas, LA.

With love and hope that I have, in my own way, continued his legacy of social justice work, I offer this book in the memory of Mr. O-geese who was my first and only needed model of how to "…live woke."

Foreword

North Carolina State University Student in Dr. Nacoste's "Interdependence and Race" course, reaction to the assigned reading:

Tim Tyson's (2003) *Blood Done Sign My Name* (NY: Three Rivers Press)

November 2015

Upon reading Dr. Tim Tyson's account of the street battles in Oxford, NC, in the 1960s and '70s, I could not help but draw comparisons between those and the recent riots we saw in our society; Baltimore and Ferguson immediately jumped to mind. Dr. Tyson wrote, "Oxford was a tinderbox and matches were not short in supply." This sentence stuck with me as I continued to read about the riots.

Much like the riots of Baltimore, the battles became a nightly occurrence by both youth and the more mature. Troopers fired into crowds, injuring protestors and warning rioters that they had "better prepare to meet their maker." Reading this section, I felt nauseous.

These race riots, rooted in hatred, prejudice, bigotry, and racism, had occurred so long ago, yet I remember seeing reflections of them on my daily news stations just a year or two earlier. Perhaps this tinder from the battles so long ago had yet to completely defuse.

I remember asking myself, "How had we come so far, just to be in the same place again?"

1. What's the Question?

"Violence is not the answer."

June 12, 2016, Orlando Pulse Club. Fifty shot dead in a "safe haven" for gays and lesbians.

July 5, 2016, weeks later in Baton Rouge, Louisiana, Alton Sterling, a black man, is killed by white policemen.

July 6, 2016, a day later in Falcon Heights, Minnesota, Philandro Castile, another black man, is killed by a white policeman. The incident is live-streamed on Facebook.

Protests erupt all over America.

July 7, 2016, another day later in Dallas, a black sniper kills five policemen at one of those peaceful protests against police shootings of black men.

"Violence is not the answer," America cried out that summer of 2016.

America was in shock.

I was in shock.

After all that I have seen and lived through, even I was in shock the weekend of July 5, 2016. A black male born in 1951 in deep-South Jim Crow legally segregated Louisiana, I have seen so much. I was 12 when President John F. Kennedy was assassinated in November 1963. I was 15 when the Civil Rights Act and the Voting Rights Act were put into national law.

April 4, 1968, I was 17 years old, lying on the couch that evening as my mother walked out the door to head to Holy Ghost Catholic Church to play bingo. News said Martin Luther King Jr. had been assassinated. I ran to the door and called out at my mother. She had the driver's side door open and was about to get in our car. When I called out, she stopped and looked up at me. I said "...they killed him." That's all I said.

My mother knew exactly what I was talking about.

I was still 17 when presidential candidate Robert (Bobby) Kennedy was assassinated that June 1968. In the Navy in 1973, at 22 years of age I served onboard the aircraft carrier USS *Intrepid* (CVS 11) that exploded into a race riot that lasted for three days at sea.

All that, and yet, the summer of 2016 I was reeling. Along with the rest of America, I was in shock. Then my expertise as a social psychologist and sense of social responsibility both kicked in. For me, being shocked was not enough. Yes, same as other Americans, I wondered ...*How can I help? What can I do?* Well, I knew it wasn't going to be as a protester, not at this point in my life. My help would be to use my expertise to show America what was really going on, to help Americans ask and seek answers to the right questions. In my teaching, I was already doing that as a professor.

I teach one of the only, if not the only college course that can help individuals have productive social interactions in these difficult days of neo-diverse America. You see, today we are living in the difficult days that Martin Luther King Jr. prophesied in 1968 in Memphis, TN. In that last speech-sermon he said, "I don't know what's going to happen now. We've got some difficult days ahead."

At North Carolina State University (NCSU), my Interdependence-and-Race course is the only one in the world that shows people how to understand and analyze what is going on in their everyday interpersonal interactions in these difficult days of bold prejudice and bigotry. I say that mine is the only course that can do this because I know of no other that begins by describing the current interpersonal-intergroup situation of America. Courses taught by others in my discipline or from other disciplines either go straight into individual psychology or broad social-structural issues and dynamics. That is why courses not grounded in the concept of neo-diversity leave people with only vague ideas ("post-racial") and ways of talking ("white privilege") that shut down rather than open up authentic dialogue. Without describing the everyday interpersonal-intergroup situation people are being confronted with; without then analyzing those interpersonal-intergroup situations, you cannot give people the interpersonal guidance (how am I supposed to interact) they are in need of and are struggling to find. That is the first goal of my course. To state it bluntly, my course is the only one in the world that asks and answers this question:

How is an interpersonal interaction influenced when one or both people are or become aware that the two people are different from each other by some group identity? Race yes, but and/also religion, sex-of-person, bodily condition, gender identity, ethnicity, sexual orientation, mental health condition, age, money condition, political affiliation, etc.?

Turns out, you see, not knowing how to have respectful social interactions with a person "not like me" is what is tearing at the soul of America.

#Starbucks #MeToo #Syracuse #BlackLivesMatter #YaleWhileBlack #Sendherback

Created by me in 2006, in my unique "Interdependence and Race" course, I take social-psychological research and translate it into strategies for productive neo-diverse social interactions that anyone can learn. I was able to create my course by combining my scholarship with my past real-world experience of intense intergroup experiences in the U.S. Navy. During my military service, with racial tensions swirling throughout, I was trained to and became a facilitator of racial dialogues to help the Navy deal with racial problems that sometimes reached the level of riot aboard ships.

Race riots aboard Navy ships carrying weapons of mass destruction. Imagine that.

On U. S. Navy shore stations and ships-of-war, including aircraft carriers, racial unrest rose to the level of riot. Black sailors trying to hurt white sailors. White sailors trying to hurt black sailors. Sometimes these riots happened at sea during Vietnam wartime operations. Most of that racial unrest occurred from 1970 to 1975.

I served in the U.S. Navy from June 1972 to March 1976. In fact, as a sailor with Air Anti-Submarine Squadron 27 (VS-27), I was on board the USS *Intrepid* (CVS 11) during the race riot of January 1973 – 5,000 men on a ship carrying warplanes and tons of munitions. While at sea, there were some black sailors and some white sailors randomly attacking each other by race.

That riot and other racial incidents in the Navy are documented, and recounted, in John Darrell Sherwood's extraordinary book *Black Sailor: White Navy*.[1] Often, I have thought of those years of racial turmoil. Not only thought of, I have used stories of that time and my experience when teaching my students about the social psychology of racial tension. When I have described the race riot aboard the aircraft carrier USS *Intrepid*, my students have looked at me in disbelief that such things could happen in one of the armed forces set up to protect American interests. Oh, I convince my students, but not because I have had a published source to point them to. Since 2006, though, I have had a source.

Sailors know that sometimes a ship has been in port too long. Then it's time to hoist anchor and move out onto the always-challenging ocean. Sherwood's book took me back to that tumultuous period in the Navy when Admiral Elmo Zumwalt ordered the Navy to lift anchor on the old racial port and set out to the uncharted sea of new race relations. Sherwood is right to call the admiral's policy changes a revolution (Chapter 3). As the Chief of Naval Operations, Zumwalt used his power to begin to bring the Navy in line with modern society. Zumwalt knew that for those changes to make a difference, he had to have the Navy pull up anchor from the old racial mud. Sherwood (p. 42) quotes Zumwalt as saying that the most important change, "… was to throw overboard once and for all the Navy's silent but real and persistent discrimination against minorities." In a number of strong statements, Z-grams, that were sent to each and every Navy unit and put in the hands of each and every officer and enlisted person, Zumwalt made the policies and the philosophy of the new Navy clear. Spectacularly, in December 1970, Zumwalt wrote (p. 47):

…We are counting on your support to help seek out and eliminate those demeaning areas of discrimination that plague our minority shipmates. Ours must be a navy family that recognizes no artificial barriers of race, color, or religion. There is no black navy, no white navy – just one navy – the United States navy.

For a long time, I wanted there to be a public telling of the story of that unruly time in the Navy. My desire had always been there, because for me as a young black man, that time, those events were a crucible in my life. I was just 21 years old when I went in, and just 25 when I got out. I learned so much. Those experiences led me to my profession. I found Social Psychology in the Navy.

Zumwalt's revolution, you see, was not just words yelled out over the fleet. Zumwalt put in strong regulations and created mandatory race-related programming. In Chapter 11, Sherwood documents and describes the Navy's action to raise racial awareness. Understanding Personal Worth and Racial Dignity, UPWARD, "…was primarily a racial awareness course…that required 'skilled and experienced trainers'…and relied on part-time racial awareness facilitators (RAFs) to teach UPWARD courses."

After my service with VS-27 onboard the *Intrepid*, I was one of those trained as a Racial Awareness Facilitator. Being trained as a RAF, facilitating over 20 seminars, and working special human relations duties was a catalyst for the rest of my life; I experienced an awakening. In 21st century vernacular, I went from being awake to being "woke."

My interest in group dynamics, race relations, and social justice was piqued. I sought out higher education and training. I became a social psychologist. Since 1981, as a social psychologist I have been publishing research articles on intergroup relations. One of the courses I have recently created is "Interpersonal Relationships and Race."

December 2006, I got wind of and ordered Sherwood's then new book. When it came to my door, for a day and a half, I sequestered myself in my house, reading. Chapters one thru four of Sherwood's book sets the racial context of the Navy. In Chapters 4 through 10, Sherwood tells of particular racial incidents (see Chapter 10 for the story of the *Intrepid*) and how those 350 major racial incidences were managed and later investigated.

As a scholar, I was impressed with Sherwood's documentation, interviews, and summaries of what he found and learned. More personally, in vivid ways, *Black Sailor, White Navy* took me back to that important time both in the Navy and in my life. Sherwood tells of that time with truth. Sometimes, I had to stop to let my emotions be a storm at sea. Sometimes I stopped to reflect on a memory that was rocking me from port to starboard; left to right.

Being a witness to this time and those events, what matters most to me is that Sherwood gives respect to all the players in the racial unrest. He discusses each party's strengths and weaknesses, and their goals (good and bad). He shows how the Navy misunderstood its own racial climate. Yet he gives respect, long due, to Zumwalt's revolution. Especially important to me, even when their tactics were clearly wrongheaded, Sherwood gives respect to my fellow black sailors. He did this by always focusing on the history and state of race relations in the Navy up to that time. On that point, Sherwood documents and says plainly (p. 226) that "…there were indications of institutional racism in many of the episodes."

Sherwood's book is a true history. It is well done. And when a job is "well done" in the Navy, we say, "Bravo Zulu."

####

I did the work to create my "Interpersonal Relationships and Race" course because I knew that what I would teach would help my students come out of anxiety and avoidance to engage in authentic social interactions with people "…not like me." Years ago, I had done that kind of social justice work in the Navy. I had done that with sailors, aboard ships at sea. No doubt, I could create a course that would help college students lift their heads into changed lives by showing them how and why they have made mistakes and how to do better. At the end of the Spring 2018 course, a student wrote:

> I have now been given the tools to analyze and think more deeply about the dynamics of interpersonal-intergroup interactions and not rush to dismiss people. I am an American, and I am so thankful that this course has opened my eyes to the inclusive breadth of what that truly means.

Not just in my classroom, I also see positive effects of teaching young people about neo-diversity even when I just give a one-shot guest lecture. After my April 12, 2018, College of Public Health Ramsey Lecture at the University of Georgia, a student wrote:

> One thing I appreciated about Dr. Nacoste's lecture was that he took the time to define a few terms that are thrown around so often in our society today, I think we have lost sight of what they mean. He talked about racism in the terms of structure, which is often overlooked in pop culture and media, who would rather blame individual entities for inequity because it is more sensational and easier to comprehend. He also defined 'bigoted' as having a negative

view of an entire group of people. This was definitely a good reminder for me to watch how I think about and generalize about other people.[2]

Hear me then: We can save the soul of America. But, to do so we must all face the unavoidable realities of neo-diversity. And, we must see our way to ask and address the questions that that neo-diversity brings into our everyday social interactions.

"Violence is not the answer," went out the cry Summer 2016. Wait, what is the question? We need to know the question before we can find the answer.

"Who are among the 'we' and who are among the 'they?'" is the neo-diversity question haunting the soul of America. Fading in and out of our lives, every day, all day, that is the question. Charles Blow says:

> We seem caught in a cycle of escalating atrocities without an easy way out, without enough clear voices of calm, without tools for reduction, without resolutions that will satisfy. There is so much loss and pain. There are so many families whose hearts hurt for a loved one needlessly taken, never to be embraced again. There is so much disintegrating trust, so much animosity stirring. So many—too many—Americans now seem to be living with an ambient terror that someone is somehow targeting them.[3]

Asked what is great about America, General Colin Powell said it was this statement from our Declaration of Independence:

> "We hold these truths to be self-evident, that all men are created equal, that they are endowed by their Creator with certain unalienable Rights, that among these are Life, Liberty and the pursuit of Happiness."

Diversity, then, is the first American promise. That makes diversity *the* American value. A place where all are considered to be, and are interacted with as equals; that really would be a place anyone and everyone would want to live. True, for a long time in America, the whole country said that those words did not apply to someone with my dark skin. But as General Powell points out,

"This beautiful statement was not the reality of 1776, but it *set forth the dream* that we would strive to make a reality...Governments belong to the people and exist to secure the rights endowed to *every* citizen."[4]

We are, and have always been, in a struggle for the soul of America. "...We hold these truths to be self-evident, that all men are created equal..." is that soul. Our American struggle, then, is how to live in that spirit every day as we encounter and interact with each other.

"Can we all just get along?"

When in despair and lamentation, Rodney King asked that question. He was thinking of the tensions between blacks and whites in Los Angeles in 1992. Without that racial question ever being answered for Los Angeles, or for the whole of America, the American intergroup situation changed.

America just ain't what it used to be.

America is no longer a society where our racial contacts are controlled and restricted by law. We no longer live in an America where the law makes one racial (or gender) group more powerful than another racial (or gender) group. Not only that, but nowadays, every day, each of us has some occasion to interact with a person from another racial, sex, ethnic, bodily condition, religious, gender identity, mental health condition, or sexual orientation group. Today our interpersonal encounters with Americans of other groups are not just in black and white, not just diverse by race and gender, but neo-diverse.

We are living, working, playing, and otherwise interacting in the same desegregated, multi-group, neo-diverse spaces.

Can we all just get along?

Neo-diversity has come upon us very fast. Rapid social change has put each of us in situations where we have to interact with people on an equal footing, but with people who do not look like, sometimes do not sound like, sometimes do not worship like, and sometimes do not love like "us."

America's 21st century struggle is interpersonal. For far too many, that everyday neo-diverse situation creates anxiety about how to interact with other people. Problem is that too many Americans are being stalked by their own neo-diversity-driven interaction-anxiety. "Who are among the 'we' and who are among the 'they?'" is the question that drives that anxiety.[5] Why?

Well, we rid ourselves of the unconstitutional, immoral laws of racial segregation. Understand, though, that legalized, regulated and enforced racial segregation and oppression had been doing something very specific in American life. Segregation made it very clear who was 'we' and who was a 'they' by specifying what members of which groups could go where and when. With those laws of bigotry gone, we now live in a time when interacting with someone who does not look like, may not sound like, may not worship, may not love like 'us' is unavoidable. Now we struggle with neo-diversity anxiety that is causing some of us to want to keep other people living in America in the category of 'they' and 'them.'

All the changes, all so fast, has thrust Americans into the same situation as Dr. Seuss's *Sneetches*. In today's America, no one is any longer able to say "…well they can't come in here. They can't come to our frankfurter parties." Too many of us are grumbling, as did the Starbelly Sneetches[6]:

"Good grief!" groaned the ones who had stars at the first…

"We're still the best Sneetches and they are the worst.

"But, now, how in the world will we know?" they all frowned,

"If which kind is what, or the other way 'round?"

Old racial, gender, ethnic rules do not apply. Without laws and social understandings prohibiting who can go where, we all find ourselves interacting with people from other American racial, ethnic, gender, and religious groups. We struggle, then, with the question, "Who are among the 'we' and who among the 'they?'" Caught off guard by the changes, we struggle with neo-diversity anxiety in our interpersonal interactions. We are all Sneetches wondering[7]:

"Whether this one was that one... or that one was this one.

"Or which one was what one... or what one was who."

Not trivial.

At work, running errands, going to a sports bar, sitting in a classroom, taking the bus, at the movies, in a park, at the public swimming pool, many feel that neo-diversity anxiety. No matter whether the situation is formal or informal, our struggles today are interpersonal-intergroup challenges of encountering and interacting with persons from many different American groups. In whatever social setting you find yourself, the interaction struggle is interpersonal.

Not trivial.

Interacting with other people is the most fundamental, most human thing we do. To work, to play, to compete, to cooperate, to friend, to love, to live well, we must interact with other people. It is bad enough when we are anxious about interacting with a particular person. Worse if we are tied-in-knots about how to interact with whole sets of people, because then we do not know how to get along at all. Not trivial, because in some people that interaction-anxiety creates a free-floating anger.

Deah Barakat

Yusor Abu-Salha

Razan Abu-Salha

February 10, 2015, one current student at, and two American graduates of N.C. State University who were born and grew up in the communities of Chapel Hill, Durham and Raleigh, NC, and who also happened to be Muslim, were murdered execution style. Indications are that the murderer had trouble interacting with these young people. Many believe that the social-interaction trouble the murderer was having was the fact that, by their behavior and dress, the three were visibly Muslim.

Not trivial.

Americans are being targeted by their 'other' group membership.

August 12, 2012. Sikh Temple, Oak Creek, Wisconsin. Six Sikh people murdered.

June 17, 2015. Emanuel African Methodist Episcopal Church massacre. Nine black parishioners murdered.

June 12, 2016. Orlando Pulse Nightclub massacre. Forty-nine mostly gay and lesbian people murdered.

July 7, 2016. Dallas, TX. Five police officers targeted and killed.

July 17, 2016. Baton Rouge, LA. Police officers ambushed, three (3) dead, three wounded.

Not trivial.

Finding it difficult to interact with or just be around people is always a problem. Today in America, finding it difficult to interact with or just be around other Americans because of their group membership is a clear and present danger because we are not the same, old America.

Then who are we?

Who do we want to be?

What kind of America do we believe in?

What kind of America do we want to live in?

What kind of America do we want for our children?

2. America, the Haunted

Two unrelated events are haunting the American identity, making us jump at our own shadows. First came 9/11.

September 11, 2001. On that 21st century "…day that shall live in infamy," at 1:30 p.m. at N.C. State, I was to teach my 200-student section of Introduction to Psychology. By that time of that day, all air travel had been halted, both towers had collapsed, and no civilians knew the real whereabouts of the President of the United States.

Rather than go through with my scheduled lecture on "Research Methods in Psychology," I opened the class by reciting John Donne's poem "No Man Is an Island." Then I said to my students, "Let's talk about what has happened in our country today." Some students revealed that they had family in New York City who they had been trying to, but could not reach. From there the discussion in the class was somber, angry, fearful, and sometimes bizarre. One exchange between students was intense.

"I think we should nuke 'em," a student yelled out.

Five or six of my students that semester, who often came to class in uniform, were in the U.S. Marine Corps, Navy ROTC. When the "let's nuke 'em" exclamation was yelled out, one of the young Marines threw up his hand and without waiting for my acknowledgement turned in the direction of that voice and loudly said,

"…nuke who? You don't know what you're talking about! Who do we aim nuclear weapons at; were we attacked by another country today! That's just silly!"

It was a blistering exchange and critique. Yet, all of the complex mood in the room was captured by my students who said,

"I don't understand how the world works anymore."

"I don't feel safe anymore."

We are still living in that psychological confusion, tension, and anxiety. What now? How does the world really work?

OBAMA WINS

Leading up to the 2008 Election Day, in my life there was interpersonal electricity. I felt like I had become a lightning rod for an electrical storm.

A 6 feet 3 inches tall, 250-pound, dark-skinned black man – white people, black people, young people, old people, acquaintances, friends and strangers all seemed to have a need to talk to me about the election. Carrying around my own thoughts, excitement, concerns and questions, I was becoming fatigued. Part of that, too, was that I was teaching my course "Interpersonal Relationships and Race." No respite, for I was observing and thinking about the campaign and associated events not just from a personal standpoint, but from a professional, social-psychological, and analytic standpoint. There was no way for me to avoid the general and the interpersonal electrical storm that was the 2008 Presidential campaign.

OBAMA WINS

When the election results flashed and thundered across the night sky, some Americans celebrated in joy, and some Americans cringed in fear. People cried, laughed, threw up their arms, danced, collapsed, shook hands, hugged each other, and held their mouths, all in belief, shock, disbelief, joy, and fear that this had happened in America. A black man had been elected President of the United States.

I was up late that night. The next morning, groggy, I made my way to the campus of North Carolina State University where I am a professor. Before getting to campus, I had tried to buy a copy of *The New York Times*, *The Washington Post*, and *USA Today*. I had no luck; all sold out. Then I had the idea that maybe in our campus bookstore there might be those newspapers. No. So I made my way to the Talley Student Center and again, no luck, but I did run into Dr. Tom Stafford, a white man, who was Vice Chancellor for Student Affairs.

"Hey Tom, how you doing?"

"After last night, I was doing real well, but now…"

He started walking toward me.

"What's going on?" I asked.

"We just found some racial graffiti in the Free Expression Tunnel. Real ugly stuff."

"I'm not really surprised," I said.

He leaned toward me, and just above a whisper he said,

"No this is real ugly. *Obama-- Shoot that nigger in the head,*" he whispered.

Tom was shaken. I could see it.

"It's being painted over right now, but what if the black community hears about that?"

Really, there was nothing to say. Tom went on with the business at hand. I started walking to my office. As I walked, I began to think about what Tom said, "…What if the black community hears about that?" As I walked, I thought so much has changed about race in America that the issue is not how will the African American community react when the word gets out. The real issue is how will the multi-group, neo-diverse, campus community react?

Our second haunting event was the election of Barack Hussein Obama to the presidency of the United States. Wait! What! Suddenly we had a black president. Well, kinda. Wasn't he raised by his white mother and grandparents? Wait, what's his name? So, a multicultural president. Well what do you mean multicultural? Is he a real American?

Although President Obama was duly elected through the American democratic process, because his identity is hard to pin down in the usual racial, religious ways, many Americans seemed to panic. Too many seemed to react with an uncertainty.

"I don't understand how the world works anymore."

No surprise that there was so much foolishness about President Obama's American citizenship and his religion.

"He's a Muslim, isn't he? Obama does rhyme with Osama."

Even after we elected him to a second term, we were still being haunted. February 2015, former NYC mayor Rudolph Giuliani said out loud:

"I know this is a horrible thing to say, but I do not believe that this president loves America. He doesn't love you. He doesn't love me. He wasn't brought up the way you were brought up and I was brought up; to love this country."

Along with many others, *The New York Times* columnist Charles M. Blow commented on Mr. Giuliani's statement. Mr. Blow's statement is noteworthy because he puts Mr. Giuliani's anxieties in context. He wrote:

[President Obama] "…not only ran for office on the idea of change, but his presence—in both visage and values—is the manifestation of change. He not only represents a very real affront to the status quo and traditional power but is also not shy about pointing out where America can improve."

Shocked and traumatized by 9/11, shocked by our own election of a black person to the Presidency, reactions to psychological ghosts spread across America: Intergroup anxiety. "…Whether this one was that one or what one was who," started making us look under the bed in broad daylight. Our Americanism, our ideas about who is a 'we' (real American) and who is a 'they,' is uncertain. Everywhere we go, in every physical space we walk into, we encounter Americans who used to be a 'them' or are the new 'them.' Uncertainty and anxiety have moved across the land because of our nation's neo-diversity.

"Come on, really?" you say. Well, yes. October 2013, an Esquire-NBC News survey reported that one in five Americans said that diversity makes them "very anxious."[5]

Haunted. We are haunted. Made skittish at our own shadows, we jump to social interaction strategies to make ourselves feel safe. Talk about being haunted, people actually say "…I don't see color."

3. Great Pretenders

Percival Everett has written, indirectly, about how we are managing neo-diversity. In his novel *Wounded*,[1] the main character is a black man, John Hunt, whose calling in life is to be a cowboy who trains horses. It is the story of a time in John Hunt's life when things got interesting.

Not to say that life wasn't interesting, anyway, for a black man living on his 1500-acre ranch in Wyoming, where it is understood that John Hunt is the best horse trainer in 'those parts.' After all, he has a convicted killer, his Uncle Gus, living with him. There's John's white cowhand, Wallace, who John thinks is "just a little dumb." There's a mule that it seems can escape from any enclosure. Not to mention a new horse to be trained, and a three-legged coyote puppy. And there's this rancher woman, Morgan, who keeps coming around, clearly interested in John, the man. But John, the man, is working to heal his own social wounds that linger from his wife Susie's death in a horsing accident.

All that going on, things don't get really interesting until John's ranch hand, Wallace, is accused of killing a gay man. Columns in major newspapers brought publicity about the killing and a few protesters out to the range. The town was now talking about 'homosexuals' but still going about the business of their hardscrabble lives.

In the novel a lot of things do happen: a murder, a rally in support of the rights of gays and lesbians, a fatherly visit that goes awry, a kidnapping, and police investigations. In that neo-diversity array of forces, people come and go, bringing reactions of anger, foolishness, love, threat, and uncertainty, leaving dismay and hope. All those comings and goings, with and without appropriate emotion, is the point.

Wounded is a novel about the fact that our being human means that when there are a lot of social forces pushing on our identity, we are aware of our vulnerability even as we, oftentimes, try to deny that vulnerability. Denying that vulnerability doesn't change the fact that sometimes we have been, can be, and will be interpersonally anxious, scared, and hurt. In his novel, Percival Everett is showing us that being socially wounded or trying to avoid being wounded is what makes interacting with other people hard. That is especially true in the emerging 21st century characterized by neo-diversity. Like one of Everett's characters says, "This is the frontier, cowboy… Everyplace is a frontier." And out here on the neo-diversity frontier, American racial anxiety is getting worse.

I am a 6 feet 3 inches tall, 260-pound, broad-shouldered, dark-skinned black man. I am the prototype for what people mean when they whisper, "…he's a big-black-man." It is impossible not to see me walk into any room. Yet in recent semesters, students in my sopho-more-level social psychology course have been trying to act as if they haven't noticed my race.

Social influences on social interaction and interpersonal relation-ships is one of the lectures I give in that course. Lecture 10 comes about four weeks into the semester. As I lecture, for all those weeks up to that day, 200 students have been looking directly at me for 75 minutes, twice a week.

In that social influence lecture, the first social influence response I define and describe is conformity; yielding to perceived group pres-sure. All human beings experience that kind of pressure at some point. Pressure where no one tells you to behave a certain way, but you feel that another person, or a group of others, would prefer you to act a particular way.

You feel you shouldn't but, *everybody else is having one more drink.*

After I have given the definition, using examples relevant to their own lives, I begin to illustrate the conformity pressure people can aim at another person and that a person can feel. Then, to begin to show the class how conformity pressures have come at me, I declare,

"By now you have noticed that I am a black man."

In past semesters, that statement has been met with appropriate laughter, smiles, and smirks. But in 2014 and 2015, from the 200 students, that statement was met with creepy silence.

Silence. No sound, no one moved, not even a flinch.

As my father would have said, "…you could hear a mouse piss on cotton."

Both times it happened, I was very surprised. Both times I stepped away from my podium. Both times I looked up into the auditorium and said to my students,

> "…that was supposed to be a joke. I expected you to laugh. Look, if you have not noticed my race, my dark skin color by now, then you have some serious brain-level problem or problems."

Both times I then stepped back to my podium and repeated myself, "…by now you have noticed that I am a black man." A bit of laughter came from both classes.

American racial, intergroup anxiety is getting worse. And one poor adaptation people are trying to use to avoid their own racial neo-diversity anxiety is the "I don't see color" strategy. Students tell me that it's so bad that if someone decides to mention that a person is black, that person whispers the word "black" as if it is a racial slur. That is causing more problems and solving none.

In Greenville, NC, the colorblindness mistake was made. With worldwide reaction, the board of Congregation Bayt Shalom hired Rabbi Alysa Stanton. That decision was significant because that meant that Ms. Alysa Stanton became the world's first black rabbi.

Two years down that tobacco road, that same congregation voted to not renew her contract. Such decisions about a rabbi or pastor can occur for any number of reasons, whether the congregation is Jewish or Christian. But I was struck by a statement about the relevance of race in hiring Rabbi Stanton. The article in the *News & Observer* indicated that "Members of Bayt Shalom said race was never discussed when Stanton interviewed for the job." Apparently, a past president of the synagogue board said about her race that, "…it was a non-issue."

If that was the case, the synagogue board was working way too hard not to see her race. Keep in mind that as soon as she was hired to be the congregation's Rabbi, the world came to attention.[2] And all that attention came because a white, Jewish synagogue had taken a black female as their spiritual leader. Yet the synagogue board says they gave race no thought in making their decision. That took a lot of psychological work to pull off.

I don't know, but one of the problems with that pretended color-blindness could have been that the board did nothing to prepare the congregation for this dramatic change. In fact, about the termination of Rabbi Stanton, a leading member of the synagogue said, "She wasn't a good fit for the congregation." With no discussion of race when she was considered for the position, the synagogue board's gargantuan effort not to see Rabbi Stanton's lovely chocolate dark skin left it to the congregation to adjust. As noble and mature as some think it sounds, we have not come far enough in this nation to say, "I don't see color" and to assume that means "skin color doesn't matter to people in my world."

One semester for my "Interpersonal Relationships and Race" course, an African American male wrote about being invited to an N.C. State fraternity party during rush. Knowing that the fraternity was all white, and to be clear with the white student-friend who invited him, my student asked if members of the fraternity would be all right with a dark-skinned black male coming to their rush party. He wrote that his white friend said,

"...he had told his fraternity brothers stories about me and they were all interested in meeting me. After hearing all of that I felt reassured, comfortable and excited to attend this band party."

At the party, my student wrote that he was talking sports with one of the fraternity members who suddenly asked,

"Who are you again? And who invited you?"

My student gave his name and the name of the person who had invited him. Then the fraternity brother said,

"...oh, so you're him. [Our fraternity brother] never said you were black."

Naturally, my student was feeling confused. He asked,

"...is that a problem?"

The fraternity brother said,

"...no offense but I don't think we're interested in having you as a part of this fraternity, you don't embody what we stand for, but we're glad to have you at the party."

Imagine living that moment.

Naive, the white friend of my black student had set this up. It seems that my student's friend didn't think he saw my student's skin color and that his fraternity brothers would also not see my student's skin color.

To not see skin color is impossible. Check any introduction to psychology textbook and you will learn that our sensory systems (parts of the human brain) are designed to make sure we see color variations in our environments. Knowing that, no one should pretend to be colorblind in their social interactions, because in America people still give skin color social meaning. Pretense of colorblindness can only lead to interracial wounds in any social circle.

4. Racism Insurance?

At my "Psychology Today" blog, after posting an essay on the colorblindness pretense, I was pleased to receive comments. I believe that a conversation about neo-diversity issues is what we need. So, let's do talk about what I was talking about.

One person reacting to my colorblindness essay made a striking comment that captured my point well. In the comment section of my "Psychology Today" post, "White girl" wrote:

> Noticing someone's race is not racist or prejudicial. *Judging* people based on their race is what's at issue. You seem to be confused. It's OK to notice what makes people different.... This is not a complicated concept. I always laugh when people gasp when I distinguish someone in a crowd by saying, 'the black guy' or 'the Asian girl,' as if those are slurs. And yes, if I'm pointing out a white person in a crowd where s/he is in the minority, I'll say, 'the white woman.' It's really not a big deal. I find the undercurrent of vitriol in your statement to be really unsettling. Oh, and yeah, I'm white.

If it's not a complicated concept, then why are so many people walking around fearful of being perceived as 'racist' if they give any evidence of noticing a person race, skin color? Classroom discussion with my students makes it clear that people, maybe young people in particular, are tied in knots about how to interact without being judged to be racist.

Reflecting that concern came the comment from "Hannah," who put it this way:

> It seems like us white people can never do the right thing, where race is concerned. I mean, if we notice a black person's race, then we're accused of being racist and of judging that person by their skin color. But if we ignore a black person's skin color, then they accuse us of 'being colorblind' and they rant about it like you just did. So what are us white people supposed to do, then?

Ranting?

I am not angry. I was not ranting. I am not filled with vitriol. I am sad about the way we have tied ourselves in these knots when it comes to interracial and all our neo-diverse, intergroup encounters and interactions. My advantage is that, as a social psychologist, I can analyze what is going on. I analyze with my goal being to give people strategies that will help them navigate the new intergroup tensions in America.

Analyze?

"Step Right Up Ladies and Gentlemen and Get Your Racism Insurance."

If you could buy an insurance policy that could back you up if you made a racial mistake, would you? That's the premise of a great spoof that is making its way around the internet.[1]

In the first skit, a white office worker with disbelief in his voice says to his black co-worker

"You... watch 'Game of Thrones'?"

Then the white co-worker goes on to say to his black male co-worker, "Man that's what I love about you:

you're a black dude but you don't act black."

Noticing the disapproving look in his black male co-worker's eyes, this well-meaning white man says, "You know what I mean, you don't act all thugged out."

Black male co-worker shows agitation and says, "So all black people are thugged out." At that moment the white co-worker realizes this interaction is not going the way he had hoped it would and suddenly sings, yes sings, "Oops I was raised... black guy come here." A black man appears and smooth's over the interaction.

That's racism insurance. Pretty funny until you realize Americans have been trying to buy some.

Someone says something untoward about Mexican people, Asian people, black people, and we cry out "...what a racist!" We are confused because prejudice is not bigotry, is not racism. One social psychological study has shown that when we cry out "...what a racist," we do so to distance ourselves from all that stuff. "They" are racist, "I am not." It becomes racism insurance. It seems that that is why so many Americans go so quick to the 'racist' label and skip over the concept of bigotry.

We all make prejudgments about all kinds of things. But when it comes to intergroup matters, *prejudice* is an unfair, unfavorable opinion of a whole group of people. Any judgment about a whole group of people is prejudiced because no one can interact and experience a whole group of people. Even so, having a group prejudice does not mean a person has to give evidence of that prejudice at any time or in any circumstance. If, however, that group prejudice comes out in external, observable (word or deed) behavior, that is *bigotry*.

By the way, all that smirking, yelling and screaming about a person being a racist is coloring outside the lines. Racism is never in a person. Racism is institutional and organizational. *Racism* is institutional and organizational systems that make individual prejudice and bigotry acceptable.

We try to absolve ourselves of having any prejudice by implying "I am not a racist." One commenter on my colorblindness post has lived with this in an interesting way. "Ebony & Ivory" had this to say:

> I am in an interracial, same-sex relationship (I'm black, he's white) and it drives me crazy when my boyfriend says he is 'colorblind.' After numerous conversations, I've come to understand that what he really means is he doesn't judge people by the color of their skin. But it feels patronizing when he says he's colorblind. I don't have the luxury of being colorblind. I'm reminded of my color all too frequently …

> I'm not asking for everyone to be Politically Correct, I'm asking that you see the color of my skin and realize that it comes with a whole host of experiences that someone of a different race doesn't necessarily experience. And those experiences are real and valid. While it may feel good to think of ourselves as colorblind, unfortunately the color of our skin does affect our social interactions.

Denial doesn't help. Any one of us has the potential to be a bigot. Hear me loud and clear: There are no innocent. Everybody carries around some prejudice from the way they were socialized to be an American. Everybody!

We really should talk more about bigotry. Some of the same people who call out somebody else for being a racist turn right around and engage in gender bigotry. Or engage in bigotry toward people with certain bodily conditions by avoiding those people. Or engage in bigotry based on sexual orientation through language use: fags, dykes, "that's so gay." Or engage in bigotry toward people with mental health conditions, saying out loud that someone is a 'retard.'

Focusing on 'racism in-a-person' is a dodge. It's a quick move to leave out all the other forms of bigotry in our society. We imply that if we can just stop people from being 'racist,' stop people from seeing color, then that would solve all the problems of human prejudice in our society. No, it would not.

'Post-racial' is another dodge.

We are only post-racial in that we are beginning to see and admit that racial bigotry is not the only form of bigotry active in America. With all the new face-to-face encounters and interactions between different groups in our neo-diverse America, many forms of group prejudice have the potential to be expressed in individual behavior. Every one of us has the potential to be a bigot. Nothing absolves any of us from that potential. Not even skin color.

5. Dr. Ben Carson Said What?

When Pope Francis arrived in the U.S. September 2015, he was greeted by President Barack Obama with warmth and respect. Seeing Pope Francis on American soil reminded some of us that Americans were once afraid to have a Catholic as our President. Presidential candidate John F. Kennedy, a Catholic, had to over and over again highlight his belief in the separation of church and state.

Verbal expression of resistance to an American President being a Catholic was and still is religious bigotry. Same goes for those sentiments expressed about an American Muslim.

Dr. Ben Carson was an outstanding, groundbreaking neurosurgeon. He is not outstanding as a political leader. In public, Dr. Carson was firm: no American Muslim should ever be "…allowed" to be President.

Anyone running for President should know that the U.S. Constitution says that "…no religious test shall ever be required as a qualification to any office or public trust under the United States." Ben Carson's statement, then, is not a part of our American political structure; it is religious bigotry. Yet Dr. Carson was surprised by the objections to his statement about American citizens who are Muslim. He was surprised because his is a primal bigotry; it is a group prejudice held so firm and confident that the person does not understand how anyone would disagree or feel repulsed by their statement, or even consider what the person has said to be bigotry.

Bigotry can be about any group. Nowadays, too many are confused about that fact. Anybody, you see, can be a bigot. Skin color does not prevent or absolve bigotry.

That is why talking about racism at the individual-psychological level is inaccurate, misleading and confusing. Yes, there has been a long, painful history of racism in America. Yes, there continue to be pockets, remnants and legacies of racism in America. But racism is a system of institutional and organizational patterns of law, policy, and action that gives support to and legitimizes individual prejudice and bigotry. Through the Civil Rights Movement's grass root protests and formal legal challenges based on our Constitution, we have successfully attacked and dismantled the systems of racism, sexism, and gender-ism. If we had not, a government employee who tried to violate the Supreme Court's rulings on unconstitutional (racial, gender, religious, sexual orientation) discrimination would not end up in jail like Kim Davis did.

Talking about racism as if it occurs at the individual-psychological level is what has led some to try to absolve African Americans as a people who were once subject to racially oppressive laws, of being able to be 'racist.' Problem is, like any others, black people can harbor racial prejudice that can pop up in verbal, nonverbal, and other behaviors (bigotry). Skin color does not eliminate the possibility of bigotry coming from members of any group. When it comes to an individual's feelings about people from different groups, bigotry can come from anyone. There are no innocent.

Social psychologists like me have analyzed intergroup tensions this way since the 1954 publication of Gordon Allport's classic book *The Nature of Prejudice*. Prejudice is not bigotry; bigotry is not racism. Back then, discussions of bigotry focused most on race-relations, but now the issues of intergroup tension are multi-dimensional. In today's age of neo-diversity, there are so many American groups that individuals can feel prejudice towards: homosexuals, Muslims, transgender persons, Christians, women, persons with visible bodily conditions, military veterans, persons with mental health conditions, interracial couples, and on and on.

Neo-diversity gives all of us, as individuals, lots of potential targets for anti-group feelings (prejudice) that can be expressed in behavior (bigotry). Especially in that neo-diversity context, anyone can be a bigot. Any person who believes that skin color prevents bigotry has been miseducated. Ben Carson is just one example of a person of high achievement, who happens to be black, being also a religious bigot.

6. From Anxiety to Respect

I was worried.

I knew something new was going on.

I knew something different was happening.

I knew the colors of American interpersonal life were changing.

Most Americans didn't see it coming. Few knew that our interpersonal lives would become so intergroup. No one could guess that we would be so unready when our everyday interpersonal encounters would involve people from so many different groups. Now the truth comes clear. Today our interpersonal encounters with the intergroup are not black and white, not diverse, but neo-diverse. Americans are having trouble adjusting to our nation's neo-diversity.

Not post-racial, not even post-gender, rapid social change has put all Americans in situations where we have to interact with people on an equal footing, but with people who do not look like, do not worship like, and sometimes do not even sound, like '...us.' That is neo-diversity, and that neo-diversity situation can create social uncertainty about how to interact with other people.

I saw that social uncertainty increasing among students at North Carolina State University. Given my experiences as a black person who grew up in the Jim Crow South, my experiences working on race-relations issues in the United States Navy (1972-1976), and my social psychology expertise as a scholar of interpersonal and intergroup dynamics, I thought maybe I could help. To put students in a position to figure out neo-diversity, I created a course. In 2006 I first taught the class as a special topics course "Interpersonal Relationships and Race," which is now in the North Carolina State University formal curriculum as "Interdependence and Race."

Physicist and Nobel laureate Richard Feynman has told us that one of the basic characteristics of science is technology: "…the things you can do once you have found something out."[1] As a social psychologist, I use my research, teaching, and writing to deliver not a physical-technology but a knowledge-technology to my audiences; a research based perspective that shows people what they can do to better navigate the complex situations of the social world.

Toward the end of my "Interdependence and Race" course, through the perspective of their new knowledge-technology, my students write about their interpersonal encounters with neo-diversity. At the end of the course my students' writings show a powerful, new understanding of how to interact well in the unavoidable neo-diverse environment of our campus and of America. Their writings at the end of the course made it clear to me that the course prepared my students for their upcoming travels across the neo-diversity frontier of America.

One student wrote:

My one new thought from the course is this.

Color is not invisible. We cannot erase it. We cannot pretend it isn't there. But what we can do is remember the unity, remember the common ideology we have as a people. We are a nation made up of many different groups. But we are still one nation. That's why understanding Neo-Diversity is so important.

Awareness of Neo-Diversity will not change the actions of those who want to hate. But it will change the way that the rest of us handle the incidents that separate us. We all feel the neo-diversity tension. Teaching about Neo-Diversity doesn't relieve the tension, but it explains where it comes from.

Knowledge of neo-diversity will help us to function more smoothly in society because it will allow us to change our way of thinking. Now that we know how neo-diversity can affect us, we can make a choice.

Seeing this powerful effect of the course on my students, I began to think about how to get what I teach out to a broader set of NCSU students. To push for NCSU students as a whole to understand, accept and embrace the neo-diversity of our campus, I wrote and self-published *Howl of the Wolf: North Carolina State University Students Call Out For Social Change.*[2] In that book, using writings produced by students who have taken my "Interpersonal Relationships and Race" course, I present NCSU students' voices describing their new awareness and growing understanding of neo-diversity. In their own words, these students speak out about how they have experienced the anxiety of being in interaction with a person who is not like them by race, gender, ethnicity, religion, or sexual orientation. They also speak out about how their new understanding of that anxiety has changed them and made them want to accept the reality of neo-diversity. I crafted this book so that the lessons learned in my class are voiced by NCSU-Wolfpack students. Their stories and voices are the new howl of the wolf (pack).

I called my book *Howl of the Wolf* and commissioned a red cover with wolves in howling pose in front of the moon so that students would be more likely to pick up and read this short book (119 pages). Student reaction was immediate and very positive.

Ashley Bridge, NCSU senior, November 5, 2012:

> It is currently almost midnight and I have just finished *Howl of the Wolf!* I could not have thought of a better title for this book. It's very thoughtful and meaningful. We, as students at NCSU, are one. We are the Wolfpack! We all come from different backgrounds, different ways that we define ourselves.

In this book, each one of us is figuratively a wolf in this wolfpack. Each of us have a voice, a howl per se, and we come together to voice our own experiences and our own thoughts. Each of us 'wolves' is different; different race, gender, ethnicity, and religion. However, we come together as a pack and howl out to stop prejudice and bigotry; to help each other in neo-diversity, to help each other in intergroup interactions.

I loved *Howl of the Wolf*. I could only hope that this book goes viral and becomes a must-read. This book could open the eyes of so many.

Howl of the Wolf was so well received on campus that it was used for the February 2013 NCSU Spring Diversity Dialogue sponsored by the Office of Institutional Equity and Diversity (co-sponsored by "Wake Up! It's Serious: A Campaign for Change," University Scholars Program, and the Poole College of Management). As an incentive for student attendance, it was announced beforehand that the first 100 students to arrive for the dialogue would each receive a free copy of *Howl of the Wolf*.

Appropriate, since I published the book to give it away free to NCSU students; about 5,000 copies by 2018. Right after I published the book and it was featured at that 2013 Spring Diversity Dialogue, word spread around campus and I began to get requests for copies of *Howl of the Wolf*. Valerie Ball in the College of Veterinary Medicine mentors students who are in majors related to veterinary medicine but at a community college in the state. Every so often, Ms. Ball has asked me for copies of *Howl* and has been forwarding her students' written comments about their experience reading the book to me.

One student from Edgecombe Community College wrote:

I am a Health Information Technology student at

Edgecombe Community College in Tarboro, North Carolina. I am doing my student clinical at the North Carolina State University Veterinary Hospital. I am in the medical records department. I am studying under Ms. Valerie Ball, RHIA. We are using your book as part of our student training. Before reading this book, I had no formal classes or training in diversity.

Diversity is important for students to learn before entering the job market. If these skills are not learned, it could have a negative impact on the organization that employs them. Learning about different races and cultures will enable a person to be skilled in management decision making, and the daily needs of the organization.

I also would like to teach the skills that I have learned to my child. Children are put into public schools with students from other ethnic backgrounds, without being taught how to interact with the people that seem different than they are. I hope to use what I have learned to help my daughter deal with diversity. Thank you again for the opportunity to learn about these important issues. I really enjoyed reading your book.

Another student from Edgecombe Community College wrote: Professor Nacoste's book was a very enjoyable and thought provoking read. It not only affirmed some views that I previously had, but pointed out some areas that I need to improve on personally. It made me think about my language and how my use of some words are damaging no matter the intent or context. I believe that I need to start viewing things in the light that if I am using words that would offend me if ANYONE said them to me, I don't need to say them at all. If people used that simplified rule, I believe that we would get closer to a country that was more accepting of 'neo-diversity.'

Howl of the Wolf was heard in places away from college campuses altogether. I gave copies to One-by-One, a grassroots community-action group whose goal is to improve race relations in the tobacco road, Southern hamlet of Sanford, NC. I have worked with the group since Spring 2008. That is why when I published *Howl,* I gave members of the group copies at one of their Sunday afternoon meetings.

A month later I went back to facilitate their discussion of the book. With a serious focus, these middle-aged to elderly Sanford citizens read *Howl* and then gave me a list of the things they said they learned from reading it: *learned* about neo-diversity and the anxiety it can cause during a social interaction; *learned* how to deal with that neo-diversity anxiety during a social interaction; *learned* that we limit ourselves if we don't figure out how to get along with people who are "different"; *learned* how to speak up in the face of intolerance.

Putting a fine point on their reactions, a member of Sanford's One-by-One group posted her review of *Howl* on the Lulu.com website. She wrote:

> What I find so fascinating about Dr. Nacoste's book is that it addresses the issues that most of us face on a daily basis regarding how to interact with people who are different from us and people whom we may have internalized prejudices about. This book includes astute insights from Dr. Nacoste's students whom are on the same journey that we are all on, even those of us who grew up in the 1960s. I highly recommend this book as a way to open up conversation on how our society can become inclusive and honor

our differences. – Susan Swan King (member of the Sanford, NC One-by-One Group), Oct 30, 2012.

Seeing and thinking about the impact my teaching and writing about neo-diversity was having on college students and older people of communities unattached to any college or university, I decided that I had a responsibility to go big. Realizing that the knowledge-technology I had developed about neo-diversity helped people, I began to write *Taking on Diversity: How We Can Move from Anxiety to Respect.*

Three months before the publication of that book, on January 28, 2015, I was the Convocation speaker at the Academic Magnet School, in North Charleston, SC. That came about because I received a request to come to South Carolina from a former NCSU student of mine from the 1990s. Yes, I said the 1990s. On December 3, 2014, she wrote:

> Dr. Nacoste, my name is Deborah Ware (formerly Deborah Mettler) and I am currently the Director of Guidance at the Academic Magnet High School in Charleston, SC. I am also a former student of yours, and I am certain that you would not remember me (it was the early 1990's), but I wanted to tell you that your class was, by far, the most important class I took while at NCSU.
>
> I don't know if you have heard about the recent controversy surrounding our school. It has been termed "Melongate" in the media and has upset many in our school community and in the community at large. If you are not familiar with our recent situation, I can send you some of the newspaper articles regarding our situation, and would be happy to talk with you about what occurred here at our football games. The reason that I am reaching out to you today is to invite

you to come speak to our student body. It is clear to us that we have a great deal of work to do regarding stereotypes and racial issues, and would like to bring in someone, such as yourself, who has made it his life's work to study, from a social-psychological standpoint, the impact of race and race relations in today's society. We have a school-wide convocation twice a year, and on January 28th, we will be holding our spring convocation for our students. We would love for you to come and share your knowledge with us and with our students. I can't think of a better person to help us in this process.

I hope you will consider coming to speak with our students and would be happy to provide you with any information you need regarding this event.

I responded:

You were a student of mine in the early 90s! Oh my...

I have not heard about the events at your school, so please do send some links along so that I can give this serious consideration. And I will consider it because these problems are cropping up all over America. Turns out you are getting to me at the right time. I have a new book coming out in April about these social dynamics:

Let's see what we can work out.

To do this would cost me one class meeting of my "Interdependence and Race" course. Cancelling a class period is something I do only on rare occasions, only for very compelling reasons. Once I read about the situation, I was convinced this was important enough for me to miss that one class period.

Funny thing that although the Academic Magnet High School is a magnet school, somehow it had become a predominantly white school that sits in a predominantly African American neighborhood. In that odd racial context, racial tension was being pushed by something the students themselves were doing. When playing other public high school teams that are predominantly black, members of the now predominantly white football team would bring out a watermelon at the end of the game to taunt the black players. With parents of the African American rival teams complaining, the whole North Charleston community was in an uproar with what the local media was calling "Watermelon-Gate."[3] My former student thought that I might be just the person to come to the school to help these young people understand why the watermelon-taunt had now blown up in their faces.

Because Mx Ware, my former student, contacted me before that coming semester, we were able to work it out. I agreed to head down to South Carolina to be the Academic Magnet High School's Spring convocation speaker.

Here I had an opportunity to reframe the 'American Dream' for a group of young people. Politicians have made the idea of the American Dream too concrete-financial. "A chicken in every pot" is really not on point. Nor is the Oprah-Winfrey-land surprise gift, "You get a car, and you get a car, and you get a car!" Our real American Dream is more abstract, lofty, and interpersonal. Our real American dream is respect.

Using that frame, I designed my presentation (Respect the Real American Dream) to give students a perspective on neo-diversity. I wanted those high school students to understand the racial dynamic that their school had become embroiled in when members of their mostly-white football team used a watermelon to make a joke aimed at mostly-black football opponents. A few days after I returned to Raleigh, I discovered a student write-up of my speech in their school newspaper, *The Talon*. I was impressed by the level of sophistication in

Ms. Salina Pi's reporting. I was impressed by the way this high school writer was able to be so accurate in depicting what happened. Ms. Pi wrote the piece in a way that captured my message, yes, but also my interaction with 600 middle to high school students, and the feel of that interaction.

Here is an excerpt from, "The Talon: Academic Magnet High School Newspaper; Student Reporter: Selina Pi."[4]

> Dr. Nacoste spoke at Academic Magnet High School Convocation 2015. "No man is an island," Dr. Rupert Nacoste, Academic Magnet High School's 2015 convocation speaker, spoke as he headed towards the center of the Rose Maree Myers stage. Dr. Nacoste has been teaching social psychology at North Carolina State University for twenty-seven years. Today, he taught AMHS students and teachers lessons about changing perceptions of diversity and social interaction in America and abroad. With an excerpt from a sermon by English poet John Donne, he introduced his lecture, "Respect for the Real American Dream."

> Nacoste reflected on his experiences growing up in the Jim Crow South. His eyes widened as he emphasized that segregation was law-enforced. Violent race riots, such as one he experienced himself in 1973 while serving on the USS Intrepid, reflected racial tensions.

> "How have things changed?" he asked the student body. High schoolers responded: Integration, Civil Rights, a black president. One exclaimed, "We're here right now!"

> Now, signs of racial tensions and change still exist, but they are often more subtle. Nacoste brought up

the example of slurs and stereotypes treated as jokes: Was a cartoon of President Obama as a chimpanzee "just a big joke?" Last May, the North Korean media published disparaging words about the President based on his mixed race. But where did these ideas originate [in North Korea]? Nacoste believed that this was an example of "America exporting racial stereotypes to be used as slurs against America."

He inquired again, "Is it a big joke?"

Though Americans may have disagreed with a political leader's policy, was it right to disagree with a president because of skin color? Was it right for somebody to joke about Jacqueline Woodson's watermelon allergy after she received an award for her memoir, Brown Girl Dreaming? Or for a 16-year-old in 2010 to make an announcement at Walmart for all black customers to leave the store?

Americans today are "confused because of dramatic social change," Nacoste explained. People are experiencing "confusion and anxiety about prejudice, bigotry, and racism." "None of us is without prejudice," he stated.

Growing up in Louisiana, he enjoyed a dish called Nutria. People recoiled in shock when he revealed that it was a type of rat, demonstrating prejudgment. However, while prejudice is natural to humans, Nacoste explained that it is unfair when it creates a "negative evaluation of a whole group of people" and leads to bigotry: the behavioral expression of prejudice by a word or deed. Finally, he clarified that "racism is never in a person," even though people "want to put things at a personal level." Instead, racism involves the "institutional and organizational" perpetuation of discrimination and prejudice.

He then faced the crowd, spreading his arms. "Welcome to the future. It ain't coming. It's here." In America, neo-diversity has replaced diversity at the level of black and white. Now racial, ethnic, socio-economic, bodily condition, gender, religious, and sexual orientation groups are among the different categories that make up modern neo-diversity.

In the past, legal segregation allowed people to easily determine "we" versus "they." Now, people struggle to distinguish between "we" and "they," and confusion and anxiety are starting to replace outright bigotry.

Students laughed as Dr. Nacoste recounted when a socially anxious stranger asked him, "How's it going, brother-man?" One student in the front row cried, "Ooh!" and Nacoste laughed vivaciously as well. He continued, stating that it was an example of how anxiety affected social interaction, then warned, "Never try to interact with someone as a representative of a group."

After my presentation, I met with juniors (up and coming seniors, they kept calling themselves). It was a lively Q&A. After that, I had lunch with teachers and the brave principal, Mx. Judith Peterson, who had allowed me to come in and shake up her school. It was quite a day.

My plan for after was to get to my hotel, gather my things, and then make the four hour drive back to Raleigh.

Ha!

Yeah right…

I was exhausted, too tired to do anything but get a bite to eat and then lay my … down. I would drive in the morning.

Even exhausted, I was pleased with the day I spent at Academic Magnet High School. I was pleased because I felt real, engaged responses from everyone – students, faculty, and administrators. I felt that something important could grow from the day I spent there.

The next morning I got up, cleaned up, had breakfast, and hit the highway, I-85, for the four hour drive back to Raleigh. Dead stopped traffic at 9 a.m. for about 45 minutes, but then the road opened up. I drove into the Raleigh city limits around 2:30 p.m. I got home, Navy-showered, changed clothes, got to campus, reviewed my notes and power-point, and at 4:30 p.m. walked into the auditorium where I gave my usual big "Good afternoon" greeting to the 200 waiting students enrolled in my "Introduction to Social Psychology" course. Greeting given and returned, I gave the lecture of the day.

Ms.. Salina Pi's column came to my attention the next week. Each time I read Salina's column, I see that my time at the Academic Magnet High School in Charleston, SC, was important. I am struck by the message she (and I hope the whole school) received from my brief time there. Ms. Pi wrote:

> "To achieve [the American dream], Nacoste urged the younger generation to respect the world's new neo-diverse frontiers…"

Respect is the real American dream. To create and live in a nation of people from many different groups, a nation of neo-diversity, and to do so with each person respecting the other.

Three months after my being in Charleston at the Academic Magnet High School, my new book hit the streets. Using my students' reports of their own experiences and new understandings, in addition to stories ripped from the headlines, I wrote *Taking on Diversity*. With that book, I was and still am reaching out to everyday people. My goal is to help Americans, especially young Americans, prepare to live our dream of a more perfect union. So, I really was pleased and took to heart the first customer review of *Taking on Diversity* to pop up on Amazon. Here is the whole 5-star review:

> Really useful, helpful, contains knowledge that makes me a better person. A book about diversity and race that doesn't involve expressing hate towards anyone. The how-to guide my generation really, truly needs to make it in the world today. More than that, to make the world a better place.

> Starts out with simple language, and uses that any time it can, conversational tone, but it's all firmly grounded in social psychology. Style and substance. More than exactly what I was looking for, this book was exactly what I needed.

Not long after, October 11, 2015, I got a letter through snail mail from a person who had read my new book *Taking on Diversity*. Trust me when I say that I was quite moved to read a complete stranger's positive and powerful reaction to the book. Here is what she wrote to tell me:

> Dear Dr. Nacoste, I have just finished reading Taking on Diversity. It is one of the most compelling and helpful books I have ever read -thank you so much for all the effort to write it and for your dedication to this issue and to making our country a better place.

> I am living in a sort of "bubble", the very diverse and generally tolerant community of Santa Cruz County, CA, and was shocked to read some of the bigoted statements relayed in the book. While not oblivious

to some of the bigotry reported in the media and other sources, I was under the illusion that younger people in general were more enlightened. It is truly painful to read many of the accounts of your students.

While reading your book, it was very enlightening to reflect back on instances where I have screwed up in my personal interactions (your Push Hypothesis). Growing up trying to please everyone around me, all my life I have struggled to voice my true feelings, sometimes remaining mute and other times harming the relationship. I am now 70 years old and still working on this!

Your directive about how to respond to bigotry was extremely useful. One of our friends periodically makes these kinds of remarks, even though he is married to a Filipina! I am wondering if perhaps she has not known how to respond to him, as I didn't. At any rate, I am now much better prepared, and am also committed to being more actively on the neo-diversity train." Thank you so much. Sincerely, G.D. (White, Italian-American female).

Neo-diversity train?

To write *Taking on Diversity*, I had to find a theme that would link all of the ideas and book chapters. Events conspired to remind me of my favorite song from the sixties: Curtis Mayfield's "People Get Ready." With his lilting falsetto, he sings about a train that's coming.

That was it, and I used that to set up the whole book. In the preface I call out to everyone standing in the train stations of America:

"In the station, attention, please! Your attention, please!

"People… get ready. The neo-diversity train is pulling into the station.

"In the station, your attention please. Attention!

"People… get ready!"

An Amazon customer reviewer titled their review "All aboard the neo-diversity train!"

Then the reader wrote:

> In a time where diversity is so misunderstood and beliefs about it are so controversial, Dr. Nacoste shows the reader how racial acceptance can be achieved and provides them with an in-depth grasp of what diversity is and why it causes so many people to feel anxiety. It is important to understand our ever-changing world, and not only does the book aid in this process, but it also helps the reader understand her/his own personal feelings about race and ethnicity.
>
> This book taught me how to let go of neo-diversity anxiety and how to effectively prevent people from using intolerant or offensive language in my presence. This is important for young people as the new generation of workers because America is very diverse, and once we begin our careers, we more than likely will have no choice but to interact with people who are different from ourselves. It is important to know how to effectively and properly interact with all individuals, not just those who are similar to us, and it is necessary if we hope to be the best versions of ourselves that we can be.
>
> Dr. Nacoste used examples from his students' personal lives to provide a more in depth understanding

of the concepts he presented. These make the material feel relatable to the reader and shows them they are not alone in their quest to achieve racial acceptance.

There are many who want to make the world a better, more inclusive place for everyone. Sometimes, we just need to be shown how to do it. Taking on Diversity does exactly that.

This book is an excellent resource for those who wish to truly understand and interact with the racially diverse world we live in and not just passively move through it in our socially assigned boxes.

If right about nothing else, this reviewer is right about this: "There are many who want to make the world a better, more inclusive place for everyone. Sometimes, we just need to be shown how to do it." Especially from teaching my students, I know that throughout our nation people are listening for a voice that will help them gain some perspective on all the intergroup tensions in America. *Taking on Diversity* was my first attempt to alert the nation to the dynamics of neo-diversity and to help Americans live woke in that new social environment.

I had to do something.

I have been worried, you see, about the soul of America.

7. Breeding Grounds

Americans are being catfished by thinking that comes from our segregated past.

Mystic River. Million Dollar Baby. God knows I admire the artistry, the poetic craft of some of the films directed by Clint Eastwood. Sad to say, though, that in politics, Mr. Eastwood has turned himself into a "back in my day" old-man joke. You know:

> "Back in my day we didn't have water. To get water, we had to smash together our own hydrogen and oxygen atoms." ☺

> "Back in my day, we didn't have no rocks. We had to go down to the creek and wash our clothes by beating them with our heads." ☺

In an interview, Mr. Eastwood was asked for his opinion of a few things presidential candidate Donald Trump had been criticized for saying. Part of Mr. Eastwood's response was,

> "…everybody's walking on eggshells. We see people accusing people of being racist and all kinds of stuff. When I grew up, those things weren't called racist."[1]

Born in 1930, coming to the age of maturity (21) in 1951 (the year of my birth), the 1954 Brown v. Board of Education Supreme Court decision making racial segregation of schools unlawful was yet to be heard. Still, in the future the 1964 Civil Rights Act had yet to be thought of; the 1965 Voting Rights Act was inconceivable in the

Jim Crow, segregated-by-law South. From that point in time, as if it made logical sense today, Mr. Eastwood said about bigoted statements about Mexican immigrants, about American Muslims, that back in his day, "When I grew up, those things weren't called racist."

Back in Clint's day, nothing was called racist by white America.

Americans are being catfished, tricked into believing it is OK to keep on doing things, keep on interacting in ways that come from a time where everything was set up to create and promote segregation, prejudice, and bigotry. Dangerous mistakes are being made that way.

As a professor, I look around and I see so much self-segregation on college and university campuses. How fraternities and sororities are allowed to operate gives me pause. I worry that colleges and universities are authorizing racial self-segregation and bigotry through the Greek system.

My worry is based on these social psychological truths:

Segregation breeds stereotypes.

Segregation breeds us versus them attitudes.

Segregation breeds group hate.

My concern about the segregation embedded in the organization of Greek letter fraternities and sororities at colleges and universities has intensified in recent years. I am concerned because over the years more and more of my students have, in their papers, reported stories of intergroup encounters with fraternity and sorority members that show members' of these organizations strong desires and efforts to exclude people of color.

Spring 2012, a white female student wrote:

> The interaction was between Emily (my black friend), the fraternity brother at the door and me. We begin to walk through the door when the boy put his arm across to block the door so we could not pass. I asked him what was the problem and he said they were full. I knew for a fact this was not the case so I push further to see what the issue really was. He told us that

we should go to another fraternity's party. I asked who else was having a party and he mentions a black fraternity's name. We then left because we knew we were not welcomed at that fraternity house.

Spring 2012, a white male student wrote:

The night of the party, my friend Randall (who happens to be black) and I were late getting there and walked up to a lawn full of many fraternity brothers and possible rush members. We saw some of our other friends and started to walk their way when one of the senior members of the frat stopped us and asked us to leave. When we confronted why he wanted us to leave he said, "We don't want any niggers or nigger-lovers here." I was shocked and could not understand the situation.

Spring 2013, a white male student wrote:

I have an officer-ship in a predominately white fraternity at NC State and I experience constant pressures to conform to issues regarding race. At chapter meetings, some of the members find it 'appropriate' to openly discriminate against black people, and sometimes even plot to keep 'thuggish-looking black people' from coming into our parties. Keep in mind there are about 12 out of the 35 members on the bandwagon for these types of vindictive motions.

None of these interactions happened at the University of Oklahoma. These stories came to me years before the story broke about the fraternity at the University of Oklahoma. March 2015, members of Sigma Alpha Epsilon were videotaped chanting:[2]

"There will never be a nigger in SAE.

"You can hang them from a tree, but they'll never sign with me…

"There will never be a…"

Over and over, on and on.

Use of the 'standard' racial slur for African Americans is more than offensive and troubling. To add to that, the idea of lynching is over-the-top disturbing because of the cavalier thoughts about the value of a black life. You cannot make an excuse for that hate. Yet, none of the fraternity members are racist; they are bigots.

Racism is not an individual problem. Racism is an organizational or institutional problem.

Today's colleges and universities have a tough job. Not so much the pure academic job, but the job of making sure that as an institution they are not engaged in racism, sexism, or religionism. That's a tough job, because that job is more than paying attention to the behavior of administrators and faculty. Colleges and universities must also monitor the behavior of its students.

We all know it is impossible for an educational institution to guarantee that there will be no students enrolled who harbor prejudice toward racial, religious, gender, mentally conditioned, sexual orientation, or bodily condition groups. No employer can make such a guarantee either. Even so, institutions and organizations do have the responsibility to monitor and manage their work environments. If and when individual biases come out in behavior (bigotry), the institution, organization, or employer must, within the limits of the law, strike hard and fast at the perpetrators.

And oh my, that is what happened at the University of Oklahoma. By the president of the university, Sigma Alpha Epsilon fraternity was removed from the campus and the campus house they lived in. Along with that action from President Boren, there also came a stunning and forceful statement that could not have been more appropriate. In part, President Boren said:

> To those who have misused their free speech in such a reprehensible way, I have a message for you. You are disgraceful. You have violated all that we stand for. You should not have the privilege of calling your-selves "Sooners." Real Sooners believe in equal oppor-tunity. Real Sooners treat all people with respect. Real Sooners love each other and take care of each other like family members. Effective immediately, all ties and affiliations between the university and the local SAE chapter are hereby severed.

That is how an institution must handle the public bigotry of those who live and work within that institution. To ignore, to excuse, to defend public racial bigotry would mean that the institution is engaged in racism.

Knowing that, what should colleges and universities do about the self-segregation inherent in fraternity and sorority life on our cam-puses? You see, we know the truth: Segregation breeds stereotypes. Segregation breeds us-versus-them attitudes. Segregation breeds group hate. Young Americans are starting to see how this is damaging their psychology and their lives as Americans. I am encouraged to see and hear so many start to speak out against this harm to our nation.

8. Using the Force

Radicals and hippies, people said. In the sixties, many Americans blamed student protests on radicalism. Young people and college students wanted too much too fast; they just didn't understand. They were too radical. That was the push back to say the protests weren't legitimate.

Soft crybabies, too thin-skinned, people say. In the 21st century, many Americans blame student protests on weakness. Young people and college students can't take real life; they're spoiled, never been pushed to grow up. They got no backbone. That's the push back to say the protests on college campuses today aren't legitimate.

Except that student protests in the sixties were legitimate because something old and anti-American needed to change: racial and gender oppression. Except that student protests right now are legitimate because something old and anti-American needs to be addressed and changed: leftover demeaning language of hate that is about, and that is aimed at, people from different groups by race, sex, mental health condition, sexual orientation, ethnic, gender identity, bodily condition, and religion. Leftover anti-group prejudice and bigotry aimed at America's neo-diversity.

After knocking down the most visible, structural walls of discrimination, we did not clean up the rubble. Students and the rest of America are free, but have to walk through the rubble of change, the social psychological leftovers.

Protests on college campuses in today's 21st century are about less structural, more interpersonal and yet still real, issues. Today's campus protest issues are reflecting the interpersonal issues that are a broil in the streets of America causing people to stumble and fall. With the structural walls now turned to rubble, Americans are struggling to stand without wobbling while having to interact with each other.

Rubble is in their paths. Some spots of the rubble are worse than others. Some places in America the rubble just makes walking difficult. Some locations, though, the rubble is thick, sharp-edged, high, unstable and still steaming, making our walking treacherous.

All over, Americans are tiptoeing through rubble to get to the store, to class, to work, to play, while keeping a watchful eye on those other Americans who they are now able to see since the walls of segregation have been knocked down. America is nervous about diversity.

Tiptoeing, hop-skipping over and through the leftover rubble, with their eyes multi-tasking, Americans are stumbling, bumping into each other. Pupils dilated with the strain of the search to answer the neo-diversity anxiety question "Who are the 'we' and who are among the 'they?'" when there is a stumble, a bumping, the blame is put on the group membership of the person bumped. That blame comes out in the language of intergroup hate. Anti-group slurs are proclaimed loud and proud, turning an interpersonal bump into a larger intergroup matter.

Language bigotry is an epidemic infecting all of higher education, aimed at our students or their classmates as a joke but really to try to intimidate and demean; to try to keep students from certain groups in their place. "… they don't belong here anyway." I have to ask, then, why are the adults trying so hard to teach college students to show tolerance for intolerance?

College students today live in social environments where language bigotry is all around them as an everyday occurrence. One of my students wrote:

> "I've heard "nigger, bitch, whitey," and multitudes of
> others…"

That is a female college student, not a male sailor.

Indeed, during the time I served (1972-1976), the U.S. Navy had to address the problem of language bigotry that led to 350 major racial incidences (including riots) ashore and aboard U.S. Navy ships at sea. To manage those problems, Admiral Elmo Zumwalt ordered racial sensitivity training for all Navy personnel. As U.S. Naval historian John Darrell Sherwood documents, "Racial epithets often caused racial unrest to come to the surface, lending merit to awareness training, especially if it could instruct members of the [Navy] regarding acceptable and unacceptable behavior."[1] Yet today we want to tell college students the world is a hard place, you just have to take the intolerance – "…suck it up." We did not tell Navy men that.

We seem to have forgotten that people who protest injustice have always been told "…you're just being too sensitive." Blacks have been told this; women, disabled people, homosexuals. Always, the first way to try to dismiss the importance of the issues raised was, and is to say "…they're just being too sensitive."

In higher education, too many administrators and faculty seem to forget that we have, with care, selected these young people to be citizens of our campuses. Our students are smart; they can read, they can do research, they can learn to be critical thinkers and observers. That's why we selected them. It is silly and arrogant, then, to behave as if all we have to do is just say to them that "…you're being too sensitive" and those smart young people will take that to heart and be quiet. Especially since, daily, these young people experience the leftover rubble of our nation's past intergroup history.

We have left in their way the language bigotry rubble that is reflected in the larger intergroup matters happening in the streets of America: Ferguson, Baltimore, not to mention the city of Chicago. Our college students see that connection. Our students realize the issues are the same. But we want to tell them that they are "…just too sensitive."

Look, college students are not protesting about trigger warnings. Except for saying on the first day of class, "You're not going to like this class," I do not warn my students that any of my lectures might make them uncomfortable.

As a professor, as a social psychologist, I teach about the reality of social life. Using the scientific concepts established by my discipline, I teach some hard ideas, some hard lessons, and I do so without apology or trigger warnings. In fact, I teach with a confrontational style. In a recent reflection paper from my "Introduction to Social Psychology" course, one of my students wrote:

> "Dear Dr. Nacoste, thank you for opening my eyes. I must admit you scared me, but after weeks of this semester I feel hopeful about getting into a relationship and not clashing with my partner…"

Another student wrote:

> "Every day when Dr. Nacoste would walk in and someone would suggest how one [unhealthy] aspect of a relationship might be… when he would ball a fist in anger and say 'Walk the hell away…' I knew what I had to do…"

Teaching the confrontational, challenging way I do, with student evaluations as a major criteria in the process of evaluation, I have won every major teaching award available at my university. No doubt, college students can take, and want to learn from, the hard truth.

Today's student protests are not about trigger warnings. College students' protests are about the very real problems of interpersonal-intergroup disrespect that they experience. In a reflection paper for my "Interdependence and Race" course, a female student wrote:

> "Words such as 'nigga,' 'bitch,' "slut,' 'retarded' are

words that generally young people throw around *as if they are nothing.*"

Evidence shows us that all manner of anti-group slurs is used on our campuses, on the food courts, in the libraries, in the residence halls, at fraternity and sorority parties, and at tailgates. That's the dark side of college life we have not been managing.

Being on the cusp of losing the soul of higher education, we are in danger of losing the soul of America. That should be protested, fought against. Students should demand that the intergroup dynamics of their campuses be managed better. Students should demand and other Americans should support their demand for change.

Please understand that across our country we are all in the leftover (psychological) rubble tiptoeing, stumbling and bumping into each other. Sometimes in panic, trying to catch a stumble to prevent a fall, too many of us are reaching out and ripping at the quilt of American life. We need to support the protests of our students to work to strengthen the stitching of that American fabric.

We cannot afford to let that fabric be torn to bits by our stumbling wobbles, because that fabric is the makings of the social-psychological quilt we have been sewing together all along. Sewn together, that fabric, that quilt is what we are promised as the more perfect union that will be what keeps the soul of America warm. Without that quilt, with only tattered remnants of that promise, we ourselves will become the bereft who are confused, frantic, lost, lonely and cold.

Students are protesting with good reason. Not only is it the right thing to do, it is their right to do so. Yet we are telling college students, some of America's future leaders, that they should learn to show tolerance for intolerance. Why are we are pushing future leaders of America to just accept the dark side of social life?

No one should have to tolerate in-your-face intolerance. Just as students were in the 1960s, students today are willing to risk being arrested, because too many people are trying to silence their voices and claims to a dream. For all students including, African Americans, women, Muslims, Latinos, for all the 'other' students, this is college life that was supposed to be the "...best time in their lives." But now, with public, hateful racial graffiti, shouted ethnic slurs, swastikas put in public places, sexual assaults, it's not that. Damn, the dark side of the real world is here and so the dream is deferred, if not lost.

Students, all Americans, have a right to freedom-of-speech. That includes the right to say to someone, "You cannot speak to me, or of me, or of my classmates or coworkers in that way. And if that kind of speech is pervasive in my environment, I have the right to report it to the authorities. There are statutes that prohibit the creation and maintenance of a hostile organizational environment. And if my grievance is not heard through those channels, I have the right to protest."

Fall 2015, the University of Missouri was all over the news.[2] More than once at that university, a neo-diverse mix of students had held "Racism Lives Here" protest rallies. Hearing nothing from upper administration of the university, one student went on a very public hunger strike: Concerned Student 1950. Faculty leadership began to issue statements of support for the students' concerns. Some academic departments also raised their voices of common concern. Twenty African American members of the University of Missouri football team threatened to boycott games; white teammates joined the boycott. Then the voice of the governor of the state of Missouri joined in speaking against 'racism' on the campus. Sudden and abrupt the resignations started: the president of the system, then the chancellor of the campus.

A dream deferred leads first to anxiety and frustration, but anxiety and frustration lead to anger. At the undoing of their college dream of innocence, students today say in anger "...oh it's on..." No empty threat, those social motivations can be a powerful and effective force, as they were at the University of Missouri.

Today, student voices are finally being heard.

The force is finally being used.

There has been an awakening.

9: Selma, Lord Selma

People live in situations.

Social psychology is unique in that the core focus is on analyzing situations, not individuals.

Being a sister is a situation.

Being a father is a situation.

Being a student is a situation.

Being a member of a fraternity is a situation.

Being a police officer is a situation.

Focusing on the social situation is the classic approach of social psychology. Kurt Lewin, the modern father of social psychology, argued that to understand social behavior, we must analyze the situation in which the person is acting.[1] Social behavior is part of social theatre; the story of behavior. What you are looking at, seeing as behavior is the result of a variety of situational forces pushing and pulling on the person.

I know that sounds odd, because the human tendency is to look at the person's individual psychology as the only possible cause of their own behavior. Makes sense of why we are so quick and so inaccurate to call individuals racist. In the everyday, we do this when it comes to America's racial past because we get confused by the images from the time of the Civil Rights Movement.

On the occasion of the 50th anniversary, we were inundated with images of what happened in Selma, Alabama, in 1965. Engaged in a march of peaceful protest for voting rights for African Americans as they crossed the Edmund Pettus Bridge, the marchers, majority black

Americans, were violently attacked by the Selma police force. Billy clubs and tear gas were used on unarmed American citizens. Looking at the film footage of that moment, my guess is that too many Americans want to lay the blame on each individual police officer. "… How could he?" Yet the fundamental problem was not the individual bigotry of a police officer, but the police force policies about dealing with 'Negroes.'

All over America, police forces had policies that allowed individual policemen to let their individual prejudices guide their behavior toward African Americans. These were policies that authorized prejudice-based, bigoted treatment of black Americans.

Forty-eight years after Selma, March 2013, Congressman John Lewis received an unexpected apology in Montgomery, AL. Modern police chief Kevin Murphy apologized to the congressman for the fact that in the past the Montgomery Alabama police had "…enforced unjust laws."

During that part of the Civil Rights Movement, John Lewis was a Freedom Rider. When the bus carrying the Freedom Riders drove into Montgomery, the bus and its passengers were met by a mob of white segregationists. That mob attacked the bus, pulled the Freedom Riders off and beat them bloody while the police force stood by and watched it happen.

Police chief in 2013, Kevin Murphy, a white man said:

> We're going to move forward as one Montgomery, one Montgomery Police Department. And we're going to continue to work at it. There's still a lot of work to do, we know that. We, the police department, needs to make the first move to build that trust back in our community that was once lost because we enforced unjust laws. Those unjust laws were immoral and wrong. But you know what? It's a new day. And there's a new police department and a new Montgomery here and now and on the horizon.[2]

March 2015, the U.S. Department of Justice issued a report on the Ferguson, MO, police department behavior toward its mostly African American citizens. That report indicates that individual police officers too often used excessive force in dealing with those citizens. That report indicates that the police seemed to think that any questions from a citizen showed contempt for the law and warranted a response of belligerent interrogation ending with the arrest of the citizen. That report indicates that these dynamics were set up by police policies of racial bias, and that because of those policies a culture was created and supported, through which the police were engaged in enforcing unwritten "…unjust laws."

Understand, though, that this is not just about police forces. Coming to grips with the truth that prejudice is not bigotry, is not racism, a recent student in my "Introduction to social psychology" course reflected:

> We often confuse the definition of racism with that of bigotry. In third grade, I met a white blonde boy with blue eyes who made me become self-aware and self-conscious of my race because he would always make insulting, ignorant racist jokes about my Chinese and Japanese descent. For example, he would say that all Asians are "…stupid, smelly, yellow Chinese nerds."
>
> And to our black classmates he would say that "slavery was the best thing that ever happened in this country." To our Jewish classmate, he would call her a "stupid Jew" and that "Jews got what they deserved in the concentration camps." His strong prejudice against nonwhite people appalled me. I thought that was racism.
>
> In retrospect, with new learning from this class, I

realize that what my classmates and I experienced was an example of racism not because the boy displayed such strong prejudices but because the institution, the school, permitted it and did absolutely nothing to stop such bigotry. I remember I complained to both my teachers and parents, but only my parents addressed these concerns to administrative staff, who opted to do nothing about the issue.

Third grade, mind you. Third grade this happened.

Move to higher education, and look at what happened at the University of Oklahoma (March 2015). Sigma Phi Epsilon fraternity members were caught on tape gleefully chanting a racial slur and suggesting their approval for the lynching of black men. At one level that is individual bigotry (the behavioral expression of a prejudice against a group).

But as members of a national Greek letter organization, the behavior of those students is supervised by two institutions: (1) the national office of Sigma Phi Epsilon and (2) by the University of Oklahoma through which the fraternity recruits its members and is a full participant on that campus. Had neither their national office nor the university acted to punish their behavior, by their lack of action those organizations would have been engaged in racism (organizational and institutional support for prejudice and bigotry). If they had been silent, each of those organizations would have revealed the situation of racism in which the fraternity lives and that would allow their individual prejudice and bigotry to thrive.

Any social psychologist will tell you that forever there will be (racially and otherwise) prejudiced individuals of all skin colors, gender, ethnicities, religions, and sexual orientations. No small consideration, then, to understand that we cannot afford to allow organizations and institutions to engage in institutional racism (which is the only kind of racism). All too important it is to distinguish prejudice from bigotry from racism.

Prejudice and bigotry occur at the individual, psychological level. The presence or absence of racism is the situation created by the organization that does or does not support individual prejudices where people live, go to school, to work, to play.

Social psychologists of my tradition analyze situations.[3] Racism, sexism, or any systems of regulated norms that guide human behavior, create situations that we must all understand because we all live in those situations.

10. And the Sign Said…

Neo-diversity anxiety is running amok in America.

> Something has happened. Something-- the cause of which we have not yet been made privy-- has happened. And what are we to do? How are we to react? Should we be afraid? These are uncertain times, and it's only natural to be frightened of uncertain things. But what do we do with that fear?

Jason Mott proclaims this in his novel *The Returned.*[1] In that novel, people who were dead and buried come back to life. No, this is not a zombie novel. People come back to life just as they were before, same age, same looks, habits, preferences. Back to life, and as their memories come back with them, they return to their old communities. And that's when the trouble starts.

Keep in mind, they look the same, they seem to be the same, but…

…their families know… their old neighbors know… their friends know… their pastors know… their police know…

…we know they had been dead and buried.

No surprise, anxiety rises up about these returned. Are they really themselves? Are they really like us? "Who are among the 'we,' and who are among the 'they'" becomes a living, everyday question.

Anxiety turns to fear. A "True Life" movement builds. People want to be able to distinguish the "True living" from "The returned." People want to know "…whether this one was that one or what one was who." Signs go up:

"We Only Serve the True Living"

"'Diversity' is on the rise in America and people are 'very anxious' about it, according to a sweeping new Esquire-NBC News survey." That was the lead in to the NBC news report of a new survey on diversity in October 2013. Based on a large-scale survey created by Republican and Democratic pollsters, analysis of the survey responses showed that a large percentage of Americans are "...worried about how 'increasing diversity' in America will affect the country's future, with almost one in five saying diversity makes them 'very anxious.'" In fact, "Nearly two-thirds (63 percent) believe that in respecting the rights of minorities, 'we've limited the rights of a majority of Americans.'"[2]

As Jason Mott asks in his novel *The Returned*,

> "...what are we to do? How are we to react? Should we be afraid? These are uncertain times, and it's only natural to be frightened of uncertain things. But what do we do with that fear?"

Take the neo-diversity anxiety that overtook the Indiana, Arkansas, and Mississippi legislators and drove them to pass "Religious Freedom" laws that Americans could use to opt out of providing public customer services to other Americans if providing the service offends a religious principle. To be clear, it's not just Indiana, Arkansas, and Mississippi. Some 32 states are considering "religious freedom" laws. Neo-diversity anxiety is all over the American reality of today.

Social change has come so fast in America that many Americans feel as if they are riding a modern roller coaster that spins you upside down and around with g-force. Almost out of nowhere, it seems, we live in an American social world filled with neo-diversity. Everyday each of us has the opportunity to encounter other Americans from different racial, sex-of-person, ethnic, bodily conditioned, sexual orientation, religious, mentally conditioned, or gender identity groups.

That has set up the still evolving, new American dilemma: "…Who are the 'we' and who are among the 'they?'"

Yet that seeming sudden explosion of diversity was not sudden. All that change began with our demolition of the laws of racial segregation. Once we did that, neo-diversity was inevitable, even if it now seems sudden.

Sudden, it seems, and some Americans want to put a hold on all that change. It's too fast, it's too much. Americans want to protect themselves from their own anxiety by making sure they only have to interact with people who fit their outdated expectations. Too many are trying to create a 'true living' movement that makes it easy for us to know and only interact with 'true believers' and 'true Americans' like 'us.'

Problem is that to put that anxiety into law opens the door to bigotry; the behavioral expression of individual prejudice. How would we in our democracy manage that behavioral expression in public spaces? After all, as Americans we all have the freedom to pursue happiness by walking around, by walking into any business that is open. How, then, would a 'true believer' establishment avoid all the awkwardness of having a non-believer walk in and ask for service? Would everyone who walks in be interrogated? Maybe it would be easier for the 'true believer' establishment to put up a sign.

"We Only Serve True Believers"

"We Reserve the Right To Serve Only True Believers"

"No Gays and Lesbians"

"No Transgender"

"Whites Only"

Wait, what?

Sign, sign, everywhere a sign…

Yes, there's the rub.

We have seen this before. We have lived this before.

Too many want to ignore the fact that the Constitution of these United States already prohibits that kind of discrimination in public service spaces. But coming to their senses, Indiana did a quick revision of its new "Religious Freedom" law. Put in place one week, the very next week Indiana revised the law to prohibit bigotry. The revision prohibits discrimination against groups in public customer service even if the rejection would be based on a religious belief.

Why did the original "Religious Freedom" law have to be revised? Better question: Why were the constitutional problems with the original law not noticed before it was signed into law?

Neo-diversity anxiety is why. Aside from a psychological disorder, anxiety is one of the worse psychological things that can happen to a person. Anxiety makes a person lose perspective. Looking out on the expanse of our ever-changing, neo-diverse America, the creepy-haunted feelings of anxiety grow more and more intense, turning into paranoia blinded to reality.

And the signs should say...?

11. Command and Control

"Keep them in their place."

In interpersonal social psychology, the concept is "fate-control": The ability of Person A to influence Person B no matter what Person B does.[1] This is the first form of interpersonal power that we all learn about as children.

"I don't want to go to bed," we, the child, whined. But one of our parents, one of the adults, picked us up and carried us into our bedroom and put us in bed. Our whining was shown to have no power to influence the directive from our parents, no power to influence that moment. Fate-control ruled that moment.

Fate-control, though, is a form of interpersonal power that can show up in the form of institutional power.

"Put them in their place."

North Carolina's House-Bill 2 (HB2) legislation was based on the intent to keep transgender people in their place. HB2 told transgender citizens that you have to use the bathroom that we, the government, say you must use. That bathroom is the one that goes with the biological sex you were born to, not the gender-identity you are living. No matter what anyone says, though, that legislation was not about bathrooms. A state law designed to designate which bathrooms members of a certain group have to use tells members of that group (and all citizens) how the state as institution evaluates and wants to control that group.

Anyone who says or thinks that bathrooms are not a civil rights issue doesn't know or is trying valiantly to ignore the history of racial discrimination in America. Making it possible for black people to use public accommodations was a central issue in the Civil Rights Act of 1965. Was that only about the use of bathrooms? No, it was about equal protection under the law, protection against government support of individual prejudice, bigotry, and discrimination.

The Jim Crow laws of legal racial segregation that I grew up surrounded by were not about water fountains (whites only), lunch counters (whites only), or bathrooms (whites only). Jim Crow laws that, as a black person I had to follow, were about keeping us "colored" people in our place. If any of us "colored people" tried to behave in a way not fitting 'our place' as specified by the law then the law was used to (often times violently) "...put them in their place."

Why was that so important? Well, if you use the same bathrooms, then at the most basic level you cannot say you are a better, a more important, or a more authentic citizen or human. That's why it was so important in the civil rights battle that African Americans waged and won to remove the stigma and laws that allowed white citizens to "show them their place."

Any institutional use of power to support anti-group racial feelings (prejudice) and racial bigotry is racism. That would be racism. NC HB2 legislation is institutional use of fate-control to support the fear of and other anti-group feelings toward transgender people. That is heterosexism.

HB2 was not about bathrooms. HB2 was about resisting social changes that extend equal protection under the law to transgender people.

We are living in a time of continuing change in our neo-diverse world. We are living in an America where every day there is the possibility that each of us will encounter and have to interact with a person not like us by some group category. Just that possibility causes, for some, interpersonal anxiety. But experiencing anxiety does not, necessarily, make a person a bigot.

J. Peder Zane, a contributing columnist writing in the *News &
Observer* agrees with the outrage against the NC law that controls the
bathrooms transgender people can use. Zane says,[2]

> "Let me join the chorus: HB2 is a bad law which must
> be repealed."

Going on, Zane makes another important point when he writes:

> [Still] …the ferocious attacks on HB2 help explain
> why it was passed in the first place. In these fast-chang-
> ing times, when traditional norms are being upended,
> there is a growing divide between the views of power-
> ful progressive elites and many ordinary citizens. One
> would never guess from the N&O's coverage that a
> whopping 69 percent of North Carolinians believe
> it is 'unreasonable and unsafe' to allow transgender
> people to use the bathroom of their choice, according
> to a poll conducted by Civitas Institute last month.

> Are these people simply ignorant bigots? Or are they
> folks who have not had time to consider enormous
> changes which they are told, nevertheless, they must
> embrace?

Speaking for myself, I am always uncomfortable when people demean others whom they disagree with. Name-calling is just
name-calling. We live in a quick-change world that is more and more
neo-diverse. Psychologically, human beings do need time to process and adjust to changes in their everyday walk through life. Neo-
diversity anxiety is real. But as Zane says with the title of his column,

> "Laws can't come from discomfort."

Laws should not come from discomfort and interpersonal anxiety. Putting intergroup anxiety into law means the government supports prejudice and bigotry. We know that government support of

prejudice and bigotry is what constitutes racism, sexism, heterosexism, and religionism.

With government support through public, institutional policies and laws, people, individuals then feel right to act on their group prejudice. Mindful in these times, social scientists are studying the effects of laws on incidences of hate crimes directed toward particular groups. Writing about some of his own research, Brian Levy gave us this summary of findings.[3] He wrote:

> ...we analyze how the rate of hate crimes based on sexual orientation changed each year from 2000 to 2012 in 48 states plus Washington, DC... [We found that] After a state enacts a pro-equality policy, two good things happen. First, hate crimes go down. Specifically, in the year following the implementation of a pro-equality policy, the incidence of hate crimes based on sexual orientation decreases...

> Second, once a state enacts [multiple] pro-equality laws, victims become more likely to report hate crimes that have occurred. This may seem counter-intuitive, but reports from the United Kingdom and American college campuses show similar increases in reporting following pro-equality policies. The logic is that a supportive social and political environment fosters trust in the legal system, which increases victims reporting.

Point?
Government laws and policies have real effects on real people.

I have a new son.

No, no… I have no biological children. But as a professor, I have had some students begin to treat me as a father figure. Humbly, I take on that mantle to be of whatever strength, challenge, and comfort I can be to that young person. Today I have a new son who was first one of my daughters.

I got this email:

"Hi Dr. Nacoste, it has been way too long!

I graduated from NC State almost three years ago and moved to New York City to attend Columbia school of social work. Now I am working as an adolescent counselor and school social worker in the Bronx. I am doing a lot of activism around LGBTQ justice and restorative justice.

I have experienced a lot of transitions since we last talked. I identify as a trans-man now and have recently started my physical transition. I am telling you this because you knew me as Katie; I now go by Jay. I have been wondering what you think about the recent anti-LGBT law passed in NC and recent political events in NC.

I am coming back to NC for a few days tomorrow. I wanted to see if you have any second to grab a cup of coffee at global village. That would be wonderful to see you and chat.

Let me know and I hope you are well. Your work and social psychology classes transformed my life and I have always carried what I learned from you with me.

At Cup A Joe the Sunday morning after getting his email, Jay and I reconnected. He brought his partner Sarah along, and for two hours the three of us had great conversations about life, the universe, and everything.

Jay told me that he had the thought that while he was here in NC he would get a few official documents changed to reflect his transition to being a male; he did grow up in NC after all. But Jay decided against trying that in NC, his home state, because he just wasn't sure the state of NC was prepared. He wasn't sure that the offices would be welcoming of this, his simple request. His partner Sarah was equally concerned about how they would be treated as a couple. Both made it clear that all their anxious uncertainty was being pushed by HB2.

Jay had come home for a visit anyway. And what a tremendous joy it was for me to see Jay. He told me that although he is still in his transition, he is happier and freer than he has ever been. He said, "I breathe differently now that I am not hiding my true self."

At the end of our time together, I pulled him into my arms for one of my bear hugs. He told me he loved me. I told him "I love you."

I have a new son. I want my son to be able to visit me at NC State without uncertainty and fear.

Laws, institutional fate-control of the racial social world of America did not last. Attempts at the creation and use of institutional fate-control of the gender-identity part of our social world don't stand a chance.

Word spreads too fast on the neo-diversity platform of social media. Americans have access to so much information we can see connections to our own past. As soon as HB2 was signed into law, by that first morning those of us not in Charlotte got the full story. We learned that the Charlotte, NC, ordinance giving transgender people the right to choose the bathroom that fit their gender-identity had gone through a long process that included opportunities for much public comment. With little to no opposition from the citizens of

Charlotte, the ordinance was passed. Yet in Raleigh, the state government of NC went wild with anxiety and went into emergency session to enact in one night a law striking down what the citizens of Charlotte approved. That is HB2.

> "HB2, or the 'bathroom bill' as it is commonly called, made North Carolina the first state to ban people from using government-owned restrooms and locker rooms that do not match the gender on their birth certificates."[4]

Too many Americans have learned to recognize the intergroup anxiety and contempt that motivates these attempts to "…put them in their place." We have seen this before.

Water fountains and bathrooms for "colored" and "white" to 'protect' white citizens. We know that the current attempts aimed at transgender people are not about bathrooms. We know that these are fate-control attempts to resist social change, attempts that are designed to "…keep them in their place."

We also know these are fate-control attempts driven by neo-diversity anxiety. Trying to fight against the intense protest roiling over NC because of HB2, NC Sen. Buck Newton (R) said this at a political rally:

"Go home, tell your friends and family who had to work today what this is all about and how hard we must fight to keep our state straight."[5]

He might as well have proclaimed, "My god… they're everywhere!

"Gays and lesbians and transgender… oh my!"

12. High Anxiety

Cowardly Lion's problem was not about him being physically weak. Cowardly Lion's problem was paranoia. Everywhere was danger. Everywhere! Even when there was nothing visible, there was danger. That's the problem with anxiety. Left to grow, left unchecked, anxiety turns to paranoia.

When it comes to the growing diversity of our country, Americans are anxious.[1] That American intergroup anxiety is really about our growing neo-diversity. In fact, one of the problems is that we need a new language for diversity.

For some it seems a long time ago. For some, not having been born, you can have no recollection of the days when Americans were talking about the "...Negro problem." From there, moving into the sixties, we began to talk about "race-relations," but then with the emergence of the "sexual revolution," to include "women's issues" we began to talk about "diversity."

None of those labels captures the multitude of groups demanding equal treatment today in 21st century America. To capture that social reality, I have introduced the concept of neo-diversity. We need this new language to give us a better calibrated lens through which to see and understand the current situation in America.

Some, though, have been confused by my concept of neo-diversity. Most of that confusion occurs because people are using their old understanding of diversity to try to figure out neo-diversity. Past usage of the term "diversity" was about making sure we were including members of particular groups that were in need of anti-discrimination protections. Hearing the word "neo-diverse," and "neo-diversity," some have asked "…well, who qualifies as neo-diverse?"

Neo-diversity is not a "…who."

Neo-diversity is a "…what."

Neo-diversity is the current *interpersonal situation* we live in today where all of us have encounters and interactions with people who are not like us on some group dimension (e.g., sexual orientation, race, religion, bodily condition, gender identity, mental health condition, sex, and ethnicity). This is a new situation in American history because, before now, we had all kinds of visible and invisible forms of segregation. For example, why are there all-women's colleges in America? Well, because for a long time women weren't allowed to go to college with men.

Why, you might ask, is neo-diversity important to analyze? Simply because this new *interpersonal situation*, neo-diversity, can cause some people to experience intergroup anxiety, a discomfort about interacting with people "not like me." Left ungrounded, left unchallenged, that anxiety will make a person lose perspective. Looking out on the expanse of uncharted interaction-situation, creepy-haunted feelings can grow more and more intense, that high anxiety becoming paranoia.

"We must fight to keep our state straight." "We must fight against the homosexual agenda."

In their important little book, Freeman and Freeman define paranoia as "…the unrealistic belief that other people want to harm us."[2] Anxiety about neo-diversity, anxiety about all of the people from different groups, can lead to exaggerated feelings of the presence of "…them." Freeman and Freeman point out the problems that this can set up. They say:

> …it's often difficult to completely rule out the possibility that a paranoid thought is actually correct. And it's precisely because it's so difficult that paranoia can thrive. Paranoia feeds on uncertainty and ambiguity.

The answer is to judge the suspicious thought on the *current evidence of threat*—and to exclude past experiences. (p. 34)

Current evidence of a threat? Take Americans' estimates of the percentage of the population of the country that is homosexual. A 2011 Gallup poll found that, on average, U.S. adults believe that 25 percent of the American population is gay or lesbian.[3] Biological and social scientists who study populations are sure that the percentage of homosexuals in any human population has never gotten as high as ten percent.

Twenty-five percent is quite an overestimation.

I got really interested in this neo-diversity anxiety-driven overestimation. At North Carolina State University, Spring 2016, as a bonus question (for research purposes), I asked both my classes to respond to this multiple-choice question:

One of the following is true. Homosexuals make up _____ of the American population:

a. 50%

b. 35%

c. 25%

d. 10%

From among the 200 students in my sophomore level social psychology course, 60 percent of the class said they believed that 25 to 35 percent of the American population is homosexual. From among the 47 more educated college juniors and senior students in my upper level course, 56 percent also estimated that 25 to 35 percent of the American population is gay or lesbian.

Biologists will tell you that is impossible because biological forces push for survival of the species through procreation. Why then are our estimates so wildly off? What is it that today makes so many people believe that the homosexual population is exploding across America?

Freeman and Freeman make this point in their book on paranoia:

> The way we think about the world, then, is hugely influenced by the number of times we hear an event and by the magnitude of its emotional impact on us. Objective facts cut much less ice. This means we're vulnerable to all kinds of irrational, unjustified fears—to paranoia, in other words. (p. 47)

No matter the estimations made by individuals, there is no epidemic of homosexuality in America, no homosexual agenda. There has been no exponential increase in transgender people in America, no transgender agenda. Our situation problem is that there was a time in America when talking about sexual orientation and homosexuality was taboo. We used to hide from the truth that Americans could be very different from each other and still be Americans.

To that purpose, the "…melting pot" idea was pushed. No doubt, the most obvious identities to be melted were racial and ethnic, but those were just the most visible. Attached to this powerful molten muzzle was also the identity of sexual orientation and (for sure) any transgender-identity.

Today we live in a different America, a neo-diverse America. Part of the neo-diversity dynamic is that people from many different groups are demanding to be heard, demanding respect. Today no one wants to be, and no one will allow themselves to be melted.

June 12, 2016, Orlando, Florida, at the Pulse Club, a known gay and lesbian bar, a man walks in and shoots and kills, assassinates as many people as possible. The number of dead: 50. Even in the midst of that terrible tragedy, seeming to have been brought on by hate of a group, LGBTQ people raised their group-voice to be heard. In the immediate aftermath, on CNN a gay man still bloody from the carnage looked into the camera and said,

"We are not going away. We have made so much progress for the LBGTQ community and this will not
stop us from speaking out. We are not going back."

Why are Americans overestimating the presence of homosexual
and transgender people in our society? We used to push, shame, and
shush people into the corners using violent-hot muzzles to keep those
people quiet. We did it to African Americans. We did it when it came
to women's rights.

But then with their own hands, members of those groups began
to take off the hot muzzles. "…We the people…" with unique voices
began to speak loud and proud. Ripping the hot muzzle off race, "I'm
black and I'm proud." Dismantling the hot muzzle on sex-of-person,
"I am woman hear me roar." Pulling off and dropping to the ground
and kicking to the side the hot muzzle that had been on sexual orientation, LBGTQ people have declared, "…Same love."

Now America is experiencing an emotional, psychological
rebound from feeling safe from 'them' to anxiety from seeing 'them'
walk out of the corners, and hearing 'them' proclaim their American
right to life, liberty, and the pursuit of happiness. Voices that had
been controlled to silence have, with courage, put their hands on the
hot muzzle, and with flesh burning ripped it off and begun to speak
up. Gay, lesbian, and transgender people who had been here all along
have begun to use their voices to cry out for humane treatment and
justice.

Remember what Freeman and Freeman said about paranoia:
"The way we think about the world, then, is hugely
influenced by the number of times we hear an event
and by the magnitude of its emotional impact on us."

Today, all kinds of voices are proud to proclaim "I too am
America, hear me roar." Quite visible and vocal, the neo-diversity
situation of America is what is causing so much anxiety across our

nation. Since it is now (and forever) unavoidable, we need to socialize people to respect that neo-diversity as America. Pushing for respect of our neo-diversity is one step we must take toward preventing anymore Wisconsin's, Orlando's, Ferguson's, Baltimore's, Dallas', Baton Rouge's, and Charleston's.

13: Hesitation in Charleston

Human being Dylann Roof hesitated.

Murderer Dylann Roof told the officers who arrested him that he hesitated. He said that after sitting through the Bible study with those black people who had, with warmth and good spirit, welcomed him, he hesitated. Influenced by the camaraderie of those people, Roof had a moment where he thought about not pulling out his gun and killing.

Tragic in that moment, he heard no voices of support for not going through with his plan to kill. He heard no voices of objection because in his interactions with his friends, no one had ever said to him, "...man, that kind of talk is not right." No friend had ever challenged his bigoted comments about African Americans taking over America. One of his friends admitted this. He said, "We thought it was just jokes... we didn't take him seriously... so..."

None of his friends ever offered a different voice. No friend offered a voice that contradicted Roof's view of America as being in danger from black people. And so, there were no alternative thoughts in his moment of hesitation, no alternative whispers, no alternative shouts, only silence. In the void that was the sound of silence from his social life, he stood, pulled his gun, and killed nine innocent, Bible-studying black people.

####

Having grown up in Louisiana in the Jim Crow time of legal racial segregation, I saw and lived through the tremendous and violent struggle for change during the 1960s part of the Civil Rights Movement. Yet even to my eyes, in recent times our nation has experienced an intergroup dynamic that has been stunning to witness.

On college campuses we have seen nooses displayed. We have learned that an anti-woman and racially bigoted fraternity notebook was found at North Carolina State University. We have seen and listened to a videotape of a University of Oklahoma fraternity singing and chanting a racial slur and in the same chant using images of lynching. Not directly on a campus, we saw the murder of the three American-Muslim University of North Carolina at Chapel Hill and North Carolina State University students. All that, and most incredible, police have been interacting with other American citizens in ways that now seem to routinely end with a fatality, sometimes with bullets in the back of the black man. We recoiled from a racial mass shooting at an historic African American church in Charleston, SC. 2017, yes 2017, America was, I certainly was, stunned by images of a public KKK, white supremacist rally in Charlottesville, VA.

America has reached a neo-diversity tipping point. This moment in history where things stand so rigid that almost anything can push the tension in the moment over into one good or bad direction. When it comes to dealing with everyday neo-diversity interactions, we have reached that tipping point.

How did we, America, get here from the civil rights revolution of the 1960s?

We got complacent. "It's all good," people said. Pushed by some who pointed to continuing racial injustice, too many white Americans became defensive. "Why do we have to keep talking about race?"

We have gotten to this tipping point because it took us too long to notice that as a nation we are well past being diverse. America is now a neo-diverse nation. But since it took us so long as a country to notice all of the social change all around us, we have been using outdated ways to try to adapt to our nation's neo-diversity.

Tolerance is not enough. Tolerance is, in fact, the problem. Tolerance gives prejudice and bigotry a pass.

As individual citizens of this nation, we have been too passive in our encounters with language bigotry in our everyday lives. "It's just a joke," people say and we take it as so. "Oh, they don't really mean that; they're just joking," we say to ourselves and others to let it pass.

But did you see, hear, or read the interview with the friend of the now confessed, not crazy, but premeditated murderer of those nine people in Charleston, SC? That friend said something like, "...yeah he used to say some racial things... make some racist jokes... but nobody took him seriously... we thought it was just jokes, but now..."

We became tolerant of intolerance. Refusing to take seriously and confront the racial, sex-of-person, and sexual orientation slurs used by friends, we let anti-group hostility slumber and grow in our communities. Left to sleep in comfort for a while, now we have to deal with what was once hibernating bigotry: anti-group prejudice feelings that people hold onto but do not express in behavior until the right stimulus comes along and wakes it up.

Knocking down the walls, dismantling the laws of legal racial segregation did not eliminate all racial prejudice. If not eliminated, then where did the prejudice and bigotry go? It didn't go anywhere; it's the leftover rubble. And do not misunderstand me, attitudes did change. We are not a nation of bigots. A great many Americans became more accepting of black people as equal citizens. But though there was change, some prejudice and bigotry just went into hibernation, hiding and sleeping in the shambles of the knocked-over walls of legal segregation.

With our "...it's all good" tolerance for intolerance, we allowed those anti-group feelings to sleep well and grow strong. In our everyday lives we encountered spoken slurs and expressions of outward hostility toward Americans from different groups and said nothing, or worse laughed along with "...the joke." We have failed to understand that letting others speak in the language of bigotry against any group allows hostility to live and hibernate. Then, when a particular circumstance shakes and wakes that hostility, no longer hibernating, that bigotry roars into social life and we have the nerve to act surprised about the police shootings, gay and lesbian nightclub shooting, or church racial murders. We act surprised, but it is we who have kept that bigotry cool and comfortable by not taking seriously the language bigotry of "…the joke."

All the recent stories of neo-diversity encounters gone bad and sometimes fatal are making it clear that we are indeed at a neo-diversity tipping point in American history. As a nation we have to engage the hibernating bigotry in our communities before it awakens and goes public with deadly consequences. Each of us must take personal responsibility for the language of hostility we allow to be used in our social interactions.

We also have to keep reminding ourselves that today the issues are not just race related, not just about diversity, but about neo-diversity. Neo-diversity is the time we live in where all of us have to encounter and interact with people from different gender, religious, bodily conditioned, sexually oriented, ethnic, mental health conditioned, and racial groups. For too many Americans that creates us-versus-them interaction-anxiety during a social encounter that can lead to dramatically bad moments.

All those awful moments of neo-diversity interactions going badly come from all of us. Yes, from all of us because we have all been too complacent, letting others speak in the language of intergroup hate. We have been letting intergroup hostility and anger grow. That is how we have come to this tipping point in neo-diverse America.

What now? Despair is wrongheaded.

Now we have to stop showing tolerance for intolerance. Too often as individuals we have tolerated language bigotry (verbal expression of stereotypes and anti-group prejudice).

All extremism starts small.

"You will not replace us!" That chant was not spontaneous in that moment in Charlottesville. Feelings and thoughts behind that chant had been expressed in small, interpersonal moments at home, at work, at play. Unchallenged in even the most gentle way, those feelings and thoughts began to seem legitimate. With no counter influence attempts, finding others with those negative thoughts about our growing neo-diversity becomes easier because rapid social change makes lots of people feel a bit uneasy.

All extremism starts small.

We have to speak up and object to the intolerance that comes up in our everyday social interactions. In that way there is a lot of hard interpersonal work to do in the midst of all the tension of the current tipping point of our neo-diverse America. Yet that work is something each of us can do in our everyday social interactions to tip us in the right direction. It is time we start to speak up and stand against stereotypes and bigotry, because stereotypes and bigotry are enemies, killers of the (real) American Dream.

"No man is an island entire of itself…" Preacher and poet John Donne wrote those words to remind us that we are all social; we are all involved in mankind. At the heart of the human condition is this truth: We all influence, and we all are influenced by, other people.

We have got to stop showing so much tolerance for intolerance. Each of us has the power of social influence in our social interactions. All social psychology textbooks and all social psychologists carry a definition of social influence. Mine is that social influence is a change in a person's thoughts, feelings, or behavior caused by real or implied pressure from another person (or persons).

Notice that by my definition, social influence requires that during social encounters people actually engage each other by listening and reacting to (putting pressure on) each other. Notice, too, the idea that the consequence of this engagement, the consequence of authentic social interaction, is some impact on thoughts, feelings, or behaviors.

Be careful, then, to understand that your social influence on another person may not occur as a change in a person's immediate behavior. Too many of us want to change people in the moment. No, that will not happen. Instead, your influence may occur as a lingering or recurring thought. I would bet that all of us have had a friend come up to us and say something like, "You know I was thinking about what you said the last time we talked and…"

Dylann Roof is not insane. Dylann Roof is not a lone wolf. Dylann Roof was not isolated. He had people he called friends, and those friends gave him a place to stay. Really, they were only pseudo friends, since his so-called friends did not engage with his expressed thoughts during their social interactions. Not insane, not a lone wolf, Dylann Roof was socially disconnected.

Social disconnection is social deprivation at its worse. Being around people who call you friend but who look you in the eyes and do not take with seriousness the thoughts you express leaves you to your own confusion, ignorance, arrogance, and brooding hate.

Roof's so-called friends made no attempts to influence his thoughts, feelings, or behaviors when he expressed his bigoted, hateful views. His brooding racial prejudice was allowed to hibernate and grow stronger and stronger. No friend took him seriously; they say they thought he was just joking.

For the record, folks, there is no innocent expression of group hate. There are no innocent racial slurs. There are no innocent anti-group jokes.

It's not just a joke.

No friend of Dylann Roof spoke to challenge his racial anger by even simply saying "…Hey, man… that's not right. Black people aren't the enemy." That is why in his moment of hesitation, Dylann Roof heard no whispers of past social influence attempts saying, "Man… what you are thinking about doing, that's not right." Roof heard no alternative, dissonant voices of attempted social influence. Quick did his moment of hesitation pass. Then he killed nine innocent people in cold blood.

There but for the social influence of real friends goes who?

14: A Question About the Confederate Battle Flag

I have been teaching social psychology at North Carolina State University since 1988. In 2006 I created my course on neo-diversity, first called "Interpersonal Relationships and Race," and (for bureaucratic reasons) now "Interdependence and Race." Over the years, students have come to trust my analyses of interpersonal and intergroup situations enough to rely on me to answer their questions.

Not just in the classroom. With my online presence, I get questions from current and former students. Via Facebook, I received this question:

> Dr. Nacoste: I was wondering, what was your reaction to the confederate flag being taken down in South Carolina? Do you think that this is the start of better racial equality and is a step forward towards neo-diversity?

I answered that question this way:

> When it comes to the Confederate Battle Flag being taken down in SC,[1] Americans should celebrate. But we must all understand what to celebrate.

> Remember, racial prejudice is not racial bigotry is not racism. Prejudice is an individual's negative feelings toward a whole group of people, in this case African Americans. Bigotry is when that prejudice is expressed

in that individual's observable behavior; use of stereotypes in conversation, use of racial slurs, avoidance of or refusal to interact with members of the group, and at its most extreme, killing black people because they are black.

For an individual to display a confederate battle flag is not necessarily a sign of that person's racial prejudice (and thus bigotry). But to have the government of SC display the Confederate Flag showed the racism of the state. Remember, that flag was the battle flag of the Southern state governments who wanted the enslavement of African Americans to continue.

Legalized slavery was the most extreme form of racism; institutional enforcement of racial prejudice and bigotry to enslave other human beings based on skin color. In the more modern history of South Carolina's government through legislation passed by that government 50 years ago, the Confederate Flag was raised at the state capitol to express symbolic disagreement with, and actual resistance to, the Supreme Court desegregation order and the progress of the Civil Rights Movement. That was racism through government bigotry.

Although that history of government bigotry was reason enough to take it down, understand, too, that the display of that flag was not just offensive to black people. The display was also offensive to America. To mourn the nine black people murdered in Charleston, the flag of our United States was flown at half-staff. At the same time, flying at the state house of SC, the Confederate Battle Flag was not flown at half-staff because it would have taken a SC legislative act for that to happen. That means for the SC state government, the Confederate Battle Flag had more official standing than the flag of the United States of America.

Historically, some individual Americans have felt, and some continue to feel, racial prejudice toward black people. Today, in their homes and in their social interactions, some of those who do harbor negative feelings (prejudice) toward African Americans as a group engage in some 'safe' forms of bigotry (use of stereotypes and racial slurs). But it was unacceptable all along to have a state government display a symbol of racial prejudice and bigotry. The display of that Confederate Battle Flag showed that the state government of SC was engaged in racism by supporting the racial prejudice and bigotry of the historic view of black people as less than human, no more than cattle.

Taking that flag down from an honored position on state government grounds was important because a symbol of racial prejudice and bigotry was removed as a display of government support. Now when any citizen looks at the symbols of the SC government, there is nothing to suggest that one racial group is more important than another in that state. As the sitting Governor of South Carolina Nikki Haley said:

"In South Carolina, we honor tradition, we honor history, we honor heritage, but there's a place for that flag, and that flag needs to be in a museum... But the State House, that's an area that belongs to everyone. And no one should drive by the State House and feel pain. No one should drive by the State House and feel like they don't belong."

Taking down the Confederate Battle Flag from the grounds of the SC State government was about recognizing that SC is not a white state. SC is a state of this union with black citizens. Same as all the states in our United States of America, SC is a state in which people of many different groups are citizens and interact with each other and the government. In South Carolina there are citizens from many different racial, sexually oriented, ethnic, bodily conditioned, gendered, religious, and mental health conditioned groups. So yes, taking down the flag was a move to show respect for that neo-diversity of the SC citizenry. That is to be celebrated. Now, the SC government and the federal government of our nation must continue to take concrete steps to ensure that our neo-diverse citizens are all shown the respect of equal rights under the law. At least that is how I analyze the situation.

Thanks for the question.

15: Language Matters

Language is social and is used to communicate between people. Language matters, too, because language reveals or directs how we see other people.

In Raleigh, a young man, a 16-year-old, is a Paralympic athlete. Desmond Jackson is a sprinter who runs the 100-meter dash with a blade to replace the missing part of his left leg. Summer 2016, Desmond competed in the Paralympic Team Trials in the hope of qualifying for the Olympics in Rio.

I learned about Desmond by reading the Saturday sports pages. I don't care about sports, but I do skim the pages for stories about issues in higher education and for human interest stories. Olga Khokhryakova did a very nice story on Desmond, making it clear that he is an outstanding Paralympic athlete and outstanding young man.[1] One thing bothered me.

Pointing out that Desmond does his workouts at Paul Derr Track at NC State University, without malice in tone or intent, Ms. Khokhryakova noted that, "[Desmond] Jackson works out at NC State with able-bodied athletes." "Able-bodied" made a gonging sound in my head.

Desmond competes in the 100 and 200-meter dashes and in the high jump, all at a competitive, Olympic level. A reasonable comparison between the physical condition in which Desmond runs compared to other athletes was done. Problem is that the language used to make the comparison was inaccurate and directs the reader to think of Desmond as not "able-bodied."

Desmond practices with athletes who are "complete-bodied" where he is "partial-bodied." That more accurate language does not push us to think of Desmond as less abled. Forgive me, but damn, Desmond has already won gold medals in the 100 and 200 meters and could out pace many, many complete-bodied teenagers his own age.

Language is one of the features of social interaction that is being pushed into transition by our growing neo-diversity. Our neo-diversity requires that we speak of each other and to each other in the language of respect.

"That's so gay," is not respectful of LBGQT+ persons and communities. It is demeaning, since we know the phrase is used to say that something weak or out of place is homosexual. I now refuse to call myself "straight" to speak of being heterosexual. If heterosexual is "straight" then homosexual is...

Somehow, though, all over America people think it is OK to say "That's so gay" in an attempt to be funny; to say "I'm straight" to be clear about their being heterosexual. But maybe after Orlando, maybe just maybe we will see that such phrases are not OK, are not funny, and are not innocent. Speaking sympathy and prayers toward LBGTQ+ persons and communities after Orlando is heartless and hypocritical if we do not change our language behavior. Our sympathy and prayers are then only a resounding gong; a clanging cymbal.

For a few years, Mark and I had crossed paths here in Raleigh. In a bookstore, library, coffee-shop, breakfast café, we would see each other, shake hands, speak a few words, and move on, him rolling along in his wheelchair, me striding through whatever place we happened to encounter each other. At one of these encounters, we decided to have a sit-down over a beer, later that week.

When we got to our table with its high stools, I watched as Mark used his muscular arms to lift himself from his wheelchair to seat himself on the taller stool. Chatting to get to know each other, he asked "…what are you teaching nowadays, professor?" I started talking about neo-diversity.

"What gave you the idea," he asked.

"All the social change in America and on our campus," I said.

"When I came to NC State in 1988, about 30 percent of the students were female at this predominantly Engineering university; I was told that some on campus thought that was a lot of '…girls.'"

"Today," I went on, "49 percent of our students are young women and that is a good thing. Also, we didn't even have a disability services office, and now DSO is one of the largest student services units on campus. With the 1995 Americans With Disabilities Act we became obligated to make reasonable accommodations for our students, and we do."

See what can happen when you ask a professor a question?

Yikes.

Anyway, I went on: "We make reasonable accommodations to students with all kinds of disabilities. In my classes, I have had students who are wheelchair bound and we simply accommodate…"

Mark's body language changed.

A gong sounded in my head.

I stopped talking.

I was looking him in the eyes and he was returning my gaze.

"I am not wheelchair bound," he said. "I use a wheelchair, but I am not bound to my wheelchair."

Of course. I had already seen that he was not in fact "wheelchair bound."

"Using a wheelchair does not define me," he said, finishing his statement.

Firm, steady and calm, he made his statement. With the change in his demeanor, he was also clear and fierce in letting me know how he felt about the language I had used.

"Thank you," I said in earnest.

Then I said:

"That's one of the things about neo-diversity. Now people who in the past did not interact and converse are in the conversation and these moments are happening. Some people handle it well, some don't. I know that I don't know everything, so when I learn something new, I am grateful. That's why I thank you, Mark."

We are in transition because of our growing neo-diversity and, as you can see, I have made my own language mistakes. There are, in fact, no innocent.

Mark and I sipped our beers. Then, professor that I am, I went on with answering Mark's original question: What gave you the idea?

"So, you see, as a black man seeing all the changes in America attached to race, all the multitude of changes I have seen on campus, I realized that students are in a new social environment that even their parents didn't experience. I started thinking about this new form of diversity, neo-diversity, and how it might be affecting social interactions."

By the way, Mark and I had a good time getting to know and respect each other. Part of any growing friendship requires managing moments of interpersonal conflict[2]. That moment between Mark and me was a necessary moment about how we can talk with each other with respect. It was also a necessary language moment of neo-diverse America.

The language we use about other people has always mattered. With neo-diversity, language matters more because language about 'others' is not spoken with 'them' far away, over there, but with 'them' in our social interactions.

Everybody's in the room. Everybody can hear what you say. When, oh dear, you use language that disrespects someone, you are going to hear an objection. That has always been true, except for the groups of people we used to treat as 'less than.'

Now, no more. Neo-diversity means that those who used to be 'less than' are now 'equal to,' and people who are equal can and will object to being spoken of, or spoken to, with disrespect.

That is human.

That is not political correctness.

That is not about 'them' being so sensitive.

That is the new social situation of America.

Welcome to the future. It ain't coming, it's here and now.

16: Cancelling Islamobigotry

Quail Ridge Books of Raleigh enlisted me to help facilitate a set of open discussions about neo-diversity issues in the Raleigh community.[1] We have had two of these "What's Going On" open forums in the bookstore. Forum 3 was to be "Islamophobia in the Raleigh Community," but that had to be cancelled because of Winter Storm Jonas.

Since I had announced Forum 3 on my Facebook page, I felt obligated to announce the cancellation. I did so with this post:

> "CANCELLED! Islamophobia discussion at Quail Ridge Books this Sunday, January 24, 2016, is CANCELLED. Too much ice, travel too treacherous. I will let everyone know when it is rescheduled. By the way, I wish we could just CANCEL Islamophobia. But it's not that easy, so always stand up for each other's humanity... that is the interpersonal answer."

Just after I posted that announcement, I found this email from a student asking for help on my university account. My student wrote:

> Dr. Nacoste, I am in your PSY 411, Interdependence and Race class. I am emailing you in hopes that you will be able to help me better respond to, and understand, a situation I found myself in this past weekend. I know that I will learn more throughout our course and if I have to wait until then it's fine! I just wanted you to know that my experience so far in your

courses has changed my mindset and I didn't notice until the situation below presented itself.

Then she described the interpersonal situation she experienced:
This past weekend I found myself spending quality time with my roommates, watching movies, when we came across the very popular film American Sniper. Now, my roommates are very right winged political advocates and thus voice their love for films such as these. I, a little more moderate, enjoy all types of films and also take pride in my country as Americans should. Thus, I thought the film would be enjoyable.

However, as the movie went on I found myself becoming quite uncomfortable and slightly angry when bigoted comments regarding the entire Islamic community were voiced by my friends. Comments such as "they should all die", "they are taught to hate us, and we're taught to tolerate them" and "they want to allow THEM into our country, they just need to LEAVE.

Being exposed to the diversity on campus, and even attending several events that allow me to interact with those who are different from me, has shown me that this type of attitude is unacceptable. I tried to intervene and focus on the fact that the actors in the movie were portraying terrorists, not the Muslim population. They didn't care. I knew I had to walk away as the anger was consuming me. I love my roommates and I know that they are all amazing people. But how can I better help them get rid of these crazy ideas and comments?

In a way I was surprised to get an email like this so early in the semester. Usually it takes a bit longer for the lessons of the course to start hitting my students, but I had already noticed that this Spring 2016 class of 46 neo-diverse (a mix of bi-racial, female, male, Arab, white, Latino/Hispanic, black, bi-sexual) students was more eager to learn than is usually the case. Early or not, whenever I get an email from any of my students about this kind of situation, I respond quickly.

To this student I wrote:

> Believe it or not, you handled that very well. Yes, as the semester goes along I will teach you and the class strategies for handling interpersonal moments like the one you described. Understand that this is the fundamental interpersonal-intergroup problem our whole country is struggling to weather, and not just ice storms aimed at our American Muslim brothers and sisters. Pick a group, say women, and somebody will let their group-prejudice blow cold into language-behavior and worse forms of bigotry (behavioral expression of anti-group prejudice).
>
> Again, you handled your situation in one of the ways I will teach. Sometimes you just have to walk the hell away. No one has to tolerate intolerance.
>
> The strategy I will teach the class avoids telling people they are wrong. That never works. The strategy I will teach you and your class is to indicate to the persons you are interacting with how much it hurts you to hear that kind of stereotype, that kind of language bigotry expressed toward a whole group of people. Just say something like, "I'm sorry, but I find that kind of language/stereotype offensive. It hurts me."
>
> That's it. If the people you are interacting with care

about you and your feelings, that kind of statement should matter.

By the way, part of what I teach is that you cannot change people in the moment. Speak for yourself, speak your feelings, and that's all you can do in the moment. If the person or persons tell you that you are wrong to feel that way, or clearly doesn't care about what you feel, don't argue, just walk the hell away.

I am very proud of the way you handled yourself. And I am so happy you are in my class.

When I posted the cancellation of the Islamophobia discussion that was to happen at Quail Ridge Books, I ended my post by saying: "By the way, I wish we could just CANCEL Islamophobia. But it's not that easy, so always stand up for each other's humanity... that is the interpersonal answer."

Knowing that what we are talking about occurs at the interpersonal (not purely psychological) level is also why I prefer to call it "Islamobigotry." Technically, a classic feature of a phobia is high anxiety and fear of the stimulus. But phobias are also uncontrollable and have no concrete origin. Phobias, then, are unexplainable and outside a person's control.

By my analysis, what is being aimed at American Muslims is not phobic but simple intergroup prejudice that is turned into bigotry by the individual's choice of interpersonal behavior. It's bigotry, same as the other bigotries:

Racial bigotry.

Gender bigotry.

Homo-bigotry.

Islamo-bigotry.

That is important to understand because unlike phobias, bigotry is concrete, can be identified and addressed in our everyday social interactions. Unlike true psychological phobias, it doesn't take cognitive-behavioral therapy to address our own or another person's bigotry in the interpersonal moment.

Anyway, cancelling the bookstore forum, getting and responding to the email from that student of mine, all happened at the time of the anniversary of assassination of three American Muslim students who each had a connection to NC State. Pained by the necessity of thinking about "Our Three Winners" Deah, Yusor and Razan, I was and still am adamant in saying we must cancel this winter storm of Islamobigotry moving across America.

Turns out, you can help quell that storm. Object to the language of stereotypes people use in their interactions with you. Since it's just another form of bigotry, you can in your everyday social interactions stand up for the humanity of all people. As Martin Luther King Jr. proclaimed,

> "The greatest tragedy of this age will not be the vitriolic words and deeds of the children of darkness; but the appalling silence of the children of light."

17: How a Mental-Health-Reveal Becomes a Trust Betrayed by Bigotry

"Have you ever considered using mental-health-condition as an example of neo-diversity?"

As other students left the lecture hall, a white female student was asking me that question at the end of the lecture day of my "Interdependence and Race" course.

"Not really," I said. Going on I said, "As you have seen, I do of course consider that mental-health-condition can activate neo-diversity anxieties, but I am not qualified to talk about features of any particular mental-health-condition."

"That's not what I mean," she said. "I mean how learning someone has a mental health-condition can push an in-group, outgroup feeling into a relationship."

This was a very sophisticated question. Taking her seriously, I told her that I could not see a way to include that idea in our class, in the remaining lectures, but would think about it.

Truth is, I was resistant to taking this on in lecture. After all, I had never done so before. Not only that, but I wasn't sure where it would fit in my lecture scheme nor whether it was important enough to take on.

My student thanked me for talking, left, and went on with the rest of her day.

I turned to my teaching assistants. Undergraduates as teaching assistants is one of my innovations for teaching my one-of-its-kind "Interdependence and Race" class. That course is a very challenging course because it digs into a topic that is so highly volatile in America: neo-diversity. Neo-diversity is the modern interpersonal situation of America where we all have to encounter and interact with people not like us on some group dimension (e.g., gender identity, religion, bodily condition, race, mental health condition, ethnicity, or sexual orientation). A central concern of the course is the why and how neo-diversity can create anxiety during a social interaction and cause interpersonal problems.

My undergraduate teaching assistants help me in many ways, in particular by observing the classroom group dynamic, especially on days when we had open discussions or when the lecture material is particularly intense (e.g., the lecture on racial slurs). Some semesters they also help me finely tune (add, subtract material from) my lectures to fit with what is going in the psychology of students in our class and/or on our campus that semester or year. My teaching assistants introduce me to inside information I cannot get without our conversations.

Spring 2019, when I asked my teaching assistants for their thoughts about the mental-health-condition question, both became pensive. Catherine, a self-described "strong Southern white woman" from Mt. Airy, NC, and Ziyere, a tall, dark-skinned African American male from the state of New York and a self-described introvert, each hesitated to think about the question. Eventually, each in their own way said they thought this was important to include in a lecture somewhere. Lo and behold, our conversation reminded me of a paper written by a student in an earlier semester. Suddenly I could see where to put the potential interpersonal dynamics of a mental-health-reveal into one of my lectures.

Through that conversation with my teaching assistants and my remembering a particular student's story, I had found a way and a place to talk about the potential neo-diversity anxiety, intergroup dynamics of a mental-health-condition reveal. I would talk about the potential dynamics of a mental-health-reveal moment in one of the upcoming lectures on language communities.

Language communities as a topic has to do with how we talk to each other from the standpoint of having different group experiences and language norms. One of the keys to productive interpersonal (and intergroup) dialogues is partner responsiveness; engaging in honest self-disclosure *and receiving a response from your interaction partner that seems to show understanding, validation, and caring.* To develop healthy relationships, this partner-responsiveness must be mutual.[1]

Turns out one of the challenges of neo-diversity is to interact with people "…not like you" and respond to those person's stories with interpersonal respect and with partner-responsiveness. Too often today in neo-diversity interactions, trapped inside their own language community, people respond with culture-centric negative social judgements: My group's way is the only way.

Now I had a way to talk about the moment of a mental-health-condition reveal and show how that moment could become an in-group, outgroup moment. You see, the semester before, one of my students had written their story of such a moment going bad. She wrote:

> In the fall of my freshman year of college, I was severely depressed. That December, I made an attempt on my life.
>
> The week I returned home from the emergency room, my best friend "B" drove over to hang out with me, since my mother didn't exactly trust me to leave the house, or be left alone at the time. He knew the gist of what had happened, but upon arriving to my house, I explained the situation further.

Let us note here that this is an incredibly intimate, honest self-disclosure. Our writer did so by trusting her best friend. Continuing with her story, she wrote:

> When I had finally gotten my story out to the one person I trusted more than anyone, he repetitively told me how disappointed he was in me. He said that my decision was selfish and stupid and that nothing in life could be so terrible.
>
> He did not understand my situation, or my depression. Lucky for him, he had never suffered from intense trauma or a mental health disorder.
>
> I tried to explain that there was a chemical imbalance in my brain, appeal to the science side of things. I thought science couldn't possibly be seen as subjective. I became emotional, and upon realizing how much he had upset me, he apologized. We watched a movie and chose not to discuss it anymore.

Not only was there no partner-responsiveness from her "best friend," his reaction to her mental-health-reveal was interpersonally brutal and demeaning. That had a powerful effect on our writer. Going on with her story, she describes the personal effect of this heartless interpersonal interaction with a "friend." She said this:

> The scars on my left arm serve as a constant reminder of the lack of understanding of mental health disorders. After this reaction, *I became closed off about what had happened.* I was hurt by my friend's reaction, and did not want to subject myself to that kind of scolding again.
>
> I knew that it was not my fault, and that I did not have a reason to be embarrassed. But *I chose not to*

share my story with others because I was unsure of how
to approach the situation in a way that could help others
learn about mental health.

In a moment of trusting vulnerability, this young person struggling with a mental-health-condition found themselves face-to-face with hibernating bigotry. Hibernating bigotry is bigotry that sleeps until the right stimulus comes along to wake it up, and then it awakens with a roar[2]:

He said that my decision was *selfish and stupid* and
that *nothing in life could be so terrible.*

Today, in a neo-diverse interaction, too often people respond with culture-centric negative social judgements that stop communication and relationship development and feelings of belongingness. When I used this story in lecture to talk about the challenge of mental-health-condition neo-diversity interpersonal interactions, my students went stiff and wide-eyed.

In that (newish) lecture I said, "You see, even a reveal of a mental-health-condition can activate an in-group, outgroup dynamic. Just in the same way as other neo-diversity (female, male; Muslim, Christian) interaction moments."

What made it intergroup? Our writer said it this way: "He did not understand my situation, or my depression. Lucky for him, *he had never suffered from intense trauma or a mental health disorder.*"

Immediately my students recognized how this mental-health-condition reveal reaction was an intergroup dynamic. Also, with their non-verbal behavior, many of my students seemed to be showing me and my teaching assistants that this was another one they had participated in some time in their past, directly or indirectly. A feeling of guilt seemed to fill the lecture hall.

I have learned to listen to and take seriously my students' comments and concerns. Even when I resist at first, I give it thought. This time with a push from my undergraduate teaching assistants, I revised a lecture. Doing so was educational for me and most importantly for my students. Now my students have a sense of how easily trust in a friend can be betrayed when it activates hibernating bigotry about mental-health-conditions.

For a variety of reasons, mental-health-conditions (e.g., anxiety, suicidal thoughts) are on the rise among young people. When those young people reach out for support from family and friends, the last thing they need or can cope with is for that interaction moment to become us-versus-them and they find themselves berated by a "friend" for the fact that they are struggling.

18: Float Like a Butterfly, Sting Like A...

Racial profiling we've heard of. You know, "driving while black."
Name profiling?

Stereotypes allow us to "...keep it simple." In ordinary times, we have the tendency to "...keep it simple." Instability in times of dramatic social change intensifies that tendency. In such times, we are especially prone to rely on stereotypes.

Like now.

We have gone from a segregated society to a neo-diverse society. In our struggle with that neo-diversity, too often to answer the question "...who are the 'we' and who are among the 'they?'" we rely on illusory correlations.[1] We give our children the impression that you can use a name to identify who might be a terrorist.

We are not preparing our children to live in 21st century, neo-diverse America. Far from it. We are teaching our children to resist the presence of neo-diversity in their individual everyday lives.

Back in 2009, I was invited to make a presentation to the 8th grade language arts classes at East Lee County Middle School in Sanford, NC. I have been a college professor for just at 30 years. I have no experience dealing with 8th graders in a classroom. Still, I was intrigued because I was told by the teacher that he had them reading *To Kill a Mockingbird* and Tim Tyson's *Blood Done Sign My Name* (a historical-memoir I have my college students read). And given that I had been working with the Sanford One-by-One race-relations community action group, I also thought this might be a good way for me to learn more about the social contexts and neo-diversity, inter-group dynamics of Sanford, NC.

I said yes to the invitation.

College students tell me that I am intimidating. Well, I am who I am as a professor and lecturer because of my Navy training as a Racial Awareness Group Facilitator. I have a certain style that includes coming on strong. Honed over the years, even when I challenge an audience I have ways of opening up the audience to dialogue.

I got those 8th graders talking. We had a lively discussion of what the experience of feeling nervous is like. When they told me about their own experiences, one of the kids said that being nervous makes people "…act goofy."

I really liked that. From that point on, in all my presentations about neo-diversity I say that neo-diversity anxiety "…makes people act goofy."

Yes, those 8th graders were intimidated by me at first. I still brought them into an honest conversation about their experiences with the neo-diversity of our time. I saw real evidence of our truthful dialogue in the written comments those 8th graders wrote about our time together in a letter their teacher sent to me later. One student wrote:

> "I loved the way you introduced the concept of confu-
> sion in the world, as far as racism goes."

Another wrote:

> "It helps to know that to not show prejudice to people
> we meet that we should…relax and not assume and
> set the conversation 'on fire.'"

Neo-diversity tensions are alive even in what appears to be a sleepy county middle school. I learned that even in middle school, some of the young people are encountering and struggling to manage intolerance and bigotry. One of the 8th graders wrote:

> "Thank you for your powerful lecture. I liked the way
> you talked about the way people judge one another
> without knowing them."

Eighth graders, yes, but already showing concern, not just about intolerance aimed at their own individuality, but about language bigotry from within their own group that is aimed outward at other groups. I had confirmed what I have been teaching my college students. In the age of neo-diversity, there are no innocent.

It was a good time. Not just fun. That racial, ethnic, and gender mixed group of very young people opened up to me. They let me in on their own anxieties about interacting with people who do not look like them. When I mentioned that at North Carolina State University we have American-Muslim female students who wear hijabs, an African American female student blurted out, "…oh they scare me."

Stereotypes are how we create monsters for our children.

Today in America we have created a social environment in which to be an American-Muslim means to some that you are not American. I say that not just because Dr. Ben Carson, a one-time presidential candidate, says that no Muslim should ever be allowed to be our president. Another early 2016 candidate was asked "…I want to know how we can get rid of them (i.e., Muslims)."

I am concerned because we are teaching our children that we can judge a person's Americanism by their religion. We are teaching our children to live by what social psychologists call an illusory correlation – a belief that two things are connected when, in fact, they are not.

As his most intense interpersonal-intergroup experience, for that writing assignment one of my college students reported this story:

> A month ago I went to my girlfriend's parents' house
> in Charlotte for the Labor Day weekend. Her family is very involved at their church, and they invited

me to help out with Sunday school. It was there – Sunday school, of all places – that I experienced the most curious interracial, dyadic interaction of my life. Here's what happened:

The lesson of the day was not to be quick to judge. We had the kids' play a game where we told them to draw something and then they would draw it and the rest of the kids had to try and guess what was drawn. Every time the kids would guess wrong, we would step in and note, "See? Judging quickly doesn't work!"

The first kid – the youngest of the group, aged five – drew Michael Jordan, and then the rest of the kids – mostly six or seven – guessed correctly who it was, relatively quickly. After three or four more kids had gone up, a boy named Cameron came up to draw his. I whispered into his ear who he was supposed to draw. He went to the back of the room, took a couple of minutes to paint his masterpiece, then returned and held his picture up for everyone to see.

The picture he had drawn was that of a gun-toting terrorist. The man had a turban, a cigarette in his mouth, and a machine gun spewing bullets in each hand. Immediately my girlfriend took the page from Cameron and said, "Cameron, that's inappropriate!"

I went up to Cameron and asked, "Cameron, why did you draw that?"

Cameron, replied, "I saw the name and I thought he was a terrorist!"

I told Cameron immediately, "Cameron that is the

most common name in the world. Not everyone with that name is a terrorist. You can't assume what people are from their name."

Cameron nodded and ran off. My girlfriend approached me and asked, "Who was he supposed to draw?"

I looked at her and revealed, "Muhammad Ali".

Stereotypes are how we dehumanize and demonize people.

Back in my day, when we heard the name "Muhammad Ali" we immediately yelled out "…float like a butterfly, sting like a bee." Now, apparently, the name means "…float like a butterfly, sting like a terrorist." We have to do better than that. Directly or indirectly we are teaching our children to judge people by the language of their names. That is a dangerous and illusory correlation.

19: Hanks Memorandum

I am a news hound and cultural observer. I read newspapers and scan news websites to keep up with news of current events and to observe cultural trends and individual missteps that are going on in the midst of all the social change our nation is experiencing.

On a typical scanning mission, I came across a website headline that stopped me from going further: "Tom Hanks' son defends using the N-word."[1] I read the short piece. After, I pulled out pen and paper and wrote, then typed, and posted a letter to Mr. Chet Hanks on my Psychology Today blog:

To: Chet (son of Tom) Hanks

From: Dr. Rupert Nacoste

Re: nigger

Dear Mr. Hanks,

What is so attractive to young white people about being able to use the racial slur "nigger"? I have had many white college students tell me that they hear the n-word used by their white peers over and over, every day. A white female in my "Interpersonal Relationships and Race" course told me, in private, that it makes her angry that she can't use the word when black people do it all the time. More in the public eye, you, an attention getting young white man, tried to defend your use of the racial slur nigger. You said, the word can be used with affection. You said, the word "…is not just for black people."

To me, this sounds like little children who don't want to have any restrictions put on their behavior. "I should be able to say or do whatever I want. I mean look… they are doing it, why can't I, Mommy?"

Well listen up, no matter whose mouth it comes out of, "nigger" is a derogatory, demeaning, dehumanizing characterization of the whole of black America. Yes, I do mean to say that black people who call each other, or anyone else "nigger," are demeaning their own group. "My nigga" is not affectionate. What it says is "I own you like a slave"; after all, you are "…My nigga." Use of the word is the epitome of racial bigotry (group prejudice expressed in word or deed).

In trying to mount your defense, you Chet (son of Tom) Hanks actually said, "I know the majority of ya'll are not gonna get this, because the history is so fresh in our country. But hip hop is not about race."[1]

Wow… so there is nothing racial about hip-hop? Even if a person was naïve enough to believe that, the question is not about hip-hop, but about the apparent great desire to say "…nigger" out loud.

I have to ask, Mr. Hanks, why is that so intense a desire? Why is your apparent need to use the word so great that you try to push pass the real truth that, as you say, America's racial history "…is still so fresh in our country." Understand this: language bigotry is rooted in group fear, resentment, hate and the desire to control 'them.' Whether it's racial (nigger), gender (bitch, slut), mental-health-condition (retard), sexual orientation (faggot, dyke), or religious (raghead, sand-nigger), ethnic (guinea, grease-ball), that language is bigotry. Whether the person using those words knows the history is irrelevant. The history of us versus them is always attached to those words.

No one can talk their way out of that social reality. No one can talk their way out of that intended group-division and hierarchy pushed by the language bigotry since that language bigotry is intended to support an "us versus them" way of thinking, feeling and behaving. There are no innocent group slurs. None are innocent or affectionate; no matter whose mouth the slur comes out of.

Ask yourself, Mr. Hanks, what is really motivating your apparent intense desire to use a word designed to support and promote the ideology of white supremacy? Is it really, as you claim, about uplifting black culture? Or is it just a guilty pleasure; a way to be able to imply that "I am still better than them"?

By your own words, Mr. Hanks, you know something about America's racial history. Given that, what is the root of your desire to proclaim the word nigger; a word you know to be rooted in the belief in white racial supremacy? Is it just because you haven't grown up enough to understand that knowing some of the truth of America's ugly, violent and still fresh racial history puts you in a position to fight for or against the perpetuation of that history? Do you actually mean to choose to perpetuate that demeaning history?

Tell us, what is really going on?

Sincerely, with questions,
Rupert W. Nacoste, Ph.D.

20: No Escaping the Othering-Hate and Dehumanizing Putdown

Language is the toughest part of my "Interpersonal Relationships and Race" course. It's that tough because that is where there are so many false claims being made that lets group hate live and thrive in America. Anti-groups slurs, racial slurs, gender slurs, all that. Toward the end of each semester in that class, I address the toughest of the toughest part, the use of the racial slur "nigger."

Today, rightly so, many people recoil from the word. But we also live in a time when people have fooled themselves into believing if you spell the word with a "...ga" rather than a "...ger" it's not the same word.

For those who don't know, there have always been whites who have refused to say the word "...nigger" in the raw. Not because they believed in the humanity of the enslaved Africans or more modern-day black people. No, aristocratic whites just felt they were too genteel to talk about blacks in such a raw, hateful way. To get around debasing themselves by being so vulgar, rather than say "nigger" outright, they said "nig-grahs" as in "...those poor, filthy nig-grahs just can't help themselves. Nig-grahs will always be nig-grahs."

Did that different pronunciation, did that different spelling, change the meaning of the word? No, not at all. Today, spelling or saying it as "...nigga" also does not change the original meaning nor the original intent of the word to dehumanize and look down upon. No matter who says it, no matter the skin color of who says it, and no matter how it is spelled or pronounced, to call anyone a nigger is to look down upon that individual as less than human.

Too many African American students are stunned by this part of that lecture. Stunned because they have been lulled into a hazy belief that it is OK for them and their black friends to call each other nigga affectionately. You know, "My nigga."

After my lecture in Spring 2016, I got an email from a black student in the class. That student wrote:

> Hello Dr. Nacoste: After looking over my notes from today's class period, I have a question for you. You told us that language has history in a group or society and all members carry it around. This made me think of how the n-word is used in the black community. Most black people know the history and roots of the word, but still continue to use it. Some try to justify it by saying "nigga" instead of nigger, however it's the same concept, right?
>
> So, my question is: what are your thoughts, as the expert, on why black people feel that it's okay to use the word between themselves, but get upset when white people use it? I've even seen instances when a Hispanic or Asian say "nigga" and it's accepted; never when a white person says it.

I replied by saying:

> You have asked a very important question. Although I will address this question in lecture, here is a brief look at what I will say.
>
> One, you are right, it is the *same* concept; somebody is better, more human, than somebody else by race.

Two, black people who use it claim they are taking the power of the word away from whites. Those black people fail to see that the meaning of the word stays the same until, of course, a white person uses it and all hell breaks loose. In that moment it is clear the word still has the same old power of racial put-down.

Three, those black people also fail to see that they are actually using the word the same way; as a racial put-down. To say to another black person, "You are *my* nigger" is to say, "I *own* you like a slave." It's not affectionate, it is dehumanizing of people of your own race and racial history.

That is why the claim of affection fails. And you should ask those black people why they want so badly to use the word anyway. African Americans know the history of the use of the word, so what makes it so attractive that some black people insist on using it? What's really going on?

In the '60s, to show pride in and affection to one another as members of the same racial group, we started calling each other "Brother" and "Sister." We young black people were also adamant about not calling each other nigger. We challenged any black person, and anyone else, who tried to get away with using the word nigger to talk to, or about, our "Brothers and Sisters."

We began to live what James Brown sang: "Say it loud...I'm black and I'm proud." You cannot live that calling each other niggers, however you spell it. You cannot live "...black lives matter," calling each other niggers, however you spell it.

"Respect yourself" is the way The Staple Singers sang it.

Respect yourself.

21: Jokes and Pokes About Other Folks

"What do you tell a woman with two black eyes?"

That's the first line of a 'joke.'

Joking is a social interaction strategy that people use to do a variety of things. Sure, even Freud would say that sometimes a joke is just a joke. I, myself, love punctuation jokes.

"A panda bear walks into a bar. Eats, shoots and leaves."

Yes, sometimes a joke is just a joke.

Even so, sometimes a joke is used in an attempt to reduce interpersonal tension between people who are interacting with each other. Sometimes, too, a joke or a costume is used to make a social commentary. In 21st century America, interpersonal tension and social comment are both often motivated by neo-diversity anxiety. Neo-diversity is the interpersonal situation all Americans now live in; a situation where every day we all have encounters (and sometimes interactions) with people from many different groups by way of sex, bodily condition, gender identity, ethnicity, sexual orientation, mental health condition, religion, and race. For some that situation brings out a neo-diversity anxiety that activates prejudice and bigotry.

Since 2008 and the election of President Barack Hussein Obama, in America we have had too many instances of racial or religious or gender bigotry go viral. I truly believe that most of us want to interact well with the people who come into our social circles of work or play. Although there is prejudice and bigotry in America, I do not believe we are a nation of bigots. But some Americans haven't figured out what it means to be living in the 21st century. Some actually think it means "I can joke however I want" until they crash into reality, sometimes with a really loud (social media) bang.

Hoisted on their own Facebook, Twitter, Instagram, or Snapchat posts, the perpetrators always claim, "We were just kidding. It was just a joke." But here's the thing: Nowadays, and too often, a joke is used to try to camouflage anti-group feelings (i.e., prejudice).

####

"I take no joy in saying this"

"In the real world"

"That's one point of view"

I had put out a call on Facebook. Here is the call:

Jokes and Pokes About Other Folks: Fighting For The Soul of America; right now, that is the tentative title of the book I will be working on in Summer-2016. For that project, I am looking for examples of how people try to hide their group prejudice and bigotry in a so-called joke or poke.

At present, I am particularly interested in finding examples of the lead-in to a "joke or poke" about other folks; about "them." No one will say those kinds of things in interactions with me. That is why I need your help. Send me examples of a lead-in that you have heard used. Do not restrict your thinking about this to any one type of group. I am interested in these jokes and pokes about a neo-diversity of groups. Classic is "…not to be racist, but…" I'd really appreciate receiving any examples you have heard used of that kind of lead-in to a "joke or poke" about any group. Thanks.

From that post, I started to get responses.
"I probably shouldn't say this"

"Don't misunderstand"

"What is it they say?"

"You may not agree"

Those are examples of lead-ins to bigoted statements that people gave me. Others, of course, had to do with the "political correctness" excuse:

"I know the PC police will get me, but…"

"I know it's not PC these days to say it, but…"

"It may be anti-PC, but…"

As a dodge from being called-out as a bigot, we all know that the "too much political correctness" excuse is in widespread use. Did you know, though, that the overuse of that excuse in social interaction is so rampant that even "Miss Manners" has been asked about its legitimacy? [1]

To that letter writer, about the political correctness gambit, Miss Manners said a number of things that stood out to me, but it boiled down to this. Trying to use the claim of bucking political correctness as a shield against having one's language behavior being identified as bigotry does not make what anyone says less than "nasty," according to Miss Manners. Quite to the point, too, was her telling the letter writer and us that in social interaction we should just listen to the words uttered and judge the words, even for, maybe especially for, political candidates.

The white man who sent me the PC examples also

made that point. He wrote:

Even people running for President can say something hurtful with that lead in. On the internet people hide behind the phrase "offended" as in "someone will get offended, but I am going to say it anyhow..." Taking offense to something means you don't have thick enough skin for the internet. And the follow up is always "this is why we can't have nice things" (because I can't make a "...it's just a joke" about rape without someone getting offended).

In my Facebook call, I said that I was also interested in "pokes," a vaguely anti-group comment followed by something like "...oh, just kidding."

One former North Carolina State University student of mine wrote to say:

As an Arab-American who chooses to branch out of the Arab community I have come across so many of the jokes that poke fun of this racial/ethnic group. On more than one occasion I have been asked in a joking manner "so you're not a terrorist, are you?" When asked this question I pause for a moment. During this pause, I think the other person who asked the question realizes that I am actually offended and then comes the *"I'm only kidding!"*

Definitely a poke.

Another former NCSU student, a black male, wrote to tell me about the identity-pokes he gets because of his light skin color. He wrote that people try to hide their 'concern' this way:

"Pardon me for asking/excuse my curiosity...but what are you mixed with?"

"Or where are you from?"

"Or sometimes, the straight up 'What are you?'"

On social media people use versions of this joking and poking as well. One current student responded to my call with a query. She wrote:

> "I've been thinking about when groups make jokes and pokes about their own groups that further stereotypes. Something like, 'I can say this derogatory thing because I belong to this group.'"

Yes, indeed, those are pokes. And pokes are destructive no matter who mouths or posts them. Destructive how, you ask?

Another former student wrote to talk about how she was pushed by others' stereotypes to speak against her own racial group. She said:

> I can remember times in middle school and high school where I began to internalize the hate for the Arab race. This manifested in me being the one to throw out the racist Arab terrorist jokes. I wanted to beat everyone to the punch line and prove to everyone that indeed I was not a terrorist, nor did I belong to 'them.'

One Facebook request and I got all those different versions of "jokes and pokes." Sure, in the past some students in my "Interdependence and Race" course had written about "jokes and pokes" in their papers. But with my Facebook request, I reached beyond the college classroom and campus and found people who were quite willing to let it be known that they had been experiencing this "joke and poke" style of social interaction.

Pervasive. Lots of people try to hide and camouflage their anti-group feelings about other Americans by using a 'joke.' Not innocent or funny, the prevalence of this strategy is a reflection of the neo-diversity anxieties gripping and squeezing our everyday social interactions. A real problem that is because our everyday social interactions are the fabric of our lives. Joking and poking, we go along ripping at that fabric and tearing at the soul of America while in camouflage.

Camouflage does not eliminate the bigotry of the 'joke.' Outward, behavioral (word or deed) expression of anti-group feelings is bigotry. No matter how it is dressed, bigotry is still bigotry.

Understand, too, that the point of that bigotry is to push group division: us versus them. Jokes about groups activate that minimal group effect—automatic categorization of people into groups with a tendency to see those groups as being in competition with each other.[2]

How do you think we ended up in North Carolina's Research Triangle with the prejudice-motivated, bigoted murders of our three American Muslim students? How did we end up in the United States with the murders of nine Bible-studying African Americans in a church? How?

We have been too passive in our encounters with language bigotry in our everyday lives. "It's just a joke," people say, and we take it as so. "Oh, they don't really mean that, they're just joking" we say to ourselves and others to let it pass.

Remember, we heard that echoed after that mass murder in Charleston, South Carolina. Friends of the now confessed, not crazy, premeditated killer of those nine people were interviewed. His friends said, "Yeah, he used to say some racial things ... make some racist jokes... but nobody took him seriously ... we thought it was just jokes, but now..."

After that horror in Charleston, SC, I posted an essay on my Psychology Today blog: "After Charleston, What Now? Stop tolerating intolerance." Discovered by Lisa Capobianco of Southington, CT, my essay provoked thoughts that she put into a column for her local newspaper. Lisa wrote[3]:

Guinea. Ginzo. Greaseball. Those are just three

derogatory names I have heard to describe Italian Americans, and even though no one has ever actually called me any of those names directly, just the sight of those words hurt.

Growing up in a neighborhood with mostly Irish and French families during the 1930s, my paternal grandmother was called a "guinea" by many of her peers who were not Italian. As a child, my grandma also was teased for the color of her skin, especially when her skin turned brown during the summer. I also think being teased for her olive skin tone played a role in my grandma's desire to bleach her skin white, which she attempted to do so many times, she admitted to me over the years.

That piece of my grandma's history has stuck with me throughout my life. Today it still surprises me how even though my grandmother was Caucasian like her French and Irish neighbors, she was made fun of by other children just because she looked "different."

We've all heard or encountered slurs and/or expressions that stereotype different racial and ethnic groups in our country. Although those children in my grandma's neighborhood may have intended to use the word "guinea" as "just a joke," should we as Americans tolerate those kinds of words in everyday language as "just a joke?"

I read an interesting article recently on Psychology Today's website by Professor Dr. Rupert Nacoste, [where he] explores how so many incidents of racial violence erupted in our nation over the last year, such as the mass shooting at a historic African American church in Charleston, South Carolina. In his essay, Nacoste makes a point I think we should all take to heart: "We, as individual citizens of this nation, have been too passive in our encounters with language bigotry in our everyday lives."

When people say, "it's just a joke," we often conclude that they really don't mean it, and we should just let the word fly off our shoulders. But doesn't the use of racial/ethnic slurs or expressions in our everyday conversations allow intolerance to persist?

People might hear my last name and say while chuckling, "Wow, you have a real 'guinea' last name." It might just be a joke for some people, but that word still has a hostile connotation, given my family's encounter with the word. It separates Italians from non-Italians, placing them in a different category. It promotes the mentality, "us" vs. "the other." The same goes for other ethnic and racial groups who have experienced other words or expressions throughout history.

It is time to start reflecting on the way we treat people in different racial and ethnic groups. We need to think about the language we use when referring to these groups, and the real meaning behind that language. Most of all, we need to start challenging ourselves to find ways to break barriers, such as speaking up when we hear a racial or ethnic slur being used."

Clearly, Ms. Capobianco got it.
An Italian joke is not just a joke, it is divisive and hurtful.

A blonde joke is not just a joke, it is divisive and hurtful.

A joke about women is not just a joke, it is divisive and hurtful.

A joke about violence against women is more than divisive and hurtful, it is demeaning and dangerous. With good reason, you might wonder, though, who would joke about violence against women. Turns out far too many college males think those jokes are funny. And not only do some college males think such jokes are funny, they are so confident that these jokes are acceptable they will tell such a joke to a female classmate. A female student in my "Interpersonal Relationships and Race" course wrote a paper about the time a male classmate told her a 'joke.' She wrote:

> In this particular class, there was one guy that I got to know pretty well, but it was strictly a classroom inter-personal relationship. To elaborate, we joked around a lot, but… one moment in particular caught me way off guard and to this day I am a little frustrated with my own response of laughing in an effort not to seem uptight. But let me tell you about the interaction …
>
> I can't remember why the class was so relaxed that day, I think we had just gotten back a test and we were waiting to go over the answers. This young man made a comment about something (to this day I still don't know what he said) and I couldn't hear him. After asking him twice what he said, he looked at me and asked, "…what do you tell a woman with two black eyes?" My response, simply enough, "…um … I don't know, what?" "Nothing, you already told her twice," and then he laughed to my face, as it turned red from embarrassment.

How could a college-educated male, how could any mature male think this was funny and acceptable enough tell a female peer? For that matter, how could any adult think this was funny and acceptable to tell anyone, woman or not? This is a more general problem than we have been willing to acknowledge. Consider the Sigma Nu fraternity at Old Dominion University.[4]

For the first day of the new semester, members of the fraternity hung giant welcome signs outside their private house where some resided. The signs of welcome were directed at incoming female students and their mothers saying:

"Rowdy and fun, hope your baby girl is ready for a good time."

"Freshman Daughter Drop Off."

"Go ahead and Drop Off Mom Too."

Many on the campus and in the nation were offended. Implied was the belief that women are only good for one thing. That group prejudice showed clear in the gender bigotry of those "…welcome" signs. Yet, some thought "Come on it's just a joke." One online commentator said:

> "These are hilarious, it's what happens in college and people just need to chill out. I can't believe they suspended the fraternity for this."

Official reactions, though, were right to be swift and condemning. Not surprising given the real concerns universities have about sexual assaults on campuses, concerns about what some call a "…rape culture." John R. Broderick, President of Old Dominion used his Facebook page to begin addressing the campus. He wrote:

> I am outraged about the offensive message directed toward women that was visible for a time on 43rd Street. Our students, campus community and alumni have been offended.

> While we constantly educate students, faculty and staff about sexual assault and sexual harassment, this incident confirms our collective efforts are still failing

to register with some.

A young lady I talked to earlier today courageously
described the true meaning of the hurt this caused.
She thought seriously about going back home.

Camouflaged or not, these kinds of demeaning jokes about groups
have real social impact on our peer citizens. Too many of us think we
should be able to say what we want, when we want, to whom we want,
especially if what is said is camouflaged as a joke. What that misses is
that in America today the camouflage is easy to see through.

We no longer live in an America where anyone can just say anything about anybody and go unchallenged. When Americans did live
in that kind of situation, it was because our country was living under
the wrong-headed belief, and with an immoral supporting social
structure, that made some groups less than other groups.

Women were less than men… *in the law.*

Blacks were less than whites… *in the law.*

Homosexuals were less than heterosexuals… *in the law.*

Through legitimate means, America got rid of and continues to
get rid of those laws (and customs). As a result, we are no longer
living separate from each other. Americans from all kinds of groups
are interacting with each other every day on equal footing, supported
by new legal statutes that give us equal-citizenship-under-the-law.
Moving into the light of the 21st century, the context of American
interpersonal life has been changed in fundamental ways as we move
toward a more perfect union. And we are not going to go back into
the darkness where camouflage can work.

We are not going back.

And that's no joke.

22: They Have Feelings Too? Really?

At the end of a semester of teaching, I always have things to ponder. Fall 2015 semester, I was reflecting on a theme that jumped out at me from the one-new-thought papers my students had written in my sophomore level course "Introduction to Social Psychology." From the beginning to the end of that course, I use social psychology to describe and explain the causes of relationship development, maintenance, and failure.

To focus their end of term papers, I ask students to describe the one-new-thought about interpersonal relationships they have had as a result of taking the course with me. I read all 200 of the one-page papers, and from them I pull quotes that I turn into my "Young Love" lecture. That is the last formal lecture I give to every class.

Having gone through that process at the end of the Fall 2015 semester, I sat at my desk editing and cleaning the lecture document. I do this to turn the document file into a PDF that I send to my students as an end of the class parting gift. Looking the "Young Love" lecture over one more time, I was quite struck, again, by the number of papers that had to do with the "theory of mind." For a person to have a "theory-of-mind" means the person is aware of and thinks about the fact that other people have thoughts, feelings, and preferences, too.

For far too many of my students, that was a new thought. It was a revelation to too many of my Fall 2015 students that other people have thoughts, preferences, and feelings, too. One student wrote:

> Sometimes…it is easy to forget about the other person's thoughts and feelings and get carried away in your own emotions. Now I can see that understanding the theory of mind has enhanced my thinking when it comes to interpersonal conflict. I have to understand that people on the other side of that tension have feelings too.

Imagine that, and then think about what that means.

College students' intergroup behaviors these days are loud and dreadful. Jokes about a person's sex, bodily condition, gender identity, race, religion, mental health condition, or sexual orientation, those kinds of jokes are told by college students with a shocking casualness. Halloween has become a 'celebration' used to mock, to make fun of 'them.' But the students making the jokes, wearing black face, or wearing fake mustaches and sombreros, are caught off guard when strong objections come their way.

Why? Well it never occurred to them that other people would not see and interpret their actions the same way they do – as harmless, "what's the big deal," fun. "Surely," they seem to think, "…everyone sees the world the way I see the world."

Yes, the jokes and costumes are forms of bigotry, yet not always bigotry rooted only in anti-group prejudice; bigotry sometimes rooted in an immature theory-of-mind. Or bigotry rooted in a theory-of-mind that does not include the perspective of people not in 'my' group. Imagine being that oblivious to all the neo-diversity around you. Imagine that.

In neo-diverse America, a theory-of-mind that does not attempt to include the perspective of people not 'like me' is faulty and maladaptive. To always default to 'people like me' is why we get so many angry protestations about political correctness. For a person whose theory-of-mind has 'people like me' as the default means for that person, having to take account of the thoughts, feelings, and preferences of 'them' takes too much effort. In fact, it's not even considered to be legitimate. With that one-group theory-of-mind, the thoughts, feelings, and preferences of 'those others' are not real, not authentic, and maybe not human.

"The only reason I have to watch my language is all this political correctness bull."

Too immature, sad, and dangerous, yet all is not lost. Once they have learned the theory-of-mind concept, my mostly 19 and 20-year-old sophomore students come to realize it's not about political correctness but about respect. One wrote:

> One concept from the course that goes hand-in-hand with Dr. Nacoste's phrase "people do not just spring into existence just because you get interested" is the concept of the theory of mind. Though both of these may seem like common sense ideas that everyone should know, I believe that many people do not quite grasp these concepts.

> If more people would attempt to understand these two ideas, they would realize that other humans are just like them; human. I know that since understanding these two concepts my interactions have been enhanced. I now understand that the person looking back at me is just a person like me.

Do notice the realization that a more inclusive theory-of-mind is something for the person to work on, to develop in order to live well in our neo-diverse world. Too many Americans are fighting against that self-development by railing against perceived "...political correctness." About that one student wrote:

The theory-of-mind definition has helped me to better acknowledge where people come from and to be accepting of people for who they are. Knowing about the theory-of-mind will help me better understand the new people I meet. Instead of getting frustrated with them or cutting myself off from them, I will try to understand their beliefs and desires.

Clearly not about political correctness. That is about having a theory-of-mind in line with our neo-diverse nation (and world).

One mistake people are making today is the mistake of believing that adjustment to university life is easy. Truth is, modern university life is filled with situations in which young people have no choice but to encounter a rambunctious, neo-diverse mix of other humans by way race, religion, sex-of-person, mental health condition, ethnicity, gender identity, bodily condition, sexual orientation, and age. Yet no one prepares young people for the day-to-day encounters they must have with neo-diversity, and that lack of preparation puts them in situations they find anxiety provoking.

About that, one of my students wrote:

> While listening to our lecture about neo-diversity, I realized that there are so many other groups besides race that you can be socially unfamiliar with, creating multiple situations of neo-diversity anxiety. I also realized that I have been mistaking the idea of being accepting of cultural diversity with empathy when it comes to my personal qualities.

> What creates the difference is that I don't interact with many people or groups of people I am unfamiliar with. I'm not prejudiced against these groups of people but I have neo-diversity anxiety. In my lifetime I haven't been exposed to a lot of different

groups of people who I encounter at this university. Due to this I don't know how to interact with people extremely different from me or what I am used to. As a result, I tend to unintentionally avoid those who I don't know how to interact with.

I never realized that I did this until our lecture on neo-diversity.

All is not lost. Coming to realize what is really going on gives a person the opportunity for self-development; to work on expanding their theory-of-mind. One of my students wrote:

Dr. Nacoste, what you said in lecture about neo-diversity anxiety genuinely enlightened me. Your words reminded me that we are all people. We are just people. At the end of the day, nobody is better than anybody. The idea that we all are longing to connect with people and belong shows that there is no reason to be afraid of anybody, because we are going to miss out on opportunities if we all shy away from each other.

When neo-diversity anxiety starts to rise up in you, I tell my students, just remember that this person who does not look like, sound like, or believe "like you" is just another student; just another human being. To be able to do that, though, my students have to work on developing a theory-of-mind that gives respect to the humanity of those other people who also have thoughts, feelings, and preferences. It is my belief that all Americans need to work on developing that mature quality in their own theory-of-mind.

23. Paris? Come On, What About Black People in America?

I was trained to be a social psychologist by Professor John Thibaut.[1] After serving in the Navy (1972-1976) and finishing my undergraduate Psychology degree at the University of Florida (1976-1978), I was admitted to the UNC Chapel Hill Social Psychology Graduate Program. I met John Thibaut on my visit to the UNC Chapel Hill to look over that program.

A white man, 5 feet 8 inches maybe, white haired, white goatee, in a suit with vest, a bow tie, smoking a cigarette in a cigarette holder, he looked up and offered me a genteel smile and a seat. His desk was slightly cluttered, but not overcome with papers. He sat in his chair, reclined back, and said,

"Tell me about yourself."

Quickly in the telling of my story, I came to my research on black student aspirations. My interest, I told Dr. Thibaut, was in black students' levels of aspirations for grades in a class. I told him of reading a paper by Kurt Lewin, Leon Festinger, and some other researchers on general levels of aspiration, and wondered if he knew anything about that research.[2]

"A little," he said. "It sounds to me, Rupert, that you have found something unique. I don't think Lewin had thought it might work that way."

There was something about the way he said the name Lewin that made me feel like Thibaut wasn't telling me all he knew about this research. Later, I would learn that at MIT this Thibaut guy had been one of the students of that Lewin guy. Kurt Lewin, the modern father of social psychology, had been his professor and Ph.D. advisor.

"Tell me about your last name, Rupert."

I started telling Dr. Thibaut of my Louisiana origins. I was telling him what I knew about the Creole origin of my...

"Do you speak French?"

"No, my parents used the Creole as a secret language. In our house they didn't spell words to hide the topic of conversation, they just changed the language."

"Yes, well..." he harrumphed. "You need to learn it to hold on to your heritage. So you will work on learning Creole-French..."

He said this in all seriousness with his genteel smile.

"Well," I said, "I'll see..."

"No, no. You must commit yourself to doing so."

Dr. Thibaut was standing up now and moving around his small office.

"Let's talk about the research you would do when you come here for graduate school."

Something important was happening and did happen in that meeting that day. When I walked out of John Thibaut's office, I knew I had met a man who was not only interested in my intellectual abilities, but in me as a person. It felt to me as if we were connected. Something had happened between us. We had laughed together.

I decided to do my graduate training at UNC Chapel Hill with Dr. John Thibaut as my major professor. Educationally I could not have asked for better. Interpersonally, with my almost daily conversations with John, it was an extraordinary experience.

Race became active in my relationship with John during the first seminar of graduate work I took with him. In his graduate seminar in which we were learning "Interdependence theory," we had just finished discussing Chapter 10, "Nonvoluntary Relationships: Frustration and Deprivation," of John's (and Harold Kelley's) book *The social psychology of groups*. As Thibaut & Kelley put it, the focus of that chapter is on "…nonvoluntary relationships which are those in which the person is forced to stay even though he would prefer not to. In terms of our analysis, the person remains in relationships of this sort only because heavy costs are in some manner associated with being in better ones."[3]

After our class meeting, as we got up to leave John called me to his office.

"Rupert, I was wondering how you felt about Chapter 10?"

"How I felt, Dr. Thibaut?"

"Yes, I was wondering how you felt about our use of the term 'Negro.'"

It was true. In Chapter 10 there were a number of spots where Thibaut & Kelley referred to "…the Negro" or "… the case of Negroes." In one of those spots, they wrote:

A person (for example, a Negro denied access to the community swimming pool) can devalue an unattainable relationship either by taking a "sour grapes" attitude toward the rewarding aspects of the interaction ("I don't get much fun out of swimming anyway") or by emphasizing the negative, cost-increasing aspects of it ("It's dangerous and takes a lot of time"). Both of these are greatly facilitated if he can control selectively the information or instigation he receives from the unattained state of affairs, keeping out evidence of pleasures that others receive and letting through evidence of high costs.[4]

"Did that offend you?"

"No, Dr. Thibaut, it didn't."

"Why not?"

Notice here that Dr. Thibaut could have let it drop. He didn't. He asked, "Why not?" John was not interested in a superficial, nice and non-threatening interaction about this racial matter. On his insistence, then, we had a real interaction-transition to work through, and it was a racial one between a white man and a black man.

When I said the use of the word "Negro" didn't bother me, John had asked, "Why not?"

"Well, because it was written when that was the accepted, respectful term. You didn't say 'colored.' And you wrote this is the '50s," I said.

"Yes… but it's out of date now."

"Yes, it is," I said. "But you're not writing that way now; you don't talk that way. Your point was analytical and the analysis was good."

"Thank you, Rupert."

"Sure, Dr. Thibaut."

John and I had encountered and managed an interaction-transition, a moment of interaction that has in it the potential for an interpersonal clash of preferences. In our then developing relationship, there would, of course, be more interaction-transitions to come. Nevertheless, from that point on, because of the fact that we managed that racial interaction-transition respecting each other, from that point on we could talk about race with openness with each other with frankness.

Over the years of my graduate training with him as my major professor and advisor, and into the years after I went on to start my career as a social psychologist, John Thibaut and I talked often in his office, and sometimes in his home. On my visits back to Chapel Hill, around town, walking to lunch, we were a striking sight, I am sure. John, this little white man, 5-foot-8, white hair with goatee, always a jacket and bow tie – me, a dark skinned, 6-foot-3, afro-haired giant. Anyone could see that we were good friends, especially since it was his preference that we now greet each other in the style of French men. I would step close and lean over for John to put a hand on each side of my face and lightly kiss me on each cheek.

John Thibaut was my teacher, mentor, and eventual friend. When John died in 1986, I felt a great loss. To this day, I miss my interdependence with him.

####

Through my time with John and his training me as a social psychologist, I learned to look at all human affairs with a focus on our social-interdependence. Originator of the theory of interdependence,[5] John said it this way: "People are interdependent and it is our interdependence that is the proper study of social psychology."

Other thinkers have also seen the core of our humanity that way. Preacher-poet John Donne (1572-1631) tried to help us understand the centrality of interdependence to our lives by saying and writing:

"No man is an island… any man's death diminishes me… for I am involved in mankind,

And therefore, never send to know for whom the bell tolls, it tolls for thee."[6]

Every semester I recite the whole poem to my social psychology classes. Students at North Carolina State University who have taken one or more of my classes know of my intense focus on our human-interdependence; that we are all involved in mankind. Even students who have only heard of me know that.

After the November 2015 coordinated terrorist attacks on Paris, through Facebook from an N.C. State alumnus who is black, I received this message and question:

> Dr. Nacoste, I have read/heard black students and professionals say that "I can't stand with France because there are issues impacting black students in America that people aren't talking about." Can you help me unpack this because I feel that lending support in a time of need doesn't mean I am standing down or not talking about from another issue of passion?

"Oh my…" was only the beginning of my response. I went on to say:

> One of the really unfortunate parts of the intergroup dynamic in America is the failure to see connections. Too many are seeing the world through a minimal-group, "…us-versus-them" lens. Too many are operating out of a "only people like me" theory-of-mind.

> "Any man's death diminishes me…"

> What was done in France was about bigotry against a people. To say that you cannot stand with others who are facing bigotry is to be a bigot. Martin Luther King Jr. said it best by saying:

> "Injustice anywhere is a threat to justice everywhere."

> Any time we do not speak out against injustice, we support an environment of injustice. In today's world where formerly, legally oppressed groups now have unprecedented opportunities to voice their indignation and objection to injustices aimed at their communities, it can be very tempting for members of

those groups to think that other injustices are less important. But the truth is that since these are human injustices, ignoring other people's pain, denying our human-interdependence, perpetuates environments of injustice. When we tell children that only "our" pain matters, we are telling them that other people are less than us. We teach children a theory-of-mind that says that people "not like us" are less than human. A moral judgment that anyone should be ashamed to make.

"Any man's death diminishes me…"

All that November 2015 weekend I felt pain for the people of Paris and the whole people of France. I felt and still feel indignation at this immoral, vicious attack on our humanity. Echoing Dr. King and John Donne, President Obama was right to say,

"Once again we've seen an outrageous attempt to terrorize innocent civilians. This is an attack not just on Paris, it's an attack not just on the people of France, *but this is an attack on all of humanity and the universal values that we share.*"

In the wake of the attack on the humanity of Paris, I, a black man who grew up in the Jim Crow legally-segregated South, I stand in indignation, sympathy, and empathy with the people of France. In words often quoted by Maya Angelou,

"I am human; nothing human can be alien to me."

No woman or man is an island. We are all involved in mankind. Those who cannot stand with other human beings in times of injustice are the reason these inter-group dynamics continue in our world in so many different forms, aimed at so many different groups.

"Any man's death diminishes me, for I am involved in mankind…"

#StandingwithParis

24: Sensitive?

All social interaction is sensitive.

When we interact with another person, right below the surface social-psychological dynamics are happening. We are moving through stages of social interaction.

> Stage I – each person assesses the situation: where, why, when, who? Where am I going? Why or for what purpose am I going there? When am I supposed to be there? Who else will be there?

> Stage II – each person assesses possible outcomes for self: How will I be treated? Will I have a good time?

> Stage III – each person tries to find a cognitive, short-cut way of understanding what might be going to happen (it's a party versus it's a funeral) or what is happening in the moment. We do this to avoid or to solve an actual or potential interaction mistake.

> Stage IV – each person experiences large or small identity concerns that can rev up emotion; each person is a little sensitive: Am I being myself? How am I coming across? What am I saying? No really, what *am* I saying?!

> Stage V – each person engages in interpersonal behavior: What is said or done. We attempt to interact

safely, in a way that is appropriate to the situation or interaction moment.

No matter the reason for the interaction, just below the surface, that is going on. Whether the interaction is set up spontaneously, formally or informally, or structured or unstructured, that is going on. Fun, friendship, competition, love, work, play, cooperation. No matter the intentions of the two people, the interaction moves through those stages.

As for me, all I wanted to do was buy a DVD.

Here's what happened.

I had been trying to track down a DVD by one of my favorite comedians, Brian Regan. In one of his stand-up routines, he tells the story about his first encounter with his new college roommate. The story[1] that Regan tells is:

> I grew up in Miami, Florida... I went to school at a small college in Ohio...
>
> My roommate my freshman year was from New Jersey...I had never met the guy... and he goes... "Hey... you wanna go halves on a pie...?"
>
> I was like... *???* ... I thought [to myself], *he wants to get a pie???*
>
> [I said]..."So, you wanta get a pie?"
>
> "Yeah" [he says]... "I figure we go halves on a pie... you know... celebrate... split a pie..."
>
> I'm still like... *???*
>
> [I'm thinking...] *Well... I hadn't really thought about that... what are you, little Jack Horner?*
>
> [I'm also thinking] *This guy wants a pie... so I wanted*

to be open minded… it's my first day in college…
you know…

I'm like… "OK… OK… let's get a pie… you seem
to like pie…"

So, we got half pepperoni and half pumpkin…

It's a funny story. And it is a good illustration of the idea of an
implicit theory of social psychology, which Philip Shaver defines as,

> "…a haphazard collection of ideas about what situa-
> tions and person characteristics are associated with
> the occurrence of particular kinds of social behavior."[2]

Many of our interpersonal expectations are set up by the implicit
(unstated) theories, assumptions, that we all carry around. Shaver tells
us, however, there two problems with relying on those implicit theories. One, our implicit theory comes from our own, limited personal
social experiences. No matter where we are from—Chicago, Illinois,
or Opelousas, Louisiana—that puts limits on our social experiences.
Two, without ever questioning it, we believe our theory to be correct.
Hard fact, God-given truth.

No wonder that the word "pie" to Miami-Florida Brian Regan
could only mean one thing. So too for his New Jersey roommate.
One word, the same word, does not always mean the same thing to
two people. Each person's social history shapes the meaning of words
and symbols. It is social meaning that ends up in our implicit theories.
There begins confused miscommunication between two people.

To have a little fun with the idea, I thought that I could show
that part of Brian Regan's routine in my "Introduction to Social
Psychology" class when I lecture on implicit theories. With that in
mind, one weekend I went into a Suncoast video store in a local mall.
It was 10:15 a.m. or so on a Saturday. Having just opened, there were
very few people in the mall. As I walked in, I saw that no one was in

the Suncoast video store except the white guy who was there to open. He was behind the counter, bent over looking down, fidgeting with the computer. He hadn't seen or heard me come into the store. I stood next to the counter for a moment and then said,

"...standup comedians."

For years my students have told me that it takes them a while to get used to the deep and big sound of my voice. Some say, "...it's intimidating." On this particular Saturday morning, since I live alone, I had not yet used my voice. My voice was Saturday-morning deep. I, of course, was not thinking about this. That would be like me thinking about the color of my eyes. To get what I wanted, I just said, "... standup comedians."

In reaction to the sound of my voice, the guy's head popped up, startled. Seeing me didn't help. You know, 6 feet 3 inches, 250lb, broad-shouldered, dark-skinned black man. The startle was in his eyes, and in his brief hesitation. I stood there and looked at him.

"I'm sorry," he said.

"...stand-up comedians..." I repeated.

"Oh... yeah... I have them over here."

He led me through the store to a rack. He pointed out the section.

"Thanks," I said.

Walking away from me, his back to me, with his left hand he pointed down a different isle and said,

"And I have black cinema over here."

He kept walking toward the front of the store.

Huh? What did he say? I thought to myself.

"What?"

His comment had stopped me.

"And I have black cinema over here."

I thought to myself, *Did I say anything about 'black' movies? No... all I said was stand-up comedians.*

I believe the guy who was waiting on me had made a racial identity belief assumption, the kind of psychological leap that is activated by feelings of intergroup anxiety. Upon hearing my voice, looking up at me, and leading me to the "…stand-up comedian section," this young white man had gone through the psychological stages of social interaction:

> Stage I – assessment of the situation; *salesperson – customer; clerk-white person interacting with customer-black male, giant.*

> Stage II – assessment of possible outcomes for self; how will I be treated? Will I be exploited? Am I safe? *intergroup anxiety.*

> Stage III – pulling up a cognitive shortcut to keep it simple; *big black man; stereotype activation.*

> Stage IV – feeling identity-concerns; emotional reactions; am I being myself? How am I coming across? Am I talking to this guy the right way? *identity-guess based on the activated stereotype.*

> Stage V – quickly deciding what to do; interpersonal behavior; *what to say; attempt to reach safety*; "…and I have black cinema over here."

Startled into an intergroup-interaction, the guy who was waiting on me was pushed to enact a "helpful" cognitive-shortcut from his implicit theory of race—a big black man likes black cinema. To be safe, to get ahead of this threatening interracial interaction, he was showing me he could cater to my preferences.

We live on a neo-diversity frontier. A lot has changed in the array of forces that was American race relations. Even racial stereotypes are not the same, but racial stereotypes have not gone away. Patricia Devine and Andrew Elliot have investigated the extent to which racial stereotypes have faded.[3] Working from the set of studies called the Princeton Trilogy, these researchers updated what we know about the stereotypes of American blacks. In the 1930s, 1940s, and 1960s, that stereotype consisted of these kinds of traits:

superstitious, lazy, happy-go-lucky, ignorant, musical

By the 1980s, those particular traits appeared to fall out of the stereotype, and some researchers thought the black stereotype was disappearing. It was not, of course, that simple. Instead what was going on was while those traits were being discounted as irrelevant (and possibly becoming out of style in wording), other traits were being added to, or reworded for, the black stereotype. In general, whites do not say they think of blacks as:

superstitious, lazy, happy-go-lucky, ignorant, musical.

Devine & Elliot found that now the stereotype is more likely to be:

*athletic, rhythmic, low-in-intelligence, poor, criminal,
hostile, loud.*

The situation of the black stereotype is even more complicated than that. Americans, white, black, and otherwise, know the stereotype. Resting quiet in our implicit theory of race are those stereotypes. In that context, Devine & Elliot ask if knowing the stereotype, does the person have to believe the stereotype is true? About this, they say that:

> …[our findings lead] us to the conclusion that the Black stereotype is not fading among Whites; rather, personal beliefs about Blacks are undergoing a revision. Results from our stereotype assessment suggest that there is a clear, consistent contemporary stereotype of Blacks and that this stereotype is highly negative in nature. Our [data on personal beliefs] however, indicate that there is an equally consistent set of beliefs about Blacks that, in stark contrast to the contemporary stereotype, is [positive].[4]

When it came to the traits a research participant personally held about blacks, more positive traits appeared:

sensitive, loyal to family, artistic, honest, intelligent,
kind.

From their data, Devine & Elliot conclude that whether a white person is prejudiced or not is irrelevant to whether a person knows the stereotype. We all know the stereotype of blacks. That does not mean a person actually holds the stereotype to be true. What, then, does this set up? Devine & Elliot say this means that not believing in the black stereotype does not stop the interaction from wobbling.

A white person who does not believe the black stereotype is sometimes in a more precarious interaction position because, for anyone, it doesn't take much to activate the stereotype. A sudden, unexpected interaction with the prototype—a big, black man—and the stereotype roars loud out of one's implicit theory of race:

And I have black cinema over here.

In my buying the DVD encounter, I believe that's what happened. By expressing the identity-stereotype leap, the interaction was shifted from a behavioral—may I help you, to an identity—I know you prefer—interaction. There is, of course, a clerk-customer interaction protocol. What the protocol requires is for the service provider to be helpful without making assumptions.

In their sales role, protocol for the sales person is to say "…if I can help you with anything else, let me know." Doing so activates the identity part of the interaction in a positive way. "… they know how to treat customers in this store."

Going off protocol requires the sales person to make identity assumptions about the customer. No surprise the customer feels that as an interpersonal intrusion, because the customer is pulled into an identity-interaction in a way that is unexpected and vague. You know what it feels like when the person waiting on you is too helpful; when that person starts to act as if they know what you like, as if they know you.

Such an identity-confused, vague-interaction is reflected in the activated thought, … *What makes you think you know me?* What the customer experiences is a sense that this person is talking to me as if we have a relationship, but we don't. For the customer Person A, this identity-familiarity is unexpected. For Person A, this level of interaction with this sales person is also without clear interaction rules. Person A, for that reason, is not sure how to react.

No doubt, my voice, my size, my dark skin adds up to me being the prototype of fear for some Americans. In my buying a DVD interaction, it felt like the clerk's behavior toward me was being guided by that stereotype. That's why I was suddenly trying to understand his motives: "What did he mean by that?" Then the interaction not only wobbles, but the scaffolding starts to vibrate, and… without buying anything, without saying another thing to the clerk, I left the store.

When I tell this story in lecture, sometimes my students ask me why I didn't say anything to correct the clerk. Well, a vague interaction at the identity-pace is dangerous. At that speed, nothing is quite stable. A person's emotions can be quick to ignite. In the case of my DVD interaction, because it was an interracial and interpersonal encounter, I am willing to admit that that social circumstance combined with his (possibly innocent) comment revved my interpersonal engine up to the identity-pace of interaction (What did he mean by that?). That's the potential effect of a comment where one or both persons in the interaction may be experiencing intergroup anxiety. The effect on the target of a real or perceived stereotype-based interaction is a quick shift that makes the target of the (real or imagined) stereotype seem "…oh-so-sensitive." You have heard the question: *Man, why are they so sensitive?*

As I tell my students, I can just imagine me going up to the counter with revved up emotion in my posture and the sound of my voice and saying "…What did you say to me?" No doubt, next I would be hearing the police sirens blaring. More important, it's not my job to try to correct a person's interaction mistakes. Not a person with whom I do not have (or hope to have) an ongoing relationship. I teach in the classroom. If I felt the interaction mistake was just too much, I would contact management of the store by letter or email to express my dissatisfaction.

To the sensitive matter at hand, it is a fundamental truth that especially in a first-time interpersonal encounter, all of us are "…so sensitive." Why? Simply that a first-time interaction with another person is vague, and we don't want to mess up. In the midst of our assessing where, when, what, and who, we are also doing something else. We are trying to guess what our interaction partner is likely to do and prefer that we do.

Sure, we know that not everybody behaves the same way in the same situation. Our special concern is to know how the person we are interacting with *right now* is going to treat this interaction *with me*. With that concern, we look for evidence of interpersonal goals. Each person is searching for signs of being valued or devalued in the interaction. That's the universal "…so sensitive" part of social interaction.

Now, add to that universal a neo-diversity dimension. Just a word, just a phrase, can rev the interaction up. From the service side of the customer service part of our neo-diversity frontier, one of my NC State students tells this story of his encounter with a fan of the rival UNC Chapel Hill Tar Heels:

> It has been my experience that no matter how you do things at a job, management can always think of a worse way that you "should" be doing things. On this particular occasion my store manager informed me that I needed to joke more with customers. Apparently, I was mistaken in my logic that people came to the Fresh Market for groceries; the reality is that they come looking for humor and friendship.

It was after this conversation with my boss that a man in a "UNC 2005 National Champions" shirt came up to my counter. Because the store is located less than a mile from the Belltower [at North Carolina State University], I decided I would take the opportunity to appease the management of the store. As the man came up to me, I looked at his shirt and jokingly said, "I guess you're shopping in the wrong part of town."

The words didn't have time to leave my mouth before I regretted saying them. The man's face immediately, and quite visibly, became filled with anger. As he spoke to me, the shaking in his voice made it clear that he was trying his best not to openly yell at me.

"I feel comfortable shopping anywhere. Why would you even say something like that?"

I was puzzled. Was this man really that devout a fan? After a brief pause, my stomach sank as the situation settled in my head. He hadn't realized I was talking about his shirt; he assumed I was referring to the fact that he was a black man in what could be considered a luxury grocery store in a more affluent and white part of Raleigh.

It would be a stretch to call my next comment coherent English.

"Your shirt…Carolina."

The same anger he had in his face quickly turned to embarrassment. He muttered, "Yeah well, umm… I'm a big fan."

We both tried our best to act oblivious to the previous exchange. We engaged in uncomfortable small talk as I hurried to get him what he wanted. It was clear to both of us that he wanted to leave and I wanted to let him.

"You have a good day."

"Yeah, you too."

I haven't joked with a customer since.

Leftover in the rubble of our segregated past is the psychology[5] that says groups have places:

"He hadn't realized I was talking about his shirt; he assumed I was referring to the fact that he was a black man in what could be considered a luxury grocery store in a more affluent and white part of Raleigh."

We are still sensitive to places. With that in our social psychology, it is no wonder that just having a person walk by can rev up an individual's sense of danger.

25. Going Home

Sensitive is as sensitive does.

Nobody wants to mess up a social interaction. To come to our expectations for how a social interaction is likely to go, to put ourselves in position to do well in a social interaction, we search for information that helps us figure out, assess the interpersonal situation we are in (or going to be in). Writers of fiction take that idea seriously.

Where is this happening?

When is this happening?

Who are the people?

Why are those people together?

Fiction writers use those questions to try to tap into what humans live every day. I know of a fiction writer, John Ed Bradley, who also grew up in the same small, bayou-Louisiana town as I did: Opelousas. We have never met.

If you knew, you might think that the reason we never crossed paths is because John Ed was born in 1959 and I was born in 1951. Yet for a town like Opelousas where everybody knows everybody's family, it's not the best explanation. Frankly, the real reason John Ed and I had no chance to meet is race. John Ed is white of Cajun heritage, and I am a black Creole.

As John Ed and I were growing up, schools were segregated by race, by law. Where John Ed would have gone either to the all-white (until 1968) Catholic school or the all-white (until 1970) public school, I went to the all-black Catholic school (graduating in 1969). John Ed would have lived in one of the white sections of Opelousas, and I in one of the black sections. Race, no doubt, was what influenced the chances of us ever meeting. But to this John Ed was not oblivious. He could not have been and have written his novel *Restoration*,[1] which is a captivating, mysterious novel of neo-diversity.

Quick and fluid, John Ed sets the cast of characters. Central to the story, Jack Charbonnet (Shar-bo-nay) and Rhys Goudeau (Go-dough) have just met and discovered their mutual knowledge of and interest in the paintings of the long-dead (fictitious) New Orleans painter, Levette Asmore. As a story of the love for art, the greed for art collecting, and the craft of art restoration, John Ed uses lively social interactions to give us an understanding of this world. Rather than lecture us, John Ed uses Jack's curious but amateur interest and questions to give us insight into what goes on there.

Jack's interest in the artist Levette Asmore developed through his father, who was a photographer and lover of Louisiana art. An art restorer, Rhys interest is both professional and personal. It is the mystery of the reasons for Levette's suicide and the discovery of a lost and forgotten mural by him that is the driving force of this novel.

In fact, a number of mysteries unfold as we follow the attempts to uncover the true story of Levette; the connection of Jack's landlord to Levette; the discovery, heisting, and restoration of Levette's mural; the trouble in the dance of romance between Jack and Rhys. And throughout, there is something, unsaid, going on that has to do with race. Jack, a white man, resists the significance of race, and at one point says to Rhys that he does not care about race. Jack is puzzled when Rhys replies, "You would make a mistake not to care about race... there is no bigger issue in my life."

Something is going on in this story that Jack, a main character, and we the reader, do not know about at first. It's hinted at, and the hints say it is important to how Jack should interact with Rhys, down to how he should talk to her. But what is that social fact? He doesn't know. We the readers don't know.

That reflects interpersonal life. The interpersonal situation exists and is before us, but we cannot see all of it, not all at once. Each social encounter requires exploration and sampling.

We start to learn this as children when we begin to learn the nuances of social interaction. Learning those lessons is how we have learned to approach new interactions with interpersonal questions. Not necessarily out of fear, just with a mature understanding that before we showed up, the other person already had thoughts, feelings, and preferences. From that, we know we should not take for granted what will happen; we should not take for granted how the interaction will proceed. We work to assess the situation. We read for the clues that the situation holds.

We do not want to mess up.

In our everyday social interactions, all of us are *Interpersonal Scene Investigators*. We are ISIs to the situations in which we come to interact. It is a cliché about detective work that, to figure out the truth of some crime, there are five things the investigator must learn: who, what, when, where, and how. But for interpersonal situations, with these questions we go at it in another order. We use the five W's. We start with where and then go to when, who, why, and what.

Where is this happening?

When is this happening?

Who is the other person?

Why are we here?

What are the appropriate behaviors for me?

We enter social situations with these interpersonal questions.

"Is this the right room?" "Am I dressed OK?"

We search ourselves to find behaviors to fit the situation before us. Sometimes, and it has happened to us all, a situation is created right before our eyes and we have to improvise. An acquaintance, a friend, a business colleague calls someone over and says, "Oh, Person A... I'd like you to meet total stranger Person B." Suddenly we are in a new interpersonal situation. What do we do? We try to assess this new situation so that we know what from our personal playbook of behaviors fits and would be appropriate to enact in this interpersonal scene.

We read for the clues in order to prepare ourselves to behave in a way or in ways that match the interpersonal context. None of us wants to make interpersonal mistakes. Worse nightmares are often feared interpersonal moments. By what circumstance do we anticipate such a moment will come to life? We expect these moments to happen when we misread, misunderstand, or for some reason do not know, the interpersonal requirements.

All I wanted to do was get to my car and go home.

Here's what happened.

For a number of years, I have been teaching my introduction to social psychology course from 4:30-5:45 p.m. In the late fall and then most of the winter, by the time I finish my lecture, answer student questions after the lecture, go back to my office to catch my breath, and gather my stuff to go home, it's dark.

I head out onto campus, which is pretty well lit, and although I know that darkness makes people a little nervous, there is nothing I can do about the size of the shadow I cast. As I heard a TV actor say, "...there's nothing I can do about the fact that I am big and black at the same time."

One particular evening after class as I approached the parking lot, I noticed a young white male, likely a student, in the parking lot, unlocking and opening a car door right next to my car. As I walked to my car, he looked up and saw me coming in his direction. I saw the anxiety rise up in him; everything about his body language changed. Moving from bending into his car, he stood up straight, squared his stance, squared his shoulders, and eyed me.

That's how quickly he had gone through his interpersonal-scene-investigation.

Stage I – assessment of the situation; *two people, night time in a parking lot; one person- white-male, watching the other person black male, giant walking toward white-male.*

Stage II – assessment of possible outcomes for self; intergroup anxiety; *motivation not to be exploited.*

Stage III – cognitive shortcut; keep it simple innovation; big black man; stereotype activation; *expectation of violence.*

Stage IV – identity-concerns; emotional reactions; *must protect self.*

Stage V – interpersonal behavior; *straighten up, square-up, use eyes to show willingness to stand ground and fight.*

Who's so sensitive?

Eyeing me the way he was, it was clear that he expected trouble as I continued to walk directly toward him. My only thought was, "…how sad."

About 10 steps from him, I pushed the button on my car key fob and the locks clicked open, and the lights of my car blinked. He heard the click, looked over and saw my car lights blink on. He looked puzzled.

I walked past him, as I had to, to get to my car, which was next to his car. I got to my car, threw my shoulder bag of student papers into the back seat, got settled behind the wheel of my car, turned the ignition, and began to back out.

By then his demeanor had changed. He had a weak smile now, and as I backed up, he leaned forward and began to wave in an exaggerated way, saying goodbye as if we had just had a pleasant conversation.

How disappointing.

How sad…

…but, what if…

…with a gun in his car, and then in his hand, me, a professor, shot dead in that parking lot.

From his point of view, from his anxiety-driven interpersonal scene investigation, he would have been able to say in truth:

"I felt threatened. I was in fear for my life."

It would have been the truth as he felt it, an irrational, paranoid truth.

All I wanted to do was get home. So too, Trayvon Martin.

###

Let's consider the interaction between Trayvon Martin and George Zimmerman. ABC news has published a timeline of the events that many observers seem to find credible.[2] Using that, here is what appears to have happened between Mr. Martin and Mr. Zimmerman.

Twenty-eight-year-old George Zimmerman, on an errand, was driving through the neighborhood. He called 911 to say that he saw a young male who was a "...real suspicious guy." Zimmerman said to the 911 dispatcher that "He's just walking around, looking about." Then Zimmerman begins to follow Mr. Martin. Asked by the dispatcher whether he was following the young man, Zimmerman indicated that he was, and the dispatcher says, "We don't need you to do that."

"OK," was Zimmerman's response.

Sixteen-year-old Trayvon Martin was on his way home to his father's house after buying some snacks at a convenience store. On the phone with his girlfriend, Mr. Martin tells her that someone is following him. After a while, Mr. Martin says "Oh, he's right behind me, he's right behind me again." Mr. Martin's girlfriend tells him to run but he says he was "just going to walk fast."

Soon after, Mr. Martin's girlfriend hears this exchange over the phone.

"Why are you following me?"

"What are you doing around here?"

Mr. Martin's girlfriend said she then heard a scuffle and then the phone call was cut off. A number of neighbors said that about that time they heard a cry for help, then a gunshot. A number of those neighbors then made calls to 911. When the police arrived, they found Mr. Zimmerman with a handgun standing over Mr. Martin, who was unarmed. Mr. Martin was dead and Mr. Zimmerman had a bloody nose and a wound in the back of his head.

Neo-diversity has created a fundamental problem for social interaction in America. Without laws of racial segregation, people who dress in all kinds of ways, people of different genders, people of different skin colors, can walk around wherever they please. Problem then is, "Who are among the 'we' and who among the 'they?'" Worried Sneetches, our neo-diversity anxiety is voices in our heads wondering:

"Whether this one was that one... or that one was this one

Or which one was what one... or what one was who."[3]

Mr. Zimmerman says that he was headed to the grocery store driving his SUV when he saw Mr. Martin, who he described to a 911 dispatcher as "...a real suspicious guy." Mr. Zimmerman then says, "He's just walking around, looking about." For Mr. Zimmerman, his interpersonal-scene-investigation, goes this way:

Stage I – assessment of the situation; *Mr. Zimmerman assesses the situation as one in which Mr. Martin isn't one of us, activating intergroup anxiety.*

Stage II – assessment of possible outcomes for self; *Mr. Zimmerman perceives Mr. Martin as out of place, raising concerns about why he is there, and concerns about the neighborhood being exploited.*

Stage III – cognitive shortcut; keep it simple innovation; *whatever in the social environment led him to that assessment and caused Mr. Zimmerman's intergroup anxiety also activates his stereotypes about "them" as a threat.*

Stage IV – identity-concerns; emotional reactions; *As reported, Mr. Zimmerman is a self-appointed*

neighborhood community watch captain; that's his iden-
tity; he is a protector of the community; he must act to
protect so his protection motivations and emotions are
revved up.

Stage V – interpersonal behavior; *To protect the*
community from exploitation by one of "them" Mr.
Zimmerman calls 911 and follows Mr. Martin. At some
point Mr. Martin challenges that following-behavior
and Mr. Zimmerman shoots him.

Trayvon Martin has bought his snacks and is on his way home.
Talking on the phone with his girlfriend, Mr. Martin notices that he is
being followed. For Mr. Martin, his interpersonal-scene-investigation
goes this way:

Stage I – assessment of the situation; *I'm being fol-*
lowed. Mr. Martin assesses the situation unstructured
and without information about why he is being fol-
lowed; it's all vague, creating anxiety.

Stage II – assessment of possible outcomes for self;
Mr. Martin wonders why is this guy following me? What
does he want? Is he going to try to hurt me? Mr. Martin's
concerns about being exploited are activated.

Stage III – cognitive shortcut; keep it simple innovation; *Mr. Martin thinks this guy's got to be up to*
something; who follows someone they don't know; who
does that except somebody looking for trouble; cognitive
shortcut-expectation of violence.

Stage IV – identity-concerns; emotional reactions;
Talking to his girlfriend on the phone Mr. Martin says
"Oh, he's right behind me, he's right behind me again."
Definitely can't let my girlfriend think I'm scared so he

tells her, I'm just going to walk fast.

Stage V – interpersonal behavior; *Mr. Martin is now filled with anxiety and confronts Mr. Zimmerman; why are you following me?!*

A cry of help is heard. A gunshot.

From all the reports I have read and listened to, that is the best imagining I can come up with of the social psychology of the interaction situation. Two people who came face to face in an interaction filled with anxiety and fear. The most important questions are not about Mr. Martin's situational assessment; he was being followed. Although it may be an impossible task, we have to try to figure out Mr. Zimmerman's initial assessment of the situation? When he saw Mr. Martin, what made Mr. Zimmerman immediately think, "This guy looks like he is up to no good."

Why was Mr. Zimmerman so sensitive, so filled with anxiety when he first saw Mr. Martin? What put Mr. Zimmerman on high alert "… wondering whether this one was that one or that one was who?"

Was it the darkness? Darkness matters.[4]

Was it Mr. Zimmerman's implicit theory, his expectancy, of who is likely to live in that neighborhood? Groups have places.

Was it Mr. Martin's race, per se? There are still bigots in America.

God knows there's been plenty of talk and outcry about the fact that Mr. Martin was a young black male. In that context of racial consideration, there has been a general outcry about the fact that Trayvon Martin is dead, and no one has been held accountable for the death of a teenager.

Many things can be said about the nation's reaction to this case. When it comes to race, one thing is that in the age of Jim Crow legal segregation, prejudice and bigotry, there would have been no outcry of the kind we had across our nation about the killing of Trayvon Martin. Yes, there would have been activists who decried what happened, but there would have been no general, mixed group outcry such as has happened. If nothing else, the tragedy of Trayvon Martin's murder shows us that the racial sensitivity of our nation has changed for the good.

Is that all that explains the outcry of a tragic interaction between two people who do not look like each other? There is, I believe, more to it than that. I think the anger expressed by all my students, I think the national outcry, is motivated by our being caught off guard by the consequences of our failure to admit and talk about the frontier reality of our time.

Many Americans are struggling with the fact that out here on this neo-diversity frontier, we can no longer use race, gender, ethnicity, or even dress to quickly judge whether another person belongs in the places we go. Continuing to try to use those shortcuts to social judgment is the shadow, the unacknowledged history of race and inter-group social change in America.

Leftover, those shortcuts through the shadow will continue to take us to dangerous alleys and dead ends because, in this age of neo-diversity, even on our way home we cannot avoid interacting with people who do not look like us. No wonder so many are so sensitive. Sad to say, but the Trayvon Martin case highlighted our precarious psychological situation. Neo-diversity, the new American frontier.

26: Home at Last

Being at home is supposed to be a safe haven. Yet at his home, Professor Henry Louis Gates, a black man, and Police Officer James Crowley, a white man, had an interaction that went viral. From what I have read, I imagine that here's what happened:

> With the help of the limousine driver who brought him from the airport, Professor Henry Louis Gates has just pushed his way in through the front door of his house.
>
> "What an idiot," he is thinking. "I knew I should have gotten that door fixed before I left."
>
> Just at that moment, a phone call has gone to the Cambridge police department saying that it appears that someone is breaking into a house.[1]
>
> "911, what's your emergency?"
>
> "Two men were pushing on the front door of a house. There were suitcases at the door. After a while one went inside. I didn't get a good look at him."
>
> "So you think it's a break-in?"
>
> "I don't know if they live there and they just had a hard time with their key. But I did notice they used their shoulder to try to barge in and they got in. I

don't know if they had a key or not, 'cause I couldn't see from my angle," the caller says.

"Two men, you say… were they black, white, Hispanic…?"

"I don't know…"

"Ma'am… were they black, Hispanic, or white…?"

"Um…well, there were two larger men. One looked kind of Hispanic, but I'm not really sure. And the other one entered and I didn't see what he looked like at all. I just saw it from a distance and this older woman was worried, thinking, 'Someone's been breaking in someone's house. They're barging in.'"[2]

Inside his home, Professor Gates is sitting when a knock comes to his door. He opens the door to find a police officer, Sergeant James Crowley, standing there.

"We have a report of a possible break in at this residence," Sergeant Crowley says.

"Well I live here."

"May I see some ID?"

"What?!"

"May I see some ID?"

"Why… because I'm a black man in America?!"

"Sir we are just trying to investigate this report. Would you bring some ID and come outside so we can talk?"

Gates shows Crowley his ID, but then demands to

know Crowley's name and badge number.

"Sir, you're under arrest for disorderly conduct."

Handcuffed, Gates was taken to the police station.

When did race become a part of this encounter between Professor Gates and Officer Crowley? From what has been made public, race entered during the 911 call, but not from the caller, from the police dispatcher. As the caller is trying to tell the dispatcher what she thinks might be going on, speaking over the caller's words, the 911 dispatcher asks, "…Are these males black, Hispanic, or white?" The caller hesitates and the dispatcher asked again about the race, ethnicity of the men. The caller says she's not sure, but maybe one of the men looked Hispanic.

From that point on we have to imagine the next interaction: that between the dispatcher and Officer Crowley. The dispatcher speaks to Officer Crowley to send Crowley's car to the scene. The caller is not sure about the race of the men, but says they could be Hispanic. Now here, as I say, we are imagining and assuming. I am assuming that the 911 dispatcher asks about race, ethnicity, to give that information to whichever officer would be going to the scene. Why else ask? Either this is a formal or informal policy of the department (or the dispatchers).

Formal or informal, in this case the information about race is not firm; it is vague. Officer Crowley does not have a piece of information he (apparently) expected to have. For Officer Crowley, race has been brought into the interaction, but race is vague. Crowley does not know what to expect at this scene. All he has is an expectation about race based on his past experiences of this affluent neighborhood. That means he expects the homeowner to be white. When he sees a black man, that's unexpected, but the man *is* inside the house, although the man seems a bit agitated. For Crowley, this is a moment of vague-interaction.

At his home, Professor Gates has finally gotten inside, but has exerted himself physically. His self-concern is active and bruised because he had to force his way into his own home.

"What an idiot," he must keep thinking.

His physiology is also revved up. He is a little out of breath and a little sweaty. Trying to relax, Gates is sitting when he hears a strong knock on his front door. He gets up, already self-agitated, now other-agitated at being taken from his needed rest. He finds himself looking at a cop.

"Why is this cop at my door?"

One of the classic situations of vague-interaction is "being pulled over by a police officer." Heart starts to race, hands start to sweat. "Oh shit," we say to our now nervous self. Even though he is at home, Professor Gates must be having some bit of these reactions in his already agitated mind and body, further revving him up.

In the case of the Gates-Crowley encounter, at this point both people are experiencing a vague-interaction (what is my role? What are the rules? What kind of relationship can I have with this person?). It's a version of neo-diversity vague-interaction because it's a black and a white man whose roles do not fit the stereotyped expectations. Black man is a highly regarded professor at Harvard. White man is a street cop. Neither man is accustomed to being challenged for any reason.

Interviewed about this incident, a 13-year veteran cop of another city said,

> "We're not going to take the abuse. We have to remain in control. We're running the show."[3]

Some have said that this encounter activated a power dynamic in this racial vague-interaction.

> "Apparently there was something about the power relationship involved—uppity, jet-setting black professor vs. regular-guy, working class cop…"[4]

Interaction speeds up. The two are now interacting at the high-speed identity pace. Whatever words either person says are subject to not just misinterpretations, but mishearing by the other person.

Activated social paranoia does that; at least that is what Freeman and Freeman might call it. They would say that in that moment, with everything moving fast, we have feelings of paranoia. Most interesting, they say that people have "anomalous experiences": thinking we heard something that actually was never said. Freeman and Freeman describe such a moment:

> So we're much more likely to respond in a distressed agitated, and—crucially—a paranoid way if we don't understand what's happening to us. Paranoia rears its head when we try to make sense of the bewildering experience (for example, people exchanging apparently whispered comments). Maybe this strange stuff is happening, we think, because other people have it in for me. *Maybe they're whispering about me.*[5]

Without knowing it, the two people have gotten on, and are now riding one of those floorless roller coasters; HYDRA- The REVENGE. Suddenly, dear reader, that roller coaster of social interaction jerks into a hither-to-fore unattained identity-paced speed. Everything is moving so fast, every movement of your head makes you feel even more wobbly, you can't focus on anything but your survival.

Am I going to get through this?

Is this it, am I going to die?

Is that me screaming?

It's intense. Even using all our interpersonal-scene-investigation strategies, we can't pick up all the details of the experience. Not being able to focus outward very well, it's not easy to know how the social interaction is going.

Crowley *says*: "Sir, would you please show me some identification."

Gates *hears*: *What are you doing here boy?*

Gates responds: "Why, because I'm a black man in America?"

Crowley *says*: "…I'd like to see some ID, sir."

Gates *hears*: "…*prove to me you live here, boy.*"

Gates *says*: "…you want me to show you my ID even though I'm in my house?"

Crowley *hears*: "*I'll show some identification to your Momma.*"

With powerful interpersonal consequences, we can become distracted by our concerns about how we are coming across and how we are being treated. We make assumptions based on either the existing or historical relationship between the groups. "May I see some ID?" is reacted to with "why… because I'm a black man in America?" And as *The Daily Show*'s "Senior Black Correspondent" put it, the challenge to the officer's authority with "why?" is heard in the outdated, stereotyping language of the very old TV show *Good Times* as "Your momma."

Today in this age of so much social uncertainty, we are prone to guess about people's identities based on the historical pattern of group interaction. Asking gives too much away. Guessing is hit, and mostly, miss.

How is this person thinking of me? How does this person see me?

Gates: Who does *he* think *he* is?

Crowley: Who does *he* think *he* is?

Self-concern is active and on alert in both people. Two people wonder, what part of my identity do I need to display in this interaction? Will Person B like the person I show myself to be? Will Person B respect me or try to demean me? Two people are no longer simply enacting behavior. Each person is now trying to understand the other's behavior at the (too sensitive) identity-pace of interaction. From Person B's perspective, Person A's behavior is no longer just behavior, but a sign of how Person A thinks about, feels about, values or devalues Person A's time and interaction with Person B. Before these two people can get off that roller coaster, Professor Gates is arrested and put in handcuffs for being belligerent on his own porch.

I know it was only one single interaction episode. True, and yet the interaction between Professor Gates and Officer Crowley was more important and diagnostic than we realized in 2009. Since then, we have seen interactions between police and citizens go down this same road with much more serious consequences: encounters between black men and police and the black man is shot dead or choked to death; then riots, peaceful protests, lack of trusts in police; then ambushing and assassination of police. How could this one episode be diagnostic of all that? What could this one episode teach us, police and citizens, about what is really going on in America?

Before Charleston, before Orlando, before Dallas, before Baton Rouge, I had this exchange[6] with an interviewer:

Question: Do you think we can get past the mentality that some have that to be a true American means you have to be white?

My answer: We have to! We're going to have to because America is becoming more nonwhite than white. In 2042, it's going to flip. It's already happening, so we either get past it, or we destroy ourselves. It's that simple.

27: Call the Police!

"Hello...police! Please have someone come to this address because..."

When we see the video, when the video or story goes viral, many Americans cringe.

Wait... what! Someone called the cops because...

An 8-year-old black girl was selling bottled water on the street to make a little pocket change.

Two black men were sitting in Starbucks, quietly waiting for a friend, but asked to use the restroom.

A black graduate student had fallen asleep in a common area of a graduate residence hall.

At Colorado State University, campus police pull two American-Indian teenage boys from a campus tour because a white parent on the tour called 911 to report that the boys were being "too quiet" and were wearing "dark stuff" and all that was suspicious.[1]

What is the culprit here? We all know the word "racist" is overused, and used mostly without accuracy. Social scientists have been pointing at that problem since the 1950s. In their classic study of prejudice and discrimination, in footnote 65 in the final chapter of their book where they discuss solutions, Simpson and Yinger say[2]:

In many ways [the concept of 'racism'] is a useful

shorthand way of saying: a complex of discriminations and prejudices directed against an alleged inferior race. Nevertheless, we [in this book] have made only minimal use of the term for two related reasons:

Racism tends to be a "swearword," not an analytic term; as such, in most of its present uses, it freezes the mind and perpetuates a vocabulary of praise and blame that we think reduces our ability to understand—and therefore to reduce—intergroup hostilities and injustices.

The second reason is closely related. Racism is often used as an explanation, rather than a description of a situation. "White racism is essentially responsible for the explosive mixture which has been accumulating in our cities since the end of World War II." (Report of the National Advisory Commission on Civil Disorders, Bantam Books, p. 10). This does not take us very far. It is equivalent to saying that we are having a serious epidemic because many people have been infected by a virus. How does the virus work to cause disease? Who is vulnerable, who immune? What situations harbor it? The tragedies associated with intergroup hostility are too severe to permit us the luxury of "medieval" explanations by naming or by lodging the cause in individual choice.

Prejudice is not bigotry is not racism. Prejudice is a negative and unfavorable set of feelings and judgments about a whole group of people. Bigotry occurs when those feelings appear in behavior (avoidance and other forms of behavioral discrimination). Racism is a system of laws or policies that support and authorize individual prejudice and bigotry.[3]

Not racism, but racial bigotry is at work because we do know these "calling the cops" incidences are racial. Still, you have to wonder why people are calling the cops for these innocuous social encounters.

Racial prejudice is not new. We all know there was a long period in our nation during which racial segregation was the rule of the day, the law of the land. Everything, in everyday life, was segregated by race. Myself a dark-skinned black man born in 1951 Louisiana, I grew up during the days of legal segregation. That is a personal, experience-based reason that I know that to say, "…everything was segregated," is no exaggeration.

People think of schools when it comes to legal racial segregation and that is accurate. At the same time, though, laws of segregation also applied to doctor's office waiting rooms, hospitals, public bathrooms, movie theaters, department stores, public parks, and pools. As a nation, we got rid of those immoral laws; we got rid of that racism. Yet, desegregation-by-law was not just simply, or immediately, accepted into the everyday behavior or psychology of individuals.

Especially given the long history of legally enforced segregation, with desegregation there were Americans who felt uncomfortable being in a park, not to mention being in a pool, with black Americans. In fact, with the dismantling of segregation, some municipalities closed their public swimming pools so that blacks and whites would not be in the same water to swim.[4] That psychological discomfort did not go away with the eventual fact of not being able to avoid being in proximity of black people at work or play.

Truth is, there still are those who feel racial prejudice that leads to a preference for social distance between white and black people, preferring to not have black people around.[5] So too is the fact that in some families that prejudice continues to be reinforced and passed on.

The Spring 2018 semester I had a white student who reported an experience of working in a summer camp. Two 7-year-old children, one black and one white, were put together to work on a project. The little white girl was clearly uncomfortable. When asked what was wrong, the 7-year-old white girl said, "My daddy says I can't play with people like them…"

That prejudice had been in family talk at home, watching TV, over meals, and by way of directives about who a child should play with by skin color. Poet W. H. Auden put it this way[6]:

"Evil is unspectacular and always human.

Shares our bed and eats at our own table."

Nurtured at home, that prejudice lived and slept in social-hibernation as long as the child stayed at home. Yet, children and grownups have to leave the house sometime. "Out there" is the neo-diversity reality of our time. Neo-diversity is the 21st century interpersonal situation where all of us have to encounter and sometimes interact with people not like us on some group dimension.

That neo-diversity reality can create a neo-diversity, interaction-anxiety; an uneasy feeling in the presence of someone from one of those "not like me" categories. Our mistake today is that rather than admit that the family talk, the family directives were inappropriate, disrespectful and un-American, too many people want to "fix" America to fit that way of talking about "them." Too many do not want to admit that the family talk has left their children and themselves unprepared for everyday encounters with neo-diversity; encounters in everyday situations with people "not like me."

Look, we know that over the last 20 years, Americans have become more anxious about diversity. To again quote the news story from 2013, "'Diversity' is on the rise in America and people are 'very anxious' about it, according to a sweeping new Esquire-NBC News survey."[7]

A concrete example is interracial dating and marriage. With its increase in occurrence, nearly 20 percent of Americans still say that interracial marriage is morally wrong.[8] That psychological stance must fill those people with anxiety as they encounter interracial couples in TV shows and commercials, walking through grocery and department stores, in parks, and at the neighborhood swimming pool.

In today's digital world, that neo-diversity anxiety is exploding through communication-technology. In the old days when a person felt anxiety about "them" being in close proximity, all a person could do was either accept it or move out of that situation. Surely you would not ask someone to call the police because you would expect that whomever you asked would ask you "…why? What's the trouble?"

Today, with a reach into your pocket and the push of three numbers, your neo-diversity anxiety is quickly and easily un-muzzled into behavior: "Hello… police…" With no need of other people, cell-phones release all of us from normal social impulse control to call the police for a "reason" that amounts to, "I feel really anxious because there are black people here…"

And hear me: No matter what the executives at Starbucks believe, what is going on is not "…unconscious bias." Most Americans have now seen the outrage-inducing video of the police taking away, in handcuffs, two black men who had been sitting quietly in a Philadelphia Starbucks waiting for a friend. With no other provocation, a Starbucks employee called the police because those two black men sitting in the store had not placed an order and asked to use the restroom.

Kevin Johnson, the CEO of Starbucks, published a public letter of apology. He says a number of things, but this line of thinking stuck out to me:

> We have immediately begun a thorough investigation of our practices… Regretfully, our practices and training led to a bad outcome—the basis for the call to the Philadelphia police department was wrong. Our store manager never intended for these men to be arrested and this should never have escalated as it did… We also will further train our partners to better know when police assistance is warranted.

That line of thinking misses the problem. To say that "Our store manager never intended for these men to be arrested" raises an important question about the manager's psychology in the moment. What was the manager's intention for "…calling the police"? To say that it was all unintentional is also how we get to Starbucks deciding to do a day of "unconscious bias training."

Unconscious!?

Refusing to admit and examine your racial or other neo-diversity anxieties does not turn those anxieties into *unconscious* bias. You know what you feel, you are just engaged in dangerous denial. It is dangerous because the neo-diversity anxiety is sleeping right under the surface of our everyday social encounters. With the right situational noise, that neo-diversity anxiety will roar awake from its hibernation, and in panic, someone will call the police.

The problem today is not race relations, per se, or unconscious bias. Too many of We Americans have become Sneetches, so frantic with worry about, "Whether this one was that one, or what one was who," that for no good reason the police are called.

The problem is getting people to admit, acknowledge, and examine the origins of and manage their neo-diversity anxiety. That is an anxiety about who belongs in what spaces. That is the anxiety of "who are among the 'we' and who are among the 'they?'" That is the anxiety that is the American intergroup problem of our time. Our newest American dilemma.

28: What Are You!?

Laws influence the psychology of citizens.

Plenty of research in social psychology has focused on the connection between how people think about social life and the laws of the land. Demonstrations of that link are easy to find. There is a journal called *Law & Human Behavior*. There are long-standing research traditions under the headings of Procedural justice, Equity-theory, and Social dominance theory.

Understanding the link between law and human psychology is important because that link explains why when you put intergroup tension into the law, those laws have long lasting effects on interpersonal psychology.[1] When you allow intergroup anxieties into law, if you later get rid of that law, it still leaves a psychological legacy that influences our social interactions.

About the role of law in America's segregated past, Gene Smith, editorial writer for *The Fayetteville Observer*,[2] put it this way:

> The Klan didn't make it all but impossible for 20th century blacks to vote in Mississippi or bar nonwhites from public universities. *The law did that.* In 1835 the N.C. General Assembly, not the KKK, decided that free blacks and Native Americans were becoming too numerous and should no longer be allowed to vote. Slavery, black codes, Jim Crow, segregation – all of it was codified and dutifully enforced.

But with clear and rightful adherence to the U.S. Constitution, through legal means of Supreme Court decisions and new congressional legislation (Civil Rights Act; Voting Rights Act), we Americans got rid of those unjust immoral laws. Yet the psychological legacy of those laws is still with us.

American's current anxiety[3] about our growing neo-diversity is a remnant of the laws that kept people of different colors away from general interaction with each other, or only in safe white-superior, black-inferior social interactions. Eliminating those laws, we have brought ourselves into our current (evolving) neo-diversity; this time and circumstance where each of us has some occasion to encounter and interact with people from many different, racial, ethnic, religious, sex-of-person, bodily condition, or gender identity groups. Yet with so much of our psychology tethered to a past of law-enforced segregation and white-superior, male-superior, Christian-superior, able-bodied superior psychology, having to interact on an equal footing with people "…not like me" creates anxiety.

Keep in mind that American laws of racial segregation were not just about who could go to school with whom. American apartheid also prohibited "race-mixing" in every possible dimension of social life. "Anti-miscegenation" laws prohibited interracial marriage until the 1967 Loving v. Virginia Supreme Court decision struck down those legal 'racial purity' statutes across the land.

In the Loving case, with a unanimous voice, the U.S. Supreme Court said:

> Marriage is one of the 'basic civil rights of man,' fundamental to our very existence and survival. … To deny this fundamental freedom on so unsupportable a basis as the racial classifications embodied in these statutes, classifications so directly subversive of the principle of equality at the heart of the Fourteenth Amendment, is surely to deprive all the State's citizens of liberty without due process of law. The

Fourteenth Amendment requires that the freedom of choice to marry not be restricted by invidious racial discrimination. Under our Constitution, the freedom to marry, or not marry, a person of another race resides with the individual and cannot be infringed by the State.

Yet in America, 50 years later, interracial dating and marriage are still frowned upon by way too many people. In 2009, a Louisiana justice of the peace refused to issue a marriage license to an interracial couple. Why? Aside from the fact that there can be no good nor certainly legal reason for refusing the couple, the justice of the peace said he would not issue the marriage license "...out of concern for any children the couple might have."[4]

Now that's an old one. "What about the children?" As if being born from an interracial couple dooms the child to some horrible existence. As I say to my students, "...what about the children? Maybe the child might become President of the United States... the way mixed race Barack Obama did."

Have no doubt, there is more going on than any genuine concern for "...the children." Laws against interracial marriage were also set up to avoid creating difficulty in identifying people by skin color. When two people of different skin color have children, the color of their offspring may not fit clearly into a stereotype of the group members. Given the history of race in America, where people were led to believe we could always identify who was black and who was white, not being able to do so creates an interaction situation filled with racial uncertainty and anxiety.

With today's increase in interracial dating, marriage and child-bearing, "Who are among the 'we' and who are among the 'they'" becomes the neo-diversity anxiety provoking question. Situations that activate that neo-diversity anxiety include those social encounters in which people cannot quickly identify other people's group membership just by their look. You see, given our history of using skin color, that was also put into laws, not being able to rely on "...the look of a person" can cause some to experience an intense psychological discomfort during the interaction. And to settle themselves in the interaction, without thinking, some people simply blurt out the question, "... What are you?"

Over the years, a number of my mixed-race college students have written about having this experience. December 2017, one such student submitted her true story that went this way:

"...we moved to North Carolina. My first day of 7th grade, I faced one of the most embarrassing interactions so far in front of a group of people. My teacher, Ms. L, asked me to stand in front of the class to tell them a little bit about myself.

"Hi, my name is J-M and I want to be a psychologist like my mom and that means I need to be in middle school and high school here..."

After a long pause, Ms. L replied, "Where did you move from Miss M?" (She mispronounced my name). So, I replied, "Its M and Tampa, but before that I lived in 29 Palms, California and before that was Virginia, and I was actually born in North Carolina but I don't remember it."

"Well you've certainly moved around a lot", she said, "You have such beautiful olive skin, where is your family from?"

"Up-state New York!" I replied without hesitation.

"I mean *what are you*? Mexican? Indian?... your ethnicity? Your last name is different from normal..." She trailed off.

I could feel my face turning red and I stuttered that I was…"

Keep in mind, this is an interaction between a teacher and a 7th grade student; an adult and a thirteen-year-old. Indeed, when it comes to the possibility of being taken over by the neo-diversity anxiety of "who are among the 'we' and who are among the 'they'", there are no innocent.

No human being should ever be asked, "*What* are you?" The problem was not the student's genetic make-up; the problem was with that teacher who felt it was absolutely necessary to know this child's race.

Before the final exam in my upper level "Interdependence and Race" course, all of my students have to put into writing what they consider to be their most intense interpersonal-intergroup experience. Then for the final exam, each student has to analyze that experience. For this student, her intense interpersonal-intergroup interaction was this "what are you" moment. She analyzed what happened using concepts she learned in my class. At the conclusion of her analysis J-M wrote:

> The first time I heard the question "What are you?" was in front of a classroom of new students, in a new state, in 7th grade. Since then I've gotten many questions and assumptions about my ethnicity from people eager to place me in a group. The embarrassment associated with this interaction, was the start of my negative experience with neo-diversity making this the most intense interpersonal-intergroup interaction I have experienced.

That is the other troubling part of this neo-diversity anxiety driven interaction dynamic. The person being asked is psychologically hit by the question, "…What are you?" My student still remembers her experience as a 7th grader and still feels its sting.

Laws matter in the psychology of a nation. Laws that separate us from each other will always leave a legacy, a monument to that time of arbitrary separation. We would do well to keep that in mind as we hear of the laws being considered for enactment that are really just potential laws that are being proposed only to keep some citizens from feeling uncertainty and discomfort in their everyday social interactions.

29. America's Hunger Games

A cannon booms.

A face is flashed across our iPhone, computer and TV screens.

Another American is dead.

We wonder, from which district? Who is left to win? Our killing competition continues.

Not willing to admit it, we still think of ourselves only as a member of a particular racial-district. But with no more legal segregation, neo-diversity means we are all encountering and interacting with people from many different groups.

Our national neo-diversity situation is causing a lot of border encounters and crossings because neo-diversity means we cannot avoid being in contact with people from the different districts. When, every now and then, we find ourselves in an unexpected neo-diversity encounter, a situation so new and so disconnected from our comfort-zone-racial-district, we go on high alert. We allow our nation's segregated history to cat-fish us into our present-day hunger games.

A Cheerios commercial with a mixed-race couple brings outrage.[1] Miss America 2013 is of India-Indian descent and oh my... the cries of disbelief and offense are loud: "If you're #MissAmerica you should have to be American."[2] Target is boycotted for supporting the dignity of transgender persons by accommodating to their human need to use a bathroom that fits their gender-identity. A movie based on the novel *The Hunger Games* becomes controversial because 'the good characters' are dark skinned.

"Why did the producer make all the good characters black?"

When the first Hunger Games movie came out in 2012, there was, in fact, that kind of reaction.[3] A stream of tweets put the outrage in sharp relief. Reporting on this for *Jezebel*, Dodai Stewart wrote: "…when it came to the casting of Rue, Thresh, and Cinna, many audience members did not understand why there were black actors playing those parts."

Before the movie, when I read the books myself, one thing that stood out to me was the descriptions of Rue and Thresh. Dodai Stewart points this out as well saying, "…On page 45 of Suzanne Collins's book, Katniss sees Rue for the first time: "And most hauntingly, a twelve-year-old-girl from District 11. She has dark brown skin and eyes…" Later… "The boy tribute from District 11, Thresh, has the same dark skin as Rue…" Putting it all together, Mx. Stewart makes this observation, "Dark skin. That is what the novelist, the creator of the series, specified. But there were plenty of audience members who were 'shocked,' or confused, or just plain angry."

Disturbing as that may be, there were worse tweets. Following the events as they unfold in the novel, Rue is killed in the competition between the teenaged district representatives. When this angelic looking little dark-skinned girl dies, as I read the book, and as I watched the movie, a mist of tears came into my eyes. But among those who thought Rue shouldn't be black anyway came this tweet: "call me racist but when I found out Rue was black, her death wasn't as sad."

Do all lives really matter?

Race is an intergroup factor of neo-diversity that is cat-fishing Americans into bigotry. We feel something is not quite right because our contact with "them" is only happening through an on-line connection. We try to figure out the situation and how we are supposed to behave. We find ourselves at a loss for how we should act in this virtual "relationship." We feel awkward. We feel fearful. We feel as if we are in the dark. But we go along trying to represent what we think is our racial district, in our American hunger games. Why?

Sociologists Eduardo Bonilla-Silva and David G. Embrick introduced the idea of a "white habitus."[4] Their hypothesis is that "… whites' socialization and isolation… creates… a racialized uninterrupted socialization process that conditions and creates racial taste, perceptions, feelings and emotions and views on racial matters." Furthermore, these researchers say that this white habitus means that "…a life centered on whites in youth will lead to a life centered on whites in adulthood." Using survey and interview data, Bonilla-Silva and Embrick establish that "…whites have very little contact with blacks in neighborhoods, schools, colleges and jobs" (even in the 2000s). From there they show that "…whites do not see or interpret their own racial segregation and isolation as a racial issue at all." That has to mean that whites are unprepared to engage in real, face-to-face interracial encounters.

Habitus is the right idea, but the focus on whites is very misleading. What we have here is a failure to communicate the whole racial-interaction picture. Yes, whites are segregated from other racial groups. So too are other racial groups segregated from whites and from each other. Even though by virtue of smaller numbers, racial and ethnic minorities come into more contact with whites than whites do with racial and ethnic minorities, that does not make that contact interpersonal and meaningful. Having frequent, informal, friendship interactions across group memberships would be the most helpful.[5] Real friendship is important because that would mean that two people have learned to be with each other as people, not as representatives of groups.

For a very long time, social psychologist Thomas Pettigrew has studied whether and how contact between members of different racial and ethnic groups leads to less intergroup tension for those in contact.[6] Gordon Allport, who trained Pettigrew, put forward intergroup contact theory.[7] That theory specifies that intergroup contact will lead to a reduction in feelings of prejudice if the situation in which the contact occurs meets these four conditions:

1. The groups in contact must be of equal status

2. The groups must have common goals

3. The groups must not be in competition

4. The groups contact must be approved of by higher authority

Over the years of his work, Pettigrew started to wonder whether "friendship" is a special case of contact that has its own unique effects. Intergroup friendship would mean more than that two people are in interaction. For the interactions to be a relationship, Pettigrew points out that there must be contact *and* interaction, *over time, with* emotional connection. That would be a friendship. With those relationship qualities, a friendship is also likely to meet the four conditions that Allport's intergroup contact theory indicates to be important to reducing negative feelings about the outgroup; equal-status, a common goal, no competition, approved by authority.

A friendship, then, brings together the power of interpersonal interaction. Powerful enough, in fact, that the evidence from research is that individuals who have a friend (not just an acquaintance) who are members of a racial outgroup show less negative feelings toward that particular outgroup.[8] Friendship, then, is a force that can reduce intergroup tensions and uncertainty in intergroup interactions.

Knowing that in this age of neo-diversity, legal segregation has been abolished, it would seem reasonable to assume that between-group friendships are happening for college students before they come to college. Again, not so; there is friendship segregation before students get to college.

Lincoln Quillan and Mary E. Smith have studied the factors that influence the occurrence of interracial friendships among students in grades seventh through twelfth.[9] Using a national sample and some sophisticated statistical methods, they found that students in schools that are not very diverse have little chance of having friends of other races.

OK, that is almost too obvious a point. But it is also true that if students of any group (white, black, Muslim) find themselves in the minority, those students are more likely to *only* have friends that are racially similar to themselves; they are more likely to have friends who are members of their own group. Actually, though, it should work the other way. In a free and open social situation, if you are a member of a small group, by probabilities you should have more friends from the larger group. But, Quillan and Campbell indicate that:

> "Disturbingly, we find especially high levels of segregation of blacks, including black Hispanics, from all other racial groups."

Coming out of a multiracial middle and/or high school *does not mean* that either white or Hispanic or Muslim, or any students have had meaningful interaction experiences with African Americans. In America, it seems, we have not simply a white-habitus but a racial-habitus for each group. My racial-habitus hypothesis is that the *racial-habitus of America is a socialization process that conditions and creates uncertainty among individuals of all racial groups about how to interact with members of other racial groups.*

Without meaningful interpersonal interactions (e.g., friendships), our racial districts of origin rule our social perceptions. Our racial districts of origin rule how we judge social interactions between people from different racial districts. Two Americans interact in a negative way, a cannon sounds, a face is flashed across iPhone screens, and all we care about is which district won. From which district did they come: black or white, homosexual or heterosexual, Christian or Muslim, civilian or police?

Who are you betting on? Do all lives really matter… to you?

Yet, love is not the answer.

We have to stop talking about "love" as the answer. Stop saying that to solve the neo-diversity problems tearing at the American fabric "…we all have to start loving one another."

Love is too distant a goal in a society of people so social-psychologically separated from each other. Love is too big and vague as an immediate interpersonal goal. Immediate love is not realistic, anyway. Love is never immediate. "Love at first sight" is not love because "want" and "love" are not the same things.

To develop a healthy interpersonal relationship requires one-to-one interaction over time and circumstances of interaction that include mutual and respectful self-disclosures. In real relationships, love grows through social interaction. For love to develop requires relationship evolution.

Love in our neo-diverse America is unrealistic because we don't know what interaction behaviors of ours will make for love in the eyes of our fellow Americans from our too often still-segregated districts. Not only that, you cannot motivate people to love others before they get themselves to respect others.

Let's work on respect.

Respect is something we can all begin working on, from a distance. Respect is interpersonal and immediate. Respect means walking by a person not like you and looking that person in the eye to give them a small kindness for the day.

"Good morning."

"How's it going?"

"Oh please… after you."

Respect from a distance is what we can start today. Respect from a distance is a realistic interpersonal goal we can all build into our everyday behaviors. Working on respect is important because respect from a distance will begin to build bridge-links between our racial districts, reducing the distance between us.

Giving each other the benefit of the doubt by assuming we all deserve a little respect, we will be able to raise our hand to wave to a person across a district boundary and see that gesture returned. Looking from ours into another district, we will then feel something new in our psychology.

"Huh… they seem friendly. Guess they're not so different after all."

We can't get there, though, relying on our one-district point of views. Nor can we get there using us-versus-them approaches that build or just reinforce psychological walls; approaches like 'white privilege.'

30: Tilting at the Windmills of White-Privilege

For years I have been pointing out the problems with relying on the flimsy idea of "…white privilege" to try to change someone's way of thinking about neo-diversity issues; to try to change a person's behavior; to try to engage in productive dialogue that allows different points of view to be expressed. March 20, 2017, my tweets @ DrNacoste carried my message again:

> #diversity/Talk about white-privilege has not weakened the allure of President Trump's anti-group rhetoric.

> #diversity/Shouting white-privilege is ineffective— the notion itself allows people to dodge responsibility for bigotry.

> #diversity/White-privilege is a Freudian claim that does not address here-and-now bigotry.

> #diversity/ Pointing to white privilege to try to stop here-and-now bigotry will never work because privilege is not about the here-and-now.

> #diversity/White privilege is crying wolf so as to not look at the bigotry in the crier's own life.

> #diversity/Wolf-crying white-privilege fails the there-

-are-no-innocent standard for having productive dialogue.

That day, I sent forth those tweets. But I was doing more than tweeting. I was doing more than using 180 characters to point out the futile tilting at the windmill of white privilege. Attached to each tweet was my then newest (March 17, 2017) and most relevant Psychology Today blog post essay, "Sometimes Bigotry is Just Bigotry." That essay reads:

> White privilege is a Freudian concept. Freudian, you say? Yes, Freudian because it is a concept that's all about the influence of what's in a person's (in this case a group's) past.
>
> Just because it's a group's past doesn't make it less Freudian. White privilege is Freudian because we are pointing to something from the past that is outside the person's awareness that we believe they have to face in order to change.
>
> Tell me, has all the talk about white privilege been effective in weakening the attractiveness of President Donald Trump's anti-group rhetoric toward some of our fellow Americans? Not at all, and you know it.
>
> Why not? It's simply because the claim of white privilege lets people off the hook. Whether we want to admit it or not, we all know that there are a lot of ways to be privileged in America. For that reason, shouting about white privilege falls on deaf ears. Surely you see that the claim of privilege fits with too many versions of the American dream (that people think are positive). America is a place where you can "…get ahead of, earn more privileges than, other

people." Sure, that ambition is no longer supposed to be racial, but… well…

Look there are too many problems with the rhetoric of white privilege for it to be effective in addressing the real and pressing intergroup issues of 21ˢᵗ century America. One of those problems is that it is a Freudian claim. We need to address the here and now to manage the new intergroup dynamic of America.

Again, what's new is neo-diversity; this time and circumstance, this new <u>interpersonal situation</u> in America where all of us have some daily occasion to encounter and interact with people not like us on some dimension. From the days of legal, racial segregation to these days of desegregation, there are now unavoidable neo-diverse social encounters at work, on campuses, in the grocery store. Given our segregated history, those neo-diverse encounters are new and provoke intergroup anxiety in people. And sometimes that neo-diversity anxiety wakes up a hibernating bigotry that roars into social interaction. That is the new intergroup dynamic of America.

To be productive in that new context, we need to leave the talk of white privilege and talk instead about the here and now. Let's address what you just did, not what things in your group's past made it easy for you to engage in anti-group behavior (bigotry); to do or say something nasty about a person because of their group membership. Not what things that you are not conscious of that let you behave the way you are behaving; that's Freudian and ineffective in changing that behavior.

What matters is what you are doing in the here and now that is bigotry – nasty, offensive, insensitive, interpersonal behavior that is directed toward a person or persons because of their group membership. The here and now is what matters, not your group's past. In the here and now, bigotry is what matters.

Here's the other Freudian problem. People who are relying on the ineffective rhetoric of white privilege to decry bigotry are also trying to distance themselves from the problems of intergroup tensions we face in America. All this talk about white privilege lets white people off the hook, but it also lets the person of color, the gay or lesbian person, the person who uses a wheel chair, feel righteous and innocent. But turns out, there are no innocent.

In today's neo-diverse America, there are many American groups that individuals can feel prejudice towards: homosexuals, Muslims, transgender persons, Christians, women, persons with visible bodily conditions, military veterans, persons with mental health conditions, interracial couples, and on and on. Neo-diversity gives all of us lots of potential targets for expressions of anti-group feelings (prejudice) that can be expressed in behavior (bigotry). Especially in that neo-diversity context, anyone can be a bigot. There are no innocent; not by skin color, sexual orientation, or religion.

There just are no innocent.

We can't let anyone off the hook for superficial reasons of group membership. We have to address any anti-group feelings (prejudice) toward any group that comes out in anyone's behavior (bigotry) in order to slow down the dangerous intergroup tensions about neo-diversity moving across our nation. Bigotry is in the here and now, and that is what we have to address. Here and now bigotry, not privilege some say has been extended to us by our group's past.

If people insist on being Freudian, then let's talk about the defense mechanism of projection. Denying your own negative tendencies but seeing those negative traits in other people, that's Freud's idea of projection.

More than once in response to my claims about the uselessness of the idea of white privilege, I have had a white person say something pretty startling to me. Spring 2016, a white student told me of her concern about the same kind of statement"

"Dr. Nacoste," she said. "I was talking to a friend, a white person, about how you taught us that the idea of white privilege isn't really productive because it's just makes young white people feel guilty. My friend responded with a bit of anger and said, 'Well, I think they ought to feel guilty.' I was shocked and confused by that statement."

My student was looking at me with that confusion on her face. I said:

"You see that's my point when I say that the idea is a claim used to attack white people; not to start a dialogue. And you are confused because it came from a white person, but I never said the attack was used only by non-whites."

Why would a white person want to use the idea of white privilege in the hopes of making other whites feel racial guilt? Projection, that's why. The particular white person knows that somewhere in the 'here and now' of their lifetime, they have had negative racial thoughts (prejudice) and that person knows that they have acted or come close to behaving with racial bigotry.

Rather than admit and critically examine these negative tendencies in their own life and learn from that awareness, the person wants to say that all white people are guilty or should feel guilty. That projection is a way to avoid self-incrimination. "It's all of the people like me, so what can I do?" As with any other Freudian defense mechanism, that's the point: to not look at our own behavior and see the mistakes we have made or are making.

Let's stop doing all of this. Let's focus on the here and now of our own behavior. That is the only way of dealing with our neo-diversity anxieties, prejudices, and bigotry in a productive way, facing the here and now of our own behavior.

Even Sigmund Freud understood the problem of overlooking actual behavior to spend time talking about unconscious motivations for that behavior. It is claimed that Freud once said, "Sometimes a cigar is just a cigar."

To deal with the intergroup tensions in America, we must tackle the thing right in front of us. We must tackle the behaviors. Otherwise, by our approach, we are (inadvertently) making excuses for the behavior, releasing the individual from personal responsibility. As we work toward a more perfect union, we cannot afford to do that.

"Sometimes, you see, bigotry is just bigotry."

31: Dear White People?

Within minutes of each other, on Thursday, March 23, 2017, I received two emails. At 2:30 p.m., the first email said:

Dr. Nacoste, I'm in need of your help. Most of my friends are aware of the research and material I have studied under your theory and many have contacted me today concerning our Union Activities Board (UAB) and want my "opinion". I'm sure you are aware of the film that will be shown *Dear White People* as part of Diversity Education Week. Many of my "white friends" are appalled. And I have tried to understand how such a loaded question filled with inter-group tension is supposed to promote diversity on campus? In the title, you can clearly see the "us vs them" dynamic. I was hoping for your insight.

I responded to that email saying:

I really don't know anything about the film, except that it has made the rounds of college campuses. But I am troubled that this is making students angry. North Carolina State University (NCSU) students, our students are defacing the posters, tearing them down. All of that is highly unacceptable, going way past just being put off by the title. Those reactions should tell you that no matter what people say they feel, those are not innocent responses to a movie title.

Everyone should check themselves to investigate why a title like this (with no racial slurs) is so emotionally provocative to them. What intergroup anxiety is it really tapping into?

By the time I finished and sent that response, I saw the second email about *Dear White People*. I put off responding to the second email because I had to finish my teaching preparation for my class at 4:30 p.m. Not only that, but I had to be sure I had the presentation ready, that I would be giving right after class (at 6 p.m.) to the Kappa Phi Lamda (Asian-American interest) Sorority for their Diversity Education Week event, which was announced this way:

> "Join the sisters of Kappa Phi Lambda and Dr. Rupert Nacoste on March 23rd, 2017 for Diversity Education Week: Revisited to have a discussion about campus diversity and social interactions! Come with personal stories, experiences, and concerns so we can address problems with cultural and diversity anxiety within our campus."

Next day, Friday, March 24, 2017 I finally got around to the second email, which said:

> I am a student in your "Interpersonal Relationships and Race" (PSY 411) class this semester. I am emailing to express my concerns over the events at Talley today, 3/23 in hopes that you will be able to help. As I was walking past Stafford Commons, I read signs that said, "Dear White People, stop dancing" and other signs that made fun of common 'white people' stereotypes.
>
> Also, the video that they were promoting by the signs was playing on the big screen, and from what I watched, the video had clips of non-white individuals

speaking stereotypes and bigoted statements that have been heard across the country and clips of white individuals yelling.

To be honest, I was caught so off guard and felt so uncomfortable I walked as quickly away from the situation as I could. Using the knowledge you have given me this semester, I am very hurt at the fact that in such a public manor, white people were being isolated as the sole perpetrators of bigotry. You have said countless times, there are no innocent, yet I feel the need to apologize for the color of my skin and the apparent bigotry that is automatically associated with it. I would be grateful for any encouragement or advice for how to deal with these emotions…

By the way, I am not just busy on the NC State University campus helping people learn how to manage themselves when these things happen. On the increase are calls to me to help other colleges and universities, to give their students a better understanding of how to interact with respect with a neo-diverse mix of people. In fact, earlier the same week of our "Dear White People" kerfuffle, I got two different requests for my help.

An administrator from Shippensburg University (Pennsylvania) wrote with a "Request for possible assistance." Her email said:

I'm currently in the middle of reading your book *Taking on Diversity* and thought now is a good time to inquire about possible ways you might be able to help our university. Last fall a vile bigoted comment was posted on social media. If you would be willing to come and assist us…

The same week I received an email with the subject, "Helping Us in Arizona." This faculty member (and administrator) said:

Right after the election we had several incidents of hate speech, defamation of property and the like on our campus. I also teach Race and Ethnic Relations and I use your book, *Taking on Diversity*. The reason I am writing you is that I have been given the 'green light' to find our Keynote Speaker for this year and I was wondering if we could get you to come to help us with these neo-diversity issues on our campus.

No one should think, then, that these are issues only at NCSU. Trust me, there are no utopias out there in America. There are no innocent places to go.

To the 2nd NCSU student who emailed me about *Dear White People* I said:

Here's what you need to understand about your reactions to this racial affront. Your response is not wrong or overly sensitive. Just like the response of African Americans to people "having fun" with stereotypes of black people (B.E.T. parties), is not wrong or overly sensitive. But part of your reaction is because you are taking my class and you are now able to articulate exactly what you are reacting to with appropriate concepts and outrage. You can now call out bigotry as bigotry. You now see bigotry in all its forms for the bigotry that it all is.

But do not "give in" to that bigotry. That bigotry, other people's stereotypes of people with white skin does not define you. Just like other's people's stereotypes of people with dark-skin color like mine does not define me. I will not let other people's stereotypes become a part of how I think of myself.

Too, it is good to know that "...there are no innocent."

I do not know the intent UAB had for using the film or promoting it the way it was done. But I do know that on our campus, in towns and cities, in Hollywood, just the same as there are white people who want black people to just shut up, there are black people who want white people to feel guilty. I cannot stop that from happening and neither can you. What we can do is see the bigotry for what it is. Understanding that, we then should know not let that make us act in inappropriate ways. We then should educate those in our social circles, about the nature of bigotry. And we then, when appropriate, should speak out against that bigotry, calmly and clearly.

Having learned of all that intergroup emotion on campus, that weekend I got to work. In fact, all of what you have just read comes from the essay I wrote for our student newspaper *The Technician*. As a guest column, my essay appeared in the newspaper that very next Monday, March 26, 2017, four days after I started getting those emails. Titled "Dear White People?" my essay became one of the most widely read of the year for *The Technician*. Toward the end of that semester and the academic year, from one of the editors I received this information:

> Your most-viewed column is "Dear White People?" with 4578 unique page-views, the 12th-most of all our articles in the 2016-17 volume, and the second-most of any article since it was published on March 26. Our Facebook post linking to [your Dear White People essay] reached 11,734 people (the second-highest of 2017).

To round out my essay, I spoke directly to our student body. I said to NC State students:

We now live in a neo-diverse America. No longer segregated from each other, on our neo-diverse campus we all have to encounter and interact with people from many different groups with many different experiences and viewpoints. Whosoever is not willing to interact with fellow NCSU students with respect, whosoever is unwilling to fight against stereotypes of any of our students, that person is just taking up space on our campus. Such a person does not deserve to be considered a member of the Wolfpack.

For the Strength of Pack is the Wolf and the Strength of the Wolf is the Pack.

To be a full-fledged member of the Wolfpack, you must believe everybody here is Wolfpack. You must support and nurture all of the neo-diverse members of the Pack no matter their [demographic] group of origin. That is the soul of the Wolfpack. #GoPack

Now to America, I say this:

Use of group stereotypes should not be offensive to you only when aimed at a group with whom you identify. If when Muslims speak out against the irrational fear of Muslims that they feel every day, and you say, "…well, they-can't-be-trusted," you show your concern about stereotypes only matters when you feel implicated. If when African American students object to white students going around in black-face at parties, or having "…dress up like a black person" parties and once again, you say, man-why-are-they-so-sensitive, you reveal your true colors. If when gays and lesbians cry out when public stereotypes of homosexuals are used or offensive anti-homosexual language ("that's so gay") is used, and you wonder why-are-they-so-sensitive you reveal that you only care about your group. If that is your approach and per-spective, you show that you have a narrow, one-group theory-of-mind.

We now live in a neo-diverse America. No longer segregated from each other, in our neo-diverse nation we all have to encounter and interact with people from many different groups. Right now, we are struggling to live up to our fundamental American values that start with, "We hold these truths to be self-evident that all men are created equal…" To save that soul of America, we must learn to interact with each other with respect.

Stereotyping is one form of bigotry. But it's not bigotry just when it is aimed at white people. All bigotry is all the same – anti-group feelings expressed in (verbal or non-verbal) behavior. Objecting to bigotry only when it is about "your group" and about your feelings means you are playing an active yet passive-aggressive role in maintaining and spreading the intergroup tension tearing at the soul of America today.

It means you are not woke.

Woke: Although an incorrect tense of awake, a reference to how people should be aware in current affairs.

Urban Dictionary (https://www.urbandictionary. com/define.php?term=Woke)

32: To Be or Not to Be Woke

In today's America, some people seem to think it is an accomplishment to claim to be "woke." Time to ask, what does it really mean to be "woke"? Looking to the online urban dictionary, for "woke" we find, "Although an incorrect tense of awake, a reference to how people should be aware in current affairs." No doubt, awareness is one thing, but knowing how to act on that awareness is another.

I have been thinking about this because I am worried. I see too many people who proclaim themselves "woke" as a fad. What, then, does it take to live woke? What should be in the social psychology of a person who is woke?

Forty-five years I have been doing the fieldwork of social justice. At the age of 22, I started doing that work in the U.S. Navy, an environment filled with danger and dangerous intergroup social interactions that included race riots aboard aircraft carriers. Under Admiral Elmo Zumwalt, to deal with these intergroup problems the Navy created and implemented an interracial dialogue intervention "Understanding Personal Worth and Racial Dignity." All sailors, officers, and enlisted were required to participate in a two and a half day session of racial sensitivity group conversations that were facilitated by trained group facilitators who were enlisted sailors.[1]

After my service onboard the USS *Intrepid*, in 1973 I was one of those trained by the Department of Defense to facilitate interracial dialogues among sailors that were anything but polite. Trained as a Racial Awareness Facilitator (RAFT), and then facilitating over 20 sessions each with 30 or so men, working special human relations duties was a catalyst for the rest of my life. With my voting-rights activist father as my model, I was awake. In 21st century vernacular, I went from just being awake to being "woke." My interest in group dynamics, race relations, and social justice was piqued. I sought higher education. I became a social psychologist. Since 1981 I have been teaching, publishing research articles, and writing books on intergroup relations as a social psychologist.[2]

To be "woke" is to be a connector of communities. That was the point of the work of facilitating interracial dialogues in the Navy: to create an environment of positive, respectful, working relationships between sailors from different racial and ethnic demographic groups. As I have lived it, to be "woke" is not a fad but a method to live by and help others understand why it is important to live by this interaction principle: Never try to interact with a person as a representative of a group.[3]

"Intersectional" is today's buzzword that has caught on with the newly 'woke.' Intersectional is a concept that is supposed to describe the fact that discrimination has overlapping, multi-group links. To talk about racial discrimination alone is to miss the complexity that people who experience discrimination are not of just one group membership. A classic case for insight into intersectionality is that racial discrimination influences black women at the same time that gender discrimination does.

For the 'woke,' that idea should mean we will not allow us-versus-them to guide our work. No surprise, not everybody who talks about America's intersectional struggles actually gets that point. On Facebook, I saw a post about feminism. It said, "…My feminism has to be intersectional." Then the attached article was "Why I hate white women," as if white women were the problem to solve.

With that, the problem is laid bare. "Intersectional" becomes an unnatural social-psychological wall. A concept that is supposed to describe interconnected struggles for fair treatment is used to push, to activate, the us-versus-them, minimal group effect; automatic categorization of people into groups that activates competition between those groups.[4] After the revolutionary work we did to knock down the walls of all kinds of American segregation, are we going to still rely on old us-versus-them thinking and feeling?

Look, there are people who voted for President Trump who now want to work against what he is trying to do. Have you seen the "I regret voting for Donald Trump" Facebook page? Have you seen the twitter stream of "@Trump-Regrets"? Have you seen the twitter hashtag "#regretvotingforTrump" with its 250,000 followers? Will you turn those people away from the social justice work that needs doing? Will you just cancel these people? Or, will you set aside your bias to really live "…woke"?

In my "Interpersonal Relationships and Race" course, I make a point of teaching my students about the work it takes to get past this old us-versus-them thinking. I let students know that in the blistering days of the "old" Civil Rights Movement, there were former Klansmen who climbed over the hot, unnatural walls of segregation to work in the movement for civil rights for African Americans. I shook hands with one or two of those former Klansmen. On the American journey toward positive social change, in our work toward a more perfect union, we must be foolish enough to take every opportunity to create coalitions and collaborations.

Spring 2017 semester, in a paper for my "Interdependence and Race" course, one of my students wrote a lament about the "woke." Reacting to my teaching about the coalition building that she had now learned went on during the "old" Civil Rights Movement, an African American student wrote:

> "Being a 'social justice warrior' is very 'in' right now. Because of this, I often find that people are quick to show how 'woke' they are by attacking someone else. Unfortunately, doing that, they miss the opportunity to teach and learn from someone else."

For close to 50 years, with much success, I have done the work of moving all kinds of people into productive dialogue toward positive social change. For me, in my work, to be woke has always been about helping to connect communities at the junction of mutual respect. Today, I will not stand by and let the newcomers to this social justice work, the newly "woke," go around ripping up the roots of the coalitions that I know we need to get through these "new" difficult days. I will not stand by and let the neophyte 'woke,' with unfocused zeal, use bigotry as a hatchet in what is supposed to be the gardening of social justice for all.

From where I stand, proclaiming yourself to be 'hella' woke means you are not woke at all. To be "woke" is to advocate for justice without putting people down; to hold to a foolish, high standard of respect for everyone's humanity. Name-calling people because of the group they happen to be born into, is not social justice work. That is just feeding the social injustice of bigotry that the 'woke' should be fighting to dismantle.

To those who claim to be 'woke,' I ask, have you educated yourself enough to know, understand and use in your work the fact that our neo-diversity situation is what has brought intersectionality to the forefront of 21st century activist work; 21st century social justice coalition building? Have you educated yourself enough to know that prejudice is not bigotry is not racism? If you have, then you would be able to address intergroup problems of today's neo-diversity in intersectionality with strategies that do not rely on name-calling.

To do our work for social justice, we must build coalitions of respect so that we can collaborate. That is what being "woke" has always meant. That is how we will survive and thrive during this period in America. That is how we will, once again, save the soul of America.

In 1960, Martin Luther King Jr. spoke directly to how difficult is the work for social justice. In a speech to young people, Dr. King said:

May I say to you as you continue your protest, you

will confront moments of difficulty. But let us realize that no great and lasting gain comes in history without suffering and sacrifice. Let nobody stop you; you are doing something that will ultimately save the soul of America.

As you advocate, as you meet to organize and develop new, innovative strategies of action, you must do so respecting everyone's humanity. If that is not your way of being a social justice worker, you are not what you are claiming. If you only care about people using stereotypes of the groups you like, if you do not check yourself from using stereotypes of people who are members of groups you think have it easy, you are contributing to the problems of social justice. To all who want to claim it, you must ask yourself whether 'tis nobler to appear to be a social justice warrior, or to suffer the slings and arrows of ridicule, to be actually 'woke.'

33. Evoke the Forms: Nine Tips to Help You Live Woke

Marriage equality. Minorities becoming the majority. What's going on? Police shootings. Racial murders. Religious murders. What is prejudice, what is bigotry, what is racism? We are anxious in our everyday walk through life. What is a disability? Is that the right word? What is gender? Why does it matter? Who gets to say what? Someone utters an anti-group slur, someone uses a group stereotype to talk about another person. Should I say something? What should I say? Change is happening every day, everywhere in America. And we, Americans, are struggling.

Everywhere in America, people are struggling to understand and manage neo-diversity. We Americans are struggling with neo-diversity anxiety even about how to interact with people who live in our neighborhoods. We are struggling with how to talk with each other, how to respect each other.

No wonder we are seeing articles that try to help us interact safely.

"Never say this to a gay person."

"Never say this to an interracial couple."

"Never say this…"

Those kinds of advice articles are showing up all over the place. But none of those articles educate the reader about what's going on that is so new that people need this kind of advice. The "…what" is neo-diversity. The "…why" is real, fast, and dramatic social change. The new problem is how to interact with each other when there are no longer barriers keeping us separate and there are no strict rules of social interaction to guide us.

Yet, there has been no apocalypse. "Who are among the 'we' and who are among the 'they?'" No matter how scary that question makes the terrain of the neo-diversity frontier feel, our world has not come to an end. Zombies do not walk among us wanting to kill us and eat our brains.

It all feels different because it is different. It seems so awful unpredictable, too; a ball of confusion.

Newtown, Ct. San Bernandino. Nice, France. El Paso – shootings, bombings, knife-attacks. With all that it can feel like the "end of days" has arrived. Maybe, then, just maybe, a message from the apocalypse would help. Maybe we would pay attention to a word of advice that comes from an end of the world perspective.

Hear, then, from the end of the world as we know it, this voice. In his apocalyptic novel *The Road*, Cormac McCarthy[1] tells us that when all that was familiar seems to be gone, we have to:

> "...Evoke the forms. Where you've nothing else construct ceremonies out of the air and breathe upon them."

Having no choice but to live on this new frontier, we must innovate. To be woke in our new interpersonal circumstances, we must be working to create new forms of interaction in the complex social situations we encounter in this new land. That is what frontier pioneers do.

###

November 2008, Senator Barack Obama is elected president, and that night racial graffiti and threat is found on my (NC State) campus. Secret Service is alerted by our university administration. Secret Service comes to Raleigh and tracks down the perpetrators. Students are in shock; many are outraged.

November 2010, another election week and racial and anti-gay and lesbian graffiti is discovered in a public space on my campus. Shock and outrage move through our students. Then, something new.

On that November 15, 2010, students at NCSU walked our campus crying out "I'm Awake," to start the Wake Up movement against bigotry on the campus. Not just an awakening for the participants, but an attempt to wake and create a movement for the whole campus community. Those students were trying to evoke a new form of social interaction between students. By the end of the next semester, word was spreading. About "Wake Up! It's Serious: A Campaign for Change," a feature article in the school newspaper,[2] ended this way:

> Over the years, racism and bigotry have made their mark on campus. Seen in classroom interactions, hidden in conversations or brazenly painted on the walls of the Free Express Tunnel, it has sparked the attention of this small group of students familiar with the pains of racial prejudice.
>
> As these individuals have been reminded of discrimination time and time again, they wish to send out a wake-up call across the University. Their ultimate message proclaims that dealing with racial intolerance includes everybody.
>
> As Mario Terry, a junior in psychology, put it, "I interpret silence as passiveness."

Likewise, in the sleepy Southern tobacco road town of Sanford, NC, the One-by-One race-relations improvement group used its voice. Seeing an opportunity, the group submitted a letter to the editor about the local incident where a supervisor at the Department of Health had used an image of a lynching to warn people there would be consequences for not turning off computers at the end of the day. One-by-One's letter caught the attention of some in the community, and *The Sanford Herald* did a feature on the One-by-One group in the newspapers' Take-5 segment. Asked whether they thought their letter had made any difference, the group's response was clear. They said:

> Whether the situation within the county's social services branch has been resolved to the satisfaction of those involved is not known, but there was a very positive result from the letter [from] One-By-One. During the meeting following the publication of [our] letter, a new participant, an African American gentleman, thanked One-By-One for the letter.

> He said: "It helps us. Otherwise, we feel alone with these issues." His statement was an eloquent validation of what One-By-One is about.[3]

Facing a new frontier, when so much of the familiar seems gone, Cormac McCarthy's advice is worth heeding. Evoke the forms. Create new, inclusive, interpersonal forms and breathe life into the new situations of interpersonal-interdependence.

In my "Interpersonal Relationships and Race" course and in my book *Taking on Diversity: How We Can Move From Anxiety to Respect*, I teach the dynamics of social interaction and relationship development. Teaching that means I am teaching students (and readers) what makes for good social interaction in this age of neo-diversity. At the same time, I am also teaching how, today, it is easier than ever for two people in social interaction to crash into each other. I put it that way because in 21st century America, social interaction crashes are the norm. It is what the narrator says at the beginning of the movie *Crash*. He says:

> "It's the sense of touch. Nobody touches anymore. I

think that we miss that touch so much that we crash
into each other just so that we can feel something."

Prejudice and bigotry exist in America. Yet we are not a nation of
bigots. Sometimes all that is going on is that in the 21st century, we
are in interaction with people from so many different groups we feel
uncertain. We try to reach out. We get nervous and distracted. Two
people reaching out nervous and distracted too often these days crash
into each other.

In my course, I teach students about why neo-diversity can
have these effects on people in social interaction. My students not
only learn what makes for good social interactions, they are learning
what can make a social interaction swerve so much the interaction
crashes. Through my teaching I end up giving my students tips for
how to live woke, how to interact with respect in neo-diverse situations. From my teaching, then, here are nine tips that go beyond the
"Never say this…" advice.

1. *Never try to interact with a person as a representative
   of a group.* Remember to only think of the person
   as one-individual who you are in an interaction
   with; one-individual.

2. If a group stereotype pops into your head, *acknowledge that stereotype for what it is to yourself, then psychologically set it aside*, and talk with respect to the
   person, the one-individual, who is in front of you.

3. *If the interaction is with a new acquaintance, remember to go slow. Don't rush the interaction.* Long ago,
   social psychologists discovered that self-disclosures
   should come slowly, as if peeling an onion.[4] We
   social psychologists agree with Shrek when he says
   Ogres and onions have layers; so too human beings.

4. *Self-disclosures should also be asked for gradually as a relationship develops.* As we adjust to neo-diversity, sometimes desires rooted in the age of race-relations flair up in our psychology. Today in social interaction, sometimes people feel that they have to know about a person's race or ethnicity before all else. But just because you are burning with curiosity about a person's race, ethnicity or religion does not give you the right to ask intrusive, disrespectful, questions like, "…What are you?" No human being should ever be asked "…What are you?" If that person wants you to know, they'll let you know when they are ready to reveal this (whatever that "this" is) about themselves. Self-disclosures should be asked for slowly.

5. If the interaction is with a new acquaintance and you find you need to ask one or two questions to get or keep the conversation going, *ask an open-ended question. Don't ask a stereotyped-based question;* for instance, saying to a tall person, "…play a lot of hoops?" Tall people, like all people, are a neo-diverse group, which means some tall people like me don't do sports at all. *Don't ask a narrow question* – What do you do for a living? Here are two open-ended questions you can ask a new acquaintance: "…What keeps you busy?" "…How do you spend your days?"

"What kind of work do you do?" Too much has changed about the roles people can inhabit in our social world to assume that is the best way to start a conversation. I never ask a new acquaintance "…What do you do for a living?" I ask, "…What keeps you busy?" And every time I ask that question of a new acquaintance, I find myself in an interesting, fun social interaction.

6. Lots of people have alerted me to the fact that one of the tough interaction struggles in America today is what to do when in conversation someone uses offensive anti-group language (gender slurs, slurs about people with mental health conditions, religious slurs, racial slurs, all manner of stereotypes). What should you do? *Let the person know your standards for continuing to interact with you. When the person you are interacting with uses the language of bigotry, do not be silent; speak into the moment; do not argue, yet speak into the moment and object.* Here's what works.[5] Speak into the moment using you inside voice to say, *"I'm sorry, I would prefer not to hear that kind of gender/ethnic/racial slur/stereotype. I find that kind talk offensive. It hurts me."* If the person continues to engage in the use of language bigotry, don't continue to argue. You have pointed out that this kind of language hurts you, and by ignoring your preference for a continuing interaction, they are telling you they care nothing about your feelings. Keep your dignity and walk the hell away.

7. *If you find yourself in an intense (heated) social interaction, don't attack (even if you are being verbally attacked).* Settle yourself into the good standards for behavior you have set for yourself. If you believe you are a kind, considerate person, then behave that way even as you make your case for your point of view.

8. *If you are in an intense (heated) social interaction, speak into the moment but follow the basic rules of good social interaction.* For instance, turn-taking means giving the other person the chance to speak from their point of view (while you listen). Also, speak for yourself. In other words, use "I" not "you."

9. *If this is a work-related (and heated) interaction, follow Tips 7 & 8 and know and speak for yourself through the policies and procedures specified in that workplace for handling the problem at hand.* If that doesn't work, seek mediation immediately.

Take these tips as the foundation for developing for yourself good policies for your social interactions in neo-diverse America. If we work to interact by policy, we will, indeed, have a chance to get along.

Sometimes, out of the blue, a former student lets me know that my tips do help. July 2016, I received this email:

Dear Dr. Nacoste, my name is B. Y. I am an NC State graduate. I took your social psychology class three years ago I believe. The events that have and continue to take place in our society leads to the reason why I am writing you. I simply just want to say thank you. While I am a white male, and come from a family where I was taught the color of your skin does not matter, society is trying to teach my generation it does. I know every event that has taken place all revolves around race. I personally wanted to thank you for your educational knowledge on this topic. It has and continues to keep me grounded and look past everything society says.

The things I learned in your class have allowed me to not get caught up in this wall of racial divide that is being built. You taught me that being acknowledged as a black or white person is a way of letting that person know they are seen and exist. You believed that this was not a bad thing, and I can tell you I learned a lot from that. That point has allowed me to have great conversations with people who are not white that I will remember for the rest of my life.

As I mentioned before that the color of a person's skin does not bother me, but it is incredible to have education and knowledge to overcome what society continues to illustrate. Thank you for opening my eyes and teaching me to not fall into this hole that continues to get deeper. Your famous phrase "walk the hell away" comes into play for me. Once again, thank you so much for the knowledge you shared while teaching my class.

No doubt we should all try to interact by policy, not just instinct, not just by impulse. We must try to live woke. To do so, we must work to evoke new positive forms of social interaction. If we use good social interaction self-directed policies to control our first impulses, our interpersonal lives will be better because we will have fewer interpersonal crashes.

"I don't know what's going to happen now...

...we've got some difficult days ahead."

Martin Luther King, Jr.

April 3, 1968

Memphis, TN

34: The Grabbers

When the audio recording of presidential candidate Donald Trump went public, America was shocked. On audio, Mr. Trump talked about his interactions with women in a way that went well beyond so-called (and always inappropriate) "locker room talk." Back in 2005, as he was getting ready for an appearance on "Access Hollywood," Mr. Trump proudly said:

"I've gotta use some Tic Tacs, just in case I start kissing her. You know I'm automatically attracted to beautiful — I just start kissing them. It's like a magnet. Just kiss. I don't even wait. And when you're a star they let you do it. You can do anything…Grab them by the pussy. You can do anything."

Shocking, yes, but when it comes to disrespect of all things woman, Donald Trump is no "lone grabber." Something wicked is rising across America, rising in everyday social interactions, rising on college campuses.

Statistics on sexual assaults on college campuses are disturbing. Those statistics are reported with frequency on our news feeds because there is an epidemic of sexual bigotry.

Painful for me is that I do not only encounter that social reality through the abstraction of statistics. I encounter the social reality of sexual assaults of young women in a much more personal way. I encounter that social reality in the personal stories young women trust me with in their papers at the end of my "Introduction to Social Psychology" course.

As a requirement for that course, I have students write a one-page paper to describe "…what one new thought" about interpersonal relationships had come to them as a result of taking my course. Each semester, to get credit for their paper I require students to use one concept from the class that their new thought was provoked by and revolved around. Finally, I have students write about how this "one new thought" would help them to function better in their interpersonal relationships. Yes, all that in one page.

Most of my students do very good papers; true, personal, hard-lessons learned written with vividness and clarity. Spring 2016, I was stunned by the number of papers by females and males that had to do with my students experiencing abuse in their relationships.

All abusers are carrying around a psychological mix of insecurity and superiority. That mix is dangerous because it means the person will be manipulative. It means this is a person who will try to take advantage of any social situation where they think they can get what they want and get away with it.

Here I was further stunned by the number of papers on fate-control, abuse of power, from my young female students that were papers describing sexual assaults at the hands of young males. One of my students wrote:

"I was raped while on a date."

Another wrote:

A kiss seemed just like a kiss. He made gestures indicating he wanted to try more but my verbal protests slowed his progress. Three no's; I said three no's but he kept going. My best friend of seven years raped me. There was no gray area; there was no questionable body language, just my body clenched up beneath him, uncomfortable, disrespected, and shocked.

All of this is unimaginable and horrible. What is behind the increase in date rape and sexual assaults of American high school females and sexual assaults and rapes of young women on college campuses? We are in the grip of an epidemic of sexual disrespect of women. Here's what I mean. One student wrote:

> After "dating" for a few weeks, he asked me out to dinner. Once we finished our meal, he took me back to my house, where we sat in the car talking. We kissed for a few minutes and then I noticed his hands moving in places I did not think they should be going. I pushed his hands away, yet they came back again, and then once more I stopped him and this time I asked him what the deal was.
>
> He replied he wanted to have sex with me. I replied that this is not something I was interested in right now. This made him really angry.
>
> He yelled that I had led him on; it was my fault, how stupid I was, how he wasted money on me, and how I was selfish."

Something wicked has come into our sexual relationship dynamics. Sexual arrogance and bigotry have become prevalent in the world of dating. And yes, I mean to use the concept of bigotry.

Bigotry is anti-group feelings of superiority expressed in behavior. Bigotry rests on the belief that the other group is inferior and so subject to any behavior the bigot feels the whim and unilateral power to enact. Sexual bigotry is a form of feelings of supremacy – male supremacy, giving males the license to get what they want; just grab if you feel like it.

OK, so an epidemic of sexual bigotry, but the question is why?

Sociologist Barbara Dafoe Whitehead, co-director of the National Marriage Project at Rutgers University, showed that there has been a major shift in the way society manages romantic interpersonal relationships. In her book, Dr. Whitehead shows that shift has been from a marriage-dating system to a relationship-dating system.[1]

The marriage-dating system brought two never-married single people together for life-long marriage. That system had courtship expectations and rules. But now American society has moved away from that system and a new system has emerged: the relationship-dating system.

How does this new system work? Very simply, the relationship-dating system is set up to make sure people have intimate relationships. That's the end of the sentence. People, never married or not, are expected to have intimate relationships, but not necessarily marriage, and certainly not life-long marriage. In the relationship-dating system, there are no courtship expectations and rules, and break ups are expected. I mean come on, how long can two people be expected to stay together… get real.

Reading Dr. Whitehead's book over a weekend in 2003, I understood the claim of a shift. I was excited to bring that idea into my classroom. In fact, that semester I created a new lecture to describe and discuss this idea in my sophomore level "Introduction to Social Psychology" course. To get into that discussion I asked my students, "What are the goals of dating nowadays?"

Asking that every semester since 2003, I learned that a major consequence of the shift from a marriage-dating system to a relationship-dating system is that modern dating motivations are all over the place. Here is a typical list of things said in that one class period where I ask my students about the goals of dating. On the goals of dating these days, they say:

Sex

Experience: figure out what you want in a relationship

Figure out your type

Not be lonely

Get attention

Have fun with someone new

Status: showing off to friends that you have a date

Learn more about someone

Have someone to do stuff with

*Feel obligated to: stigma attached to being single for
long amounts of time*

To fit in

Marriage: "benefits:" legal, monetary, etc.

To feel wanted

Pity the other person

Emotional support

Revenge

To not be bored

Familial expectations/obligations

You like them

Fulfillment in helping someone else reach their goals

Money

Help figure out who you are

To be happy

Rebounding from a failed relationship

To become more open minded

To fall in love

To have fun/ To go on fun dates

As I facilitate my 200 students giving their opinions on the goals of dating these days, I am waiting for someone to say "…to find the person you are going to marry." Trust me. That always comes up late and in some classes is never mentioned.

Dating goals nowadays are all over the place. Not only that, but there are no rules of dating. When I use the word "…courting" with my classes, I tease my students by saying, "When I say courting, you have no idea what I'm talking about." They smile and grimace as they shake their heads to agree with me.

No rules leaves an open door to all kinds of behavior in the arena of dating. The manipulative person can have a field day in that unstructured social world.

One female student wrote:

> I find it sad that after I have been hanging out with a guy for a long or short period of time, I find it necessary to say, "…hey, I do not have sex with anyone unless I am dating them." The reactions I have gotten from that statement range from a look of confusion, a look of disgust, to on the rare occasion, a look of respect.

> Throughout my college experience I have found it extremely frustrating that the majority of people my age do not correlate sex and relationships together.

As a social influence on young people in particular, the relationship-dating system is setting young people up for crashes in their attempts to build long-lasting romantic relationships. One put it this way:

> "It seems as if the relationship dating system has turned the focus on less about finding someone to date, court and marry and more about finding someone who can be fun 'for the moment.'"

Yeah, but once educated young people start to see the truth of the way it really is. One wrote:

> It took me a long time to realize that I am worth a whole lot more than the bull^%$# I put up with from my ex-boyfriends. As I look back on my past interpersonal relationships, I can see that I let a lot of things slide that I would not put up with today. I let boys use me for my body without giving me the intimate level of personal connection that I know I needed.

Donald Trump is not patient zero. Our dating social system is the swamp in and from which the epidemic of sexual disrespect grew. Donald Trump is just one male. But as a visible, prominent example, Donald Trump's bragging about grabbing is an indirect social influence pushing into a social system that is already filled with uncertainty about what is appropriate dating behavior. That makes Trump's bravado even more of a dangerous virus.

What now? We have to teach young people to pay attention, to develop strategies in order to develop healthy dating and more long-term relationships. Myself, I try to inoculate my students from the virus of sexual disrespect in my lecture on the dating system. I use this quote from one my female student's papers from Spring 2016. Aloud I read,

> "He [told me] he wanted to have sex with me. I replied that this is not something I was interested in right

now. This made him really angry.

He yelled that I had led him on; it was my fault, how stupid I was, how he wasted money on me, and how I was selfish."

Then, with no trigger warnings given, I roar at the males in the lecture hall:

Wait, wait and… oh hell no! That is beyond out of control, inappropriate, and disrespectful.

Young males! If you don't know, let me tell you. Just because a woman spends time with you, does not obligate her to have sex with you.

Men know that! Boys do not!

Look, I'm an optimist about young people. Young people just need the opportunity to learn. Today's generation is no different than any other generation when it comes to that. I believe we can put them in a position to do better. That's on us the adults, though. It's not on them.

September 27, 2018, I lectured on modern dating dynamics. At the usual point where I roar my outrage at the male students in the class about them feeling owed sex because a young woman has spent time with them, something happened. Although it was on my mind, I didn't anticipate how it would influence me during lecture. But because that was the day of the hearing of sexual harassment claims against Supreme Court nominee Mr. Brett Kavanaugh, my roar went to another level. My students heard and saw me shake with anger and disgust when I said,

"Young males! If you don't know, let me tell you. Just because a woman spends time with you, does not obligate her to have sex with you. Men know that! Boys do not!"

To put a fine point on it, I shook the auditorium with my roar: "We must put a stop to this sexual disrespect of women."

The next morning, Friday, September 28, 2018, I received this email:

> Dr. Nacoste, I wanted to thank you for your lecture. As a woman, I have rarely felt a man in power advocate for my safety, for my rights to my body, and for my rights as a human. Today, I heard it powerfully from you.
>
> I was reflecting on the Kavanaugh case just now, and I needed a break from reading the different news stories, I went onto Twitter and saw your tweet. Once again, I felt the comfort your lecture gave. A friend of mine who is also in your class and I discussed your words, and how grateful we are that you said them. You have influenced future leaders- and nothing is more important than those seeds of change.

Reading that email at my desk, I was in tears because it told me I was right to roar. We must put a stop to all this sexual disrespect of women. We've all got work to do.

Still, in the case of Mr. Trump, we are talking about someone who, at the time, wanted to be president of the United States. So much for that candidacy… right? I mean, how could he possibly win once the American people heard the tape of his statement?

How?

35: Wait… What?
He Won?!?

One-time presidential candidate is now President Donald Trump. But how in the world did Mr. Donald Trump connect to enough Americans to win the presidency?

Pundits got it wrong. Many people misunderstood Mr. Trump's campaign. President Trump did not win on a campaign of bigotry. Yes, he made bigoted statements. But whatever his particular statements about groups, Mr. Trump had one clear message and it was not "Make America Great Again," it was let's "Make America simple again."

Turns out that, "…make America simple again…" was the subtext and core message underlying the mix of statements that made up Mr. Donald Trump's campaign.

"Drain the swamp." "Lock her up." "Build a wall." "America First."

Human psychology prefers simplicity. We carry in our brains a cognitive economic motivation that pushes us to use cognitive short-cuts. No matter who we are, what our station in life, we carry around with us a cognitive economic system: "…those cognitive processes that serve to reduce and simplify the vast amount of information that floods most people's lives, thus allowing efficient processing and avoiding an otherwise overwhelming overload."[1]

We prefer the"…keep it simple" rule. Problem is that in times of rapid social change, the real world is complex. That real-world complexity requires complex information processing that puts a strain on our human psychology. That is why in times of rapid social change, as are these times in which we are living, we are drawn to simplifying messages.

It is in that way that the psychology of Mr. Donald Trump's winning presidential campaign has been misunderstood. "Make America Great Again" has the side effect of unleashing simple emotions and awakening hibernating bigotry. Still, that is but a side effect, not the main social-psychological dynamic. Turns out Mr. Trump was elected to make America simple again. You see the idea of making America simple again easily connected with the intergroup anxiety that lots of Americans are feeling. That intergroup anxiety is attached to the neo-diversity situation of America in which all of us have to encounter and interact with people from many different groups.[2]

An ironic part of today's complex, digital world is that we can customize and streamline the flow of information we expose ourselves to; we can keep ourselves in a stream of information of only like-minded voices. *New York Times* columnist David Brooks put it this way:

> The threat of terror hasn't united Americans, but divided them. The globalization of trade has sparked nationalistic backlashes. The revolution in communications technology has brought media segmentation, as people seek out newspapers and shows that reinforce their preconceptions.

Mr. Brooks' point is that we have available to us: MTV, Food Network, GodTube.org, Rush Limbaugh, NPR, Fox News, MSNBC, PBS, DIY (do it yourself TV channel). These and other media cater to interest groups. Nowadays a person has the option of only paying attention to broadcasts that match that person's particular interests, politics, or cultural and religious beliefs. Our social uncertainties, our search for simplicity, motivate us to shelter ourselves.[3] But much to our dismay, we can't control the people we see on the street, in Walmart, going into the movies, in television commercials, or eating at a restaurant.

Americans are struggling. Spring 2018, one of my students reported her most intense interpersonal-intergroup story. She wrote:

A little background information before the story: I work at a restaurant/entertainment venue in North Hills, an area surrounded by upscale high-rise apartments and condos. In the venue I work at the front desk but also bounce around from serving and bar tending as well. The area was known in the past for being very "white" but in the last few years as Raleigh has grown, so has the diversity in the community. We now get more people of color coming through our doors than ever before.

Here's what happened:

I was gathering some menus at the front desk when a white man (perhaps in his late forties or early fifties) wandered over to me with his plate of Buffalo wings, leaned in, and stated "you know, this place used to be really classy."

Knowing there was a complaint coming I began mentally searching for the patience to handle whatever was about to come out of his mouth because it was a Saturday, we were on a three-hour wait list, and this guy looked like someone ready to rant. I simply smiled and asked, "What do you mean 'used-to-be?'"

He then gestured to a group of black women checking in at the desk next to me and said, "It was classy before *those* folks found out about this place. My wife and I used to come here all the time when it was just decent folks like me and you coming in. Now it's just ghetto-city in here."

I didn't really know what to say. I wanted to make it known that just because I am white does not mean I share any views of his and, moreover, I wanted him to know just where he could shove his outdated opinions. But I also didn't want to be fired. I was speechless and before I could get a word in, he continued:

"Ugh! There go more of 'em!" he exclaimed as he gestured toward a black family just having a pleasant dinner together. "You see what I mean? They're everywhere."

Unfortunately, my patience only extends so far so in response I calmly said "…well, then you can leave."

He looked at me for a second in confusion, scoffed, slammed his drink onto the counter in front of me, grabbed his wife, and walked out the door, leaving his unfinished plate of wings for me to clean up.

Look, the 21st century desire for the simple "way things used to be" has been with us for a while. How else to explain vitriolic responses to TV commercials with interracial couples? Sure, it's easy enough, simple enough to see the bigotry of those responses. But what motivates the bigotry? Bigotry, you see, is not free-floating. Bigotry is always activated, motivated, and supported by something in the social world. Could it be so simple (so to speak) that it all has to do with the new structure of our society?

We got rid of Jim Crow laws of racial segregation. With that dramatic change, a number of simple group-certainties began to disappear.

Things were simple when homosexuals were less… *in the law.*

Things were simple when women were less… *in the law.*

Things were simple when blacks were less… *in the law.*

Things were simple when transgender persons were less… *in the law.*

Now all those groups legally demand public respect. Members of all those groups speak out when others use offensive language about their group membership; when others try to tell them where to use the bathroom; when others make jokes. But then the opposing cry goes up about too much "…political correctness."

Make America simple again makes a strong, automatic psychological connection with the anxiety some people are feeling about so-called political correctness. Talking about Mr. Trump's winning campaign and the revolt against political correctness that became attached to his campaign, one columnist put it this way:

> "Political correctness is an unwritten and constantly
> changing code of forbidden language and practices
> and most Americans sense its unfairness."[3]

Rapid social changes have come to us because we have moved from a segregated to a desegregated to a neo-diverse, everyday social environment. "Constantly changing code of forbidden language" is a very telling description of the social tensions.

"Who can't I talk about now?" "What words can I not use today?" "It's not fair."

Now people from many different, once shunned groups are demanding respect. Today, no one wants to be or will allow themselves to be melted.

That's not simple.

Resistance to that complexity can easily show up as bigotry. Bigotry, you see, is based on simple thinking about group membership. Bigotry is based on the simple us-versus-them idea that is the minimal-group-bias. A demand to not have to serve homosexual people based on religious freedom is a cry for that us-versus-them simplicity.

> "Even though I do public business, I have private
> beliefs that I only want to think about. I don't want

to have to give in to political correctness."

That is the psychological struggle. Right now in America, what is motivating the desire for social simplicity is rapid social change. Social customs have fallen. Social arrangements are changing and keep changing. For some it's just too much. Some have been looking for a way to slow it all down. In that psychological struggle, "Make America Great Again" was really "make America simple again" and that was a comforting, seductive voice.

"Drain the swamp." "Build a wall." "America First."

And that voice was heard.

36: And Yet, We Are Not Done

After the November 9, 2016, election results showed that Mr. Donald Trump won our presidential election, I started to get emails. With the subject "Is this hell in a hand basket?", one email read:

> "Dr. Nacoste, I am reaching out to you because I am confused and overwhelmed by this election. How did we get to this? How have bigotry and hatred prevailed? What does this mean for every minority in this country?"

On Facebook, I found myself being tagged to commentaries filled with questions: "What can I tell my daughter? The democratic process has unfolded. And yet we don't feel safe." Another from a former student (a Muslim woman), who wrote: "I'm actually scared to leave the house tomorrow, on a real note..."

I don't do counseling.

I always tell my students that, because they ask.

After listening to my lectures on interpersonal relationships over a semester, when they absentmindedly ask me about doing counseling, suddenly remembering to whom they are talking, they want to retract the question. In that moment, they think back to my lectures and to my blunt, unnerving answers to their naïve romantic questions during the semester, and in that memory they realize their mistake.

When in response I say, "…nobody wants my version of counseling," they react with head-shaking understanding.

Still, that doesn't mean they won't still ask for my help.

Here is an email exchange between me and a student who had just finished my "Introduction to Social Psychology" course at the end of Fall 2016.

> Student: Hey, Dr. Nacoste, I am one of your students from the recent PSY 311 class and I was wondering if you could offer me advice on something. Let me first say that I thoroughly enjoyed your unique class and will be using a lot of the information I learned in my upcoming relationships. However, I have one major problem that I was wondering if you could give any advice for.
>
> So, I am not typically an anxious person, and I go about the day feeling pretty stable emotionally. However, when I am thinking about a girl I like or am about to hang out with them I get stricken with severe anxiety. My chest tightens up, my mind races, and breathing becomes difficult. I can think about them when I'm alone and feel great feelings, but when it comes time to hangout I get extreme anxiety which causes me not to act like myself. All other aspects of my life are great, but this inability to form a close relationship with a girl is having a terrible impact on my confidence and life. Any advice on how to control this would be greatly appreciated. Thank you so much for all that you have done!
>
> Me: What you are experiencing is "interaction anxiety": an exaggerated concern about how to interact without making an interpersonal mistake. Without

realizing it, the social uncertainty of the potential interaction is getting a hold of you and taking you outside of yourself.

Here's what you should do. First, admit to yourself that yes, as with any new interaction, you or she will make a small mistake that makes for a brief moment of awkwardness. That happens to everybody. No big deal, so don't go in trying not to make a mistake. If you make a mistake, don't panic; acknowledge your mistake, apologize if need be, move on.

Second, look, you are projecting too far into the future of the interaction (will we kiss at the end of the date?) and too far into the future of the (only potential) relationship (will she become my girlfriend?) Stop doing that. Just… stop it.

Just have a conversation, go on a date with an activity (not just sitting looking at each other), and just get together with somebody (in your case a girl) you just want to have a little fun with. Get outside of your imagination about what will happen, and go make something fun happen for a couple of hours.

Student: "Ah I see the part about looking too far into the future is definitely true about me. I'll try not to let those thoughts consume me anymore as well as further researching interaction anxiety. Thank you for your help!"

I don't do counseling, but I will not leave my students hanging.

####

I am an analytic scholar, by no means a counselor. Yet, on November 9th, 2016, in the hallways of the campus building that houses my office, Poe Hall, I was doing "walk-by" counseling. As I walked to the copy machine or to get to the bathroom, I was having to respond to questions, feelings of dismay, and helplessness because Mr. Trump had won our presidency.

And that was just the faculty.

How did I respond to all these emotions? I said this:

"I have seen worse." I made that statement and a few people gasped, wondering, I guess, what I could have seen that was worse. Without being asked, I explained.

> I grew up in the Jim Crow South. I, a dark-skinned black man, grew up in the Jim Crow South of legal racial segregation – a fully American, societal system that said that I and people with my skin color were not human. I grew up in an America that created, accepted and enforced that Jim Crow legal racial segregation; that accepted and enforced that way of thinking about and interacting with black people. But...we fought and destroyed that system of laws.

Today many are confused, because despite what you have been told, bringing down the walls of that system did not erase all of the attached psychology of prejudice. Since creating and teaching my "Interpersonal Relationships and Race" course in 2006, for years I have been warning students about assuming that all bigotry in America had been eradicated by the 1970s. In my general writings, in my presentations, I have been warning America about taking that for granted. I have been describing the hibernating bigotry that still lives and breathes in some (not all) in America; that bigotry that sleeps until the right stimulus wakes it up.

Presidential candidate Donald Trump awakened that once-sleeping, hibernating bigotry. Evidence of that awakening became clear in the sudden, dramatic increase in anti-black, anti-Muslim, anti-gay, lesbian, transgender graffiti; the next days after the election's sudden increase in the waving of the Confederate battle flag all over America.

Now many are seeing and realizing that there is leftover psychology from the days of Jim Crow, legally enforced racial segregation. Now it is clear that we have more work to do than many thought we had to do; more work that too many didn't expect.

But in the 2016 presidential election there was more going on than bigotry, there was economic distress. There were feelings of social isolation. There was fatigue with and distrust of all things connected to Washington politics, career politicians, lobbyists, national media. There was anxiety about our growing neo-diversity. Not necessarily hate, but anxiety and uncertainty about what that means for people's everyday lives.

Mr. Trump crafted a message that tapped into all of that. Since it was that complex, we must accept that not all those who voted for Mr. Trump voted to support his bigotry. It's just not that simple.

Let's not demonize persons who voted for Mr. Trump. Let's not demonize the American political process.

January 21, 2017, was an historic day because of the national and international marches to support women's rights, civil rights, and also to protest the inauguration of President Trump. One marcher in Raleigh, however, was concerned about the demonizing of other Americans. Twenty-year-old Emma McDonald said this:

> It's important to not villainize (Trump) if we want to understand why people did vote from him. I know a lot of people who did vote for him who are wonderful people and support (equality). If we say everyone who voted for Trump is racist or bigoted or xenophobic... we're kind of putting them into a box.[1]

Let's not make the energy-draining error of engaging in the same kind of bigotry we are trying to denounce. There is no innocent bigotry.

In my "Interpersonal Relationships and Race" (PSY 411) course, I emphasize that in order to "...save the soul of America," we all have to check our stereotypes and tendencies toward bigotry. "There are no innocent" is always a major theme in the course.

Spring 2017, after the inauguration I did a lecture in which I applied that theme to the panicked reactions some had to people who voted for the election of President Donald Trump. One of the points I made is that only objecting to stereotypes and bigotry aimed at groups of people you like is not moving us toward our goal of a "... more perfect union." Bigotry is just bigotry, I said.

The evening after that lecture I got an email from a white male student with the subject "Thank you for today's lesson" and the following message:

> Dr. Nacoste, I'm currently writing this e-mail aboard a [North Carolina State University] Wolfline bus just minutes after your PSY 411 class today. While I was waiting at the bus stop, I noticed a student walk by wearing a t-shirt that said this: "Infidel for Trump" on the front and "Make America Great, One Round at a Time" on the back with a picture of a rifle. My mind immediately jumped to this thought: *I HATE those kinds of people.*
>
> Then I remembered what you said just minutes earlier; that that kind of thinking is part of the problem. There are no innocent and I still have some growing to do. Thank you for enlightening me.

Let's respect each other and get to work. We must get to work because so much is at risk. And our work must be from a position of being educated to understand and know that prejudice is not bigotry is not racism. Presidential candidate Donald Trump expressed anti-group feelings about multiple sets of people: Mexicans, Muslims, disabled, women, people. But prejudice is not bigotry is not racism.

"They are rapists…" "…they are terrorists…" "Nasty women…"

Mr. Trump's bold modeling of bigotry on the campaign trail did something quite dangerous to American life. Around our nation, Mr. Trump's unabashed verbal bigotry awakened in some Americans their hibernating bigotry, that bigotry that sleeps until the right stimulus wakes it up.

Presidential candidate Donald Trump awakened that hibernating bigotry that had been sleeping in some Americans. Bad enough, but we must acknowledge the power Mr. Trump now has as president of the United States. As president, Mr. Trump is in a position to propose and push for policies that mirror his campaign rhetoric of prejudice and bigotry.

As early as January 28, 2017, we had already seen that through executive orders and through members of his cabinet, Mr. Trump was quick to begin proposing and pushing for policy legislation and law that would support and institutionalize bigotry at the national and international levels. If he is successful in that approach, President Trump will not only taint the office of the presidency, but he will have created a new, more inclusive American Jim Crow; a new multi-group caste system; a system of laws that authorize group prejudice and bigotry toward America's neo-diversity.

Racism, you see, is a system of organizational and institutional patterns of behaviors that support and authorize prejudice and bigotry. To engage racism, to engage in any groupism, requires power at the organizational and institutional level.

With the power of the presidency to shape the enactment of policies for our country, President Trump is in a position to advocate national policies that if enacted will not take us backward. Wielding the power of the presidency in 21st century neo-diverse America, President Trump will be in a position to advocate for policies of discrimination that would be aimed at multiple groups.

A Muslim registry. Religious freedom acts that allow businesses to not serve gays and lesbians and whomever else the business person says offends her or his religious beliefs. And the sign will say, "...no ____s allowed; we don't serve ____s."

Should such ideas and practices be put into law, America will not be going backward to old ways. Oh no. America will be moving into the future with a shining new, more inclusive American Jim Crow caste system; a new multi-group apartheid. It will be new because of the neo-diversity in color and culture of the groups subject to national, institutional patterns of behavior that support and authorize prejudice and bigotry.

Prejudice is not bigotry is not racism. Understanding the differences is important for all of us who care about social justice issues. You see, accurate definitions of prejudice, bigotry, and racism will allow those working toward "...equal justice for all" to develop action strategies that focus on the actual problem dimension that can be addressed at the right policy level.

Asked the question, I answer:

"America is not done. We ARE NOT going to hell in a hand basket."

True, we are in the basket, but we can stand up, reach up, and then climb out. As my father, Mr. O-geese, always said: "...The only way to keep a man in a ditch is to stand there over him." The only way to keep us in this basket is for those so motivated to stay very close by and do nothing but watch us, and we let that intimidate us.

We've got some difficult days ahead. Feel your emotions. If you feel hurt, do not deny that you are hurt. Talk to like-minded people. Then reach out to any person in your social circles who is willing to have a civil conversation about how we can work to reclaim the soul of America. Lots of emotion is good if it becomes your signal to get to work, to focus that emotion into strategies to reinvigorate the true soul of America. "We hold these truths to be self-evident, that all are created equal..."

Let's focus our emotions. In our neo-diverse America, let's start developing new strategies to address the new challenges facing America. With all the trauma of violence in the summer of 2016, something amazing started to happen. Fall 2016, before the election of President Trump, Dr. Tim Tyson wrote to tell me that the work of the Moral Monday movement was spreading so much that there has been an increase in white Americans joining the NAACP. In fact, he told me that in the mountains of NC, the new Yancey-Mitchell County NAACP is the only all-white NAACP chapter in America.

Let's focus our emotions. Let's start building new neo-diverse coalitions and alliances to fight all forms of bigotry in America to work toward our goal of "...a more perfect union."

Let's get the hell up out of this basket.

37: Hope

We are not going to hell in a hand basket.

Mass killings of gay, lesbian, and transgender people, police killings of black men and women; these kinds of events are not new. What is new is the attention the events are getting and the outrage that has moved through our nation. Not just LGBTQ outrage, not just black outrage, but outrage across all kinds of racial, ethnic, religious, sexually oriented lines. Even in the face of all those 21st century negative intergroup events, yes, there is still hope. There is hope in that outrage.

Outrage, though, is not enough. We need thoughtful reflection that can lead to individual and group action. When it comes to the police shootings of black men and women, Larry Collins, my old high school classmate and a former Marine, has made this point: "Seems to me that the vetting process is lacking, or nonexistent in the police departments throughout the country."

Should members of our police forces have a bullying attitude and approach to their sworn duty to serve and protect us? Interviewed about what happened in Boston between Professor Gates and Police Officer Crowley, a 13-year veteran cop of another city said:

"We're not going to take the abuse. We have to remain in control. We're running the show."[1]

We must ask, should our municipal governments be institutionalizing police forces that manage their work by viewing the citizens it serves and protects as 'enemy combatants'? We should ask, how is it that our police forces seem to be hiring people who have the tendency to over react to black males?

"It looks like a demon."

Ferguson police officer Darren Wilson made that statement to describe his reaction to and shooting of 19-year-old Michael Brown.[2] We should ask how and why do municipalities and cities hire as police individuals who use race as a threat assessment tool that leads individual police officers to see black men and women as "its" that look like demons.

We need to be vocal and ask, "…What the hell is going on?" But our outrage must be focused on policy change. We cannot just be outraged, we have to be strategic in focusing our outrage to improve what is going on in our own communities.

We need to be raising the question of the vetting process of the people hired. We need to be raising that question in meetings of our county commissioners, in meetings of our city and town councils that control police forces.

And, let's not be distracted by cute attempts to make us feel better about police. A Facebook friend asked: "Is it just me or would you rather see police officers completing racial sensitivity, de-escalation, or non-lethal ways to take down a person training than having lip-sync battles?!"

I answered: "I keep telling people, police giving away ice-cream to kids, playing basketball with black kids, or lip-singing does not amount to training for the intense situations they have to face."

Truth is, these displays of humanity are meaningless to the moment a police officer has to decide whether to use deadly force.

In fact, these moments of police humanity are not about individual police-persons or about what police do. By design these are attempts to influence the way police are perceived by citizens. Understand that from what social psychologists know about person-perception, that is the only possibility. With these videos, citizens are put in the position of observer. As observers, we have no choice but to evaluate the behavior of the individual in the situation shown. Here the drawback is that as observers we tend to see individual behavior through the prism of the "fundamental attribution error": the tendency to disregard features of the situation and focus on individual traits as the explanation for the behavior. That cognitive tendency ends up meaning that we evaluate and make attributions about "what kind of person would do this?"

From there the attribution process takes over. We have observed a behavior. We ask and answer the question, "Is the person doing this on purpose?" With the answer being, "Yes, they are doing this on purpose," the only available attribution is that this is a nice person. After all, this person in uniform is giving children ice cream. How else to evaluate that behavior other than as a "nice thing to do for a child"?

With almost no cognitive choice, observers end up coming to the attribution that this person is nice; their internal make up is of a nice person. See, police-persons aren't bad people. See, police are nice people.

That is a disingenuous manipulation of social perception. Few people are saying police are bad people. Black Lives Matter is a social justice movement about the callous disregard for black lives. NFL players who kneel do not say in one voice police are bad. Kneeling when the cameras are rolling is their way of trying to draw attention to a *system* of policing that has too often led to the shooting of an unarmed black person. The cute videos push us away from thinking about those policy issues.

Videos of police giving out ice cream tell us nothing about revised and new police training. Situational training is what matters, situational training that includes race or skin color as one of the varying stimuli police must learn to manage in the moment; situational training that reduces the automatic tendency of some police officers to use skin color as a threat assessment tool – "It looks like a demon;"

situational training that will make for better police action that truly serves and gives equal protection to all citizens.

I say again, we are not going to hell in a hand basket. But we need more than outrage and finger-pointing blame. Unbalanced outrage led to injustice in Dallas and Baton Rouge. How could anyone think shooting police officers was a just action? That was not righteous outrage, that was unbridled rage and vindictiveness; hate. Hateful acts are never about and can never bring justice.

The targeting and assassination of police officers in Dallas, the ambush attack of police officers in Baton Rouge, show us again that there are no innocent. "Without justice, there is no peace," people proclaim. Justice, though, is not of one color. Justice is multicolored, multiethnic, multi-gender; human.

Anxiety and fear of interacting with people from "other" groups can affect anyone. There are no innocent. And yet, we are not in a hopeless situation. We are, however, living in the difficult days that Martin Luther King Jr. prophesied.

"We've got some difficult days ahead," he said in Memphis on that April 1968 night before he was assassinated. Seeming to know he would not be with us for much longer, King stood in hope in the Mason Temple (Church of Christ) headquarters. King stood and spoke in hope, not for himself, but in hope for black people as a people, in hope for all the downtrodden, in hope for America as a nation. Why? He truly believed, as he often proclaimed, that "the arc of the moral universe is long, but it bends toward justice." King believed that we can make positive change happen. He truly believed, as he said, that he was doing his work to "...save the soul of America."

Yes, we can, just not with platitudes.

"Love is the answer." "Give peace a chance." "Let's just all get along."

Platitudes are not action. Instead of mouthing platitudes, we must each engage in real conversation in our social circles. Without venom, calm but firm in conversation, object to the injustices you see. Speak your desire for Americans to respect each other no matter group membership. Do not go looking for a fight, but if you are attacked in conversation, keep your dignity. Speak humble but firm your belief in the fact that in America we have real neo-diversity problems to solve. If the other conversant does not give you respect, walk the hell away.

Keep your dignity. People will feel your resolve. That will give them pause to think.

Other strategies we must use may also seem not enough, but we have to make what moves we can as individuals. Look, I am a scholar. I could despair and say "...What good does my teaching and writing do when there is so much deadly injustice happening right now?"

I will not despair because I come from a family of day-breakers. I come from a family of people who always lived and worked to "... beat a way for the rising sun," as Arna Bontemps put it in his poem "The Day-Breakers."[4]

In deep-South Louisiana, in the Creole/Cajun world of "Laissez les Bontemps roulez," my parents were born into sharecropper poverty and hard Jim Crow, legal racial segregation. Even so, my parents became day-breakers, fighting for the dawn of social justice.

Born in 1918 with little education, Mr. August (O-geese) Nacoste fought for civil rights, for voting rights. My father, Mr. O-geese (in the Creole), drove black people to register to vote, and he drove black people to the polls to vote.[5] During the time my father ran for public office in 1966, rocks were thrown into and shattered the big living room window of the front porch of our G.I. Bill-financed, three bedroom house. Mr. O-geese did not despair; he did not let his children despair. Till the day he died he kept fighting for civil rights.

I always knew that about my father's social justice work. In fact, everyone in our small bayou town and in the area surrounding Opelousas knew about my father's work to advance the civil rights of black people. Barely a high school-educated man, my father worked as a school janitor and a school bus driver. But in 1997, the local chapter of the National Association of University Women made my father one of their first inductees into the then new Opelousas Civil Rights Hall of Fame. Especially as an adult, I was truly impressed and in awe of the work my father had done in his life that made him a day-breaker in my eyes.

Oh, I loved and was proud of my mother, too, but her work as an elementary school teacher did not really stand out to me in the same way as my father's work. Born in 1922, Mom got her GED through a correspondence course while having four children. Then attending night school with the domestic help of my father, Mrs. Ella (Malveaux) Nacoste became an elementary school teacher. My mother's teaching mission was to help black children achieve beyond the circumstances thrust upon them by Jim Crow racial discrimination.

Mom was a lady, a wonderful mix of being proper in a farm girl kind of way. Somebody might drop by our house unannounced and unexpected and Mom would still be so polite, making coffee and offering a bite to eat.

Mom did these things that as a kid I didn't understand or really pay that much attention to. One of those things was that she always seemed to be buying school supplies. She always seemed to have some kid to give them to. I thought that was nice but really didn't think much about it… not until she retired and I asked my older sister Elinor, who still lives in Opelousas, what Mom was up to in her retirement. That's when I learned my mother was a day-breaker.

In a phone conversation just talking about life, my sister told me that our mother, Mrs. Ella Malveaux Nacoste, was keeping her eye out for sales on school supplies or went to the local dollar stores and bought school supplies. I asked my sister why. Mom was retired after all, no longer a teacher.

Elinor told me our mother had always given poor children school supplies. At the beginning of each new school year, families in our neighborhood knew to bring their young children to our house to get some school supplies from "Miss Nacoste." Little things the children would need like pencils and pens, pads of writing paper, notebooks, maybe a backpack – my mother would hand out those small things.

At the beginning of every school year and during the year, a child could come to our house to get some supply their family might not be able to afford to buy for them. Turned out that even in her retirement, my mother was still a source of school supplies. My mother was a quiet educational resource for poor black children. When my sister told me all this, I was blown away.

Born into the era of hard Jim Crow laws of racial discrimination, from their seemingly powerless stations in life, both my parents fought hard for human rights. They did not despair. They worked to be day-breakers and jealous guardians of the (real) American dream.

38: The Long View of a Jealous Guardian

Too tired to continue the work to save the soul of America? Sometime in 2018, after another moment of racial bigotry went public, I saw a Facebook post where someone reacted by lamenting, and others were affirming, that "I'm tired from seeing so much of this and having to try to educate other people about these problems." Tired? I am a dark-skinned black man close to 70 years old. I have lived through the horrific time of legal racial segregation, riots, and assassinations. I have fought many fights for equality and justice for our humanity. Still, I am not yet tired because I cannot afford to be.

Do not give in to despair. Despair is the path to the dark side of inaction. We are not done. We are in a continuing fight for human rights in our country. We must not talk about "being done." We must commit to the fight. That is how I have lived my life.

October 2018, I had quite a week. Friday (October 19, 2018) evening I gave the keynote address to the 500-person audience of the regional leadership conference of the South Atlantic Affiliate of College and University Residence Halls. Sunday (October 21st) I was on a plane to Shippensburg, PA. That Monday at Shippensburg University I spoke to four different classes of first year, first semester students about neo-diversity and learning to manage the anxiety of interacting with someone "…not like you." Then that evening I gave my campus-wide lecture "Getting Along at the Table of a Neo-diverse Campus."

Tuesday (October 23rd) I was on a plane back to Raleigh, where I returned to my teaching duties on Wednesday and Thursday. That Thursday (October 25th) evening, I had the honor of moderating a discussion at Quail Ridge Books. I moderated a conversation between two of the Marjory Stoneman Douglas High School teenagers who lived through the Parkland massacre. Sarah and Delaney, who came to Raleigh, were part of the group that put together the amazing March for Our Lives event in Washington, DC. The #MarchForOurLives group has continued their organizing against gun violence and for common sense gun legislation in our country with a push to get people to vote, and educating people with their new book that we all should read, *Glimmer of Hope*.[2]

Asked by my friends at Quail Ridge Books to do so, it was my honor to be the moderator of the conversation. Even though they are still kids, Sarah and Delaney were ready for my probing questions, answering and elaborating with strength of vision, commitment, and good humor. They were outstanding ambassadors for the March for Our Lives movement. Also, for me it was wonderful to see that lots of teenagers turned out to hear and interact with Sarah and Delaney. Pictures were taken:

Sarah (on the left) and Delaney (on the right) even took one with this old but not-yet-tired jealous guardian of the (real) American Dream.

More than once a student has wondered out loud about my optimism about America. Confused by the way I teach a topic like racial slurs, a puzzled student says:

"You've seen so much ugly racial stuff Dr. Nacoste, but you never seem discouraged. How do you do it; how can you keep working on these issues, and with such a positive attitude?"

My usual answer is simple and straightforward:

"I have the long view. In seeing so much, I have seen much movement toward what we are working on; that more perfect union. That's how I do it. I know we have, and I know we can still change and improve."

That is still my answer, but I came across another way to say it that I really like, especially given my age. Watching *Criminal Minds*, of all things, the quote used at the end of one episode rang through me as a sounding bell. It resonated in my soul. Why and how do some people keep at it even when change can seem so slow? Here is what the Dalai Lama XIV says about that:

"To remain indifferent to the challenges we face is indefensible. If the goal is noble, whether or not it is realized within our lifetime is largely irrelevant. What we must do therefore is to strive and persevere and never give up."

I know we are living in a very difficult time in America, yet I will not despair because in these difficult days I know that some of the thousands of students I have taught listen for my voice. I raise my voice because I can use my voice in ways that others can't.

####

I was invited to and did speak at the United, Not Divided Rally on the evening of Monday, February 20, 2017.[1] Lead sponsor of the rally was the Muslim Student Association. This was a rally of protest against President Trump's travel ban that was clearly aimed at countries with a predominantly Muslim population. Showing that this rally was really about being united, not divided on our campus, other student organizations (e.g., Latin American Student Association, Fulbright Student Association) joined as official co-sponsors of the rally. The rally was held outside Talley Student Center on the Stafford Commons, a green area.

Picture this: A mix of young people, brown skinned, white, dark skinned, male, female, some women wearing Hijabs, some women with heads uncovered, some women wearing Abayas-, some women

in (so-called) Western clothing, a white child with a sign that read "…
diversity makes us stronger," along with a program of student, administration, faculty speakers.

As planned, after the first set of speakers (of which I was the last),
just at first dark, suddenly we heard a strong, musical voice coming
through the loud speakers. With the mix of people at the rally, an
affecting, resonant, melodic male voice echoed out over the neo-diverse group, rendering the call to Muslim prayer. The Muslim devout
began to move to the area where a tarp had been placed on the ground
for those who would kneel, bow and pray.

At the same time, people not praying kept a respectful distance
but continued their connecting to each other in conversation with
smiles, laughter, and thoughtful exchanges. Through the glass walls
of Talley Student Center, I could see, anyone could see, students of
many group categories. Some were just walking through Talley, some
sitting, eating, computers out studying, writing, and some standing in
line to buy food while back outside Muslim students prayed and other
students walked by. Also, there, outside and not too far away, students
played a running, jumping game (of some sort) in shorts and t-shirts.

Here was a true neo-diversity moment at NC State. Here was a
mix of the Wolfpack of many different ethnicities and group identities,
living and interacting in physical proximity to each other, respecting
each other's space and activities.

Like I said, I spoke in the segment of the program before the call
to prayer. For that 10-minute speech, I set my theme with words I
first heard uttered by Maya Angelou. Those words are those of an
ancient, at one time enslaved Roman playwright who wrote, "I am
human, nothing human can be alien to me." With that as the theme
throughout, early in my 10-minute speech I said:

> I am human. Nothing human can be alien to me. Not
> necessarily those words, but that philosophy guided
> the building of cross-racial, cross-ethnic, cross-reli-
> gion, coalitions and collaborations that became the

movement of unity that was the full-blown civil rights movement. People risked their lives to knock down the unnatural walls (of segregation) that had been put up to stop us from living lives at the intersections. Like you are doing today, a mix of people gathered to rally for American solidarity; for unity.

I also said:

"Approval or disapproval of each other's everyday lives, like or dislike, cannot be a part of our working vocabulary. You cannot effectively tear down unnatural walls of injustice and keep up your own unnatural psychological walls."

Going on, I said:

I am not here today to show that I approve of the Muslim faith of Islam. I also did not come here with reluctance because I disapprove of the Muslim faith of Islam. I am here because… I am human. Nothing human can be alien to me.

I do not know the words of the Prophet Mohammed… peace be upon him. When Deah, Yusor, and Razan, Our-Three-Winners, were murdered, to feel hurt and anguish, I did not need to know the words of the Prophet Mohammed… peace be upon him.

I did not need to be Muslim to feel the pain of the injustice of the murders of those three beautiful young spirits, Deah, Yusor, and Razan. I am human. Nothing human can be alien to me.

To do our work for social justice, we must build coalitions of respect so that we can collaborate. That is how we will survive and thrive during this troubled period in America. That is how we will change the world again.

So, let's get to work. Let's stop the building of unnatural walls. Let's get to work saving the soul of America. Let's get to work united, not divided.

It was quite an evening. I was proud to be part of that neo-diverse collaboration at NC State.

Trust to hope.

Have enough faith in the truth of the real American Dream to hope.

E pluribus unum – out of many, one.

On the night of his 2008 election as our president, Senator Barack Hussein Obama proclaimed:

> This is our time… to reclaim the American dream and reaffirm that fundamental truth, that, out of many, we are one; that while we breathe, we hope. And where we are met with cynicism and doubts and those who tell us that we can't, we will respond with that timeless creed that sums up the spirit of a people: Yes, we can.

Do not give up on hope; always hope. But the hope President-elect Obama was advocating, the hope I am advocating, is hope in action. In these difficult days we need people of conscience to act.

Ask yourself, what kind of America do I believe in?

What kind of America do I want to live in?

What kind of America do I want for my children and grandchildren?

With your answers as your guide, vote, march in protest, write letters and emails to your mayors, city council, county commissioners, and police chiefs. Write, email your congressional representatives.

Demand not just investigations, but demand city, county, and congressional commissions.

In his 2017 farewell address to America, outgoing President Barack Obama said:

> ...our democracy is threatened whenever we take it for granted. All of us, regardless of party, should throw ourselves into the task of rebuilding our democratic institutions. When voting rates are some of the lowest among advanced democracies, we should make it easier, not harder, to vote. When trust in our institutions is low, we should reduce the corrosive influence of money in our politics, and insist on the principles of transparency and ethics in public service. When Congress is dysfunctional, we should draw our districts to encourage politicians to cater to common sense and not rigid extremes. And all of this depends on our participation; on each of us accepting the responsibility of citizenship, regardless of which way the pendulum of power swings.

In that spirit, he went on to say:

> It falls to each of us to be those anxious, jealous guardians of our democracy; to embrace the joyous task we've been given to continually try to improve this great nation of ours. Because for all our outward differences, we all share the same proud title: Citizen.

> Ultimately, that's what our democracy demands. It needs you. Not just when there's an election, not just when your own narrow interest is at stake, but over the full span of a lifetime. If you're tired of arguing with strangers on the internet, try to talk with one in real life. If something needs fixing, lace up your

shoes and do some organizing. If you're disappointed by your elected officials, grab a clipboard, get some signatures, and run for office yourself. Show up. Dive in. Persevere. Sometimes you'll win. Sometimes you'll lose… And more often than not, your faith in America – and in Americans – will be confirmed.

By the way, no one strategy made the Civil Rights Movement a success. America's Civil Rights Movement did not win out only because of Martin Luther King Jr.'s non-violent strategy. America's Civil Rights Movement succeeded because of the multiple and multi-dimensional strategies that were all at work, all at the same time.

Even artists got involved. In protest of racial segregation, Ray Charles refused to perform where whites and blacks would be separated in the performance hall. In support of the Civil Rights Movement, Bob Dylan sang out at rallies and demonstrations, "The times they are a changin'…" In support of the Civil Rights Movement, on national TV on the Ed Sullivan Show, Curtis Mayfield & The Impressions sang, "People Get Ready."

Different strategies make it possible for each of us to find our way to be involved in the work that must be done to save the soul of America. Bob Dylan's voice in song is still relevant: "The times they are a changin'…" In the words of the Black Panther Bobby Seale, "Seize the time!" Today, the American spirit of courage inhabiting our eternal flame is once again calling out to each of us to, "Ask not what your country can do for you, but what you can do for your country." As we continue the fight to save the soul of America, look around and find a strategy you can work with and through; a strategy that fits your demeanor, style, and social situation. We should not all be doing the same things, but we should and can all be doing something.

###

People have asked me what I think about NFL player Colin Kaepernick's not standing for our national anthem in protest of racial injustice in America. A former student emailed me to ask about the issue. He wrote:

> I have become confused with the growing act of college and pro athletes sitting during the national anthem at games. I know you served in the U.S. military and have decades of experience watching America improve on race issues. In your opinion, what is the correct response to all this?

Yes, I am a military veteran. I served this country to protect American freedoms. But hear me when I say that I did not serve this country to prevent people from using their American freedom to protest injustice in this country.

America is not perfect, but America is an exemplary country because we citizens can protest to point out injustice. We, American citizens, can protest, push for and work to remove injustice from the way we do things in America. That is not true in all other countries. In some other nations, protest is prohibited and punished (with imprisonment, sometimes death). We are different, but to really live that difference requires an understanding of our citizenship that is not elementary, not simple.

America was founded on the principle that all citizens have the right to "call out" the government for (active or passive) wrong actions. That is part of the American identity. In recent times, though, too many Americans have let themselves get caught up by the minimal group effect: automatic psychological categorization of people into groups, with a tendency to see everything as group competition.

As a social psychologist, I know that we are living in a new American social context. We are living in this situation of neo-diversity where each of us has to encounter and sometimes interact with people who do not look like, sound like, worship like, love like, or promote America "...like us." Anxiety about that neo-diversity inter-personal situation is what is pushing a lot of Americans to rely on a minimal group perception of events. We are motivated to automatically categorize social events into us versus them.

We have all seen the intergroup violence that is alive in our nation. We saw that intergroup violence in unprecedented ways in Summer 2016 – a mass killing of gay, lesbian, and transgender persons, police shooting after police shooting of black men, white police officers assassinated by a black sniper. Protests emerged all over America.

Many were thankful then when the NFL season started just in time to feed our yearning for the simple. Many were just "...ready for some football." Trying to relax into the simple, straightforwardness of football, oh man, we are reminded of America's complex intergroup problems by having an NFL player not stand for the national anthem to protest racial injustice.

"How dare he? Who does he think he is? No real American would do that, right?"

Us-versus-them (minimal group) psychological motivation and anger starts to take over. "Kaepernick is not a real American; he's not one of us," people cry out. Well, turns out patriotism and protests are not in competition with each other. In fact, even while in the military I was engaged in protests movements. That is why I have been offended by the attempt of some to frame Kaepernick's symbolic, peaceful protest as an insult to those of us who served this country in the military.

I never played football. No matter because football is a game... a *game*. But I did serve my country in the U.S. Navy. You tell me which is more important to you.

Yes, I am offended that someone, anyone, would try to use my service to our country to support their elementary view of American patriotism. The very idea of classifying me and my comrade-in-arms' motivations to serve in this one-dimensional way is to use us as a stereotype. To whoever does this, I and my comrade-in-arms are nothing more than a representation of one way to feel as an American. I am deeply offended by being seen and used as a (one-dimensional) representative of such a neo-diverse and strong group of people.

Football is entertainment, a *game*. About what happens at a game, President Trump has called NFL players who kneel during the national anthem SOBs.

Again, I have never played sports. A black man, I did grow up in the deep South in the time of Jim Crow legal racial segregation. I did grow up in an activist household. I did conduct voter registration of black people in 1968. I did march and protest, including sitting during the national anthem. I did, later, serve my country in the U.S. Navy during a time of racial turmoil and change in that branch of the military. Even while I served I engaged in peaceful protest of ongoing racial inequities in the Navy. Protest and patriotism are not in conflict with each other.

Unlike the message coming from our current commander in chief, I received letters of appreciation from Navy leadership for my work to fight racial injustice in the Navy. Almost 50 years ago during my service in the U.S. Navy, I was trained to be and became a "Racial Awareness Group Facilitator," a RAFT. I did not seek out that role. In fact, I went into that role by order of my squadron commanding officer, Commander W. S. Hogkins, because of something he and the Captain of the NAS (Naval Air Station) Cecil Field saw in me. Their intuitions were right.

I have always found it difficult to articulate how becoming a facilitator of difficult racial dialogues lit up my being. How do you describe the feeling of finding your purpose that sets your soul on fire? No one can, not really.

Recently, though, I found something that, in my case, helps. Not through my own words, but with words others used to describe me back then, 1974-1976. Cleaning out a drawer in a desk at home, I came across the files from my military service that I received after being honorably discharged. Among those papers I found letters of appreciation and commendation for the work I was doing then as one of the Navy's RAFTs.

One letter of appreciation came from my first commander at Air Anti-Submarine Squadron VS-31. For my early work as a RAFT ashore, Commander W. S. Hodgins honored me with an unexpected letter of appreciation. He wrote:

> I would like to express my sincerest appreciation to you for your outstanding performance as a Squadron Racial Awareness Facilitator from April 1974 to the present (September 1974). You demonstrated your versatility during this time by serving as a member three different Facilitator Teams, assisting Air Anti-Submarine Wing-One, Carrier Air Wing Seven and VS-31. By voluntarily donating your time and energy to the UPWARD [Understanding Personal Worth and Development] Program you have made a significant contribution to the Squadron's Human Relations efforts. Your dedication and perserverance in this sometimes-thankless assignment... Your unique understanding of problems and purposes associated with Human Goals in today's Navy has been a greatly appreciated asset to this squadron.

From January 1975 there is a letter of evaluation from the newest commander of Air Anti-Submarine Squadron VS-31. Commander R. L. Parker wrote:

> Petty Officer Nacoste's performance as a RAFT has been outstanding. He has considered his RAFT duties as a collateral personal responsibility. His success in accomplishing both his (regular) personnelman and (voluntary) RAFT duties concurrently speaks well of his maturity and professionalism. Since involvement as a RAFT some short eight months ago, he has

guided some 240 Navy men through race-relations education seminars. Petty Officer 2nd Class Nacoste's interest in race relations education is such that he has applied for further training as a race relation's specialist. He is most highly recommended for this advanced training and for further assignment in this field of endeavor.

For that same time period, I received a surprise letter of commendation from the Captain of the USS *Independence* for my service on the USS *Independence's* Human Relations Advisory Team. In that January 1975 letter, Captain W. B. Warwick wrote:

> While attached to the USS *Independence* Human Relations Advisory Team and assigned to Human Relations Advisor (HRA) Watches ashore, your performance was outstanding. You demonstrated an intense desire to assist in the reduction of conflicts between personnel in liberty (free time) status, which grow out of lack of communication. You have also repeatedly demonstrated a sincere concern for fellow shipmates, through your effectiveness in calming anxious crowds and diffusing tensions at Fleet Landing and other trouble spots. Your aid has been invaluable to both Shore Patrol [Navy police] and the Liberty party [sailors on free time].
>
> You demonstrated a high degree of diplomacy and a keen insight into the problems of people. Your devotion to duty and outstanding efforts and expertise, along with your support of the Human Goals Program, were an important contribution to the morale and safety of the crew ashore, as well as being an important contribution to the United States

Foreign Relations Effort, and were in keeping with the highest traditions of the United States Navy. WELL DONE! (Bravo Zulu!) – W. B. Warwick, Captain, USS *Independence*

I was on fire. Feeling the heat of my calling, I stumbled in and embraced that heat. I went from being cool awake to being burning woke. I was on fire with awareness of the important work I could do. I was now, and truly woke. Not woke in self-declaration of being "… hella woke," but woke to every opportunity that came my way to do the work.

Taking on extra (collateral) duties to work with a number of the racial awareness teams, becoming a volunteer member of the ship's Human Relations Advisory Team, and walking ashore as a member of the ship's Human Relations Advisor Watches to keep sailors out of all kinds of intergroup troubles, I had found my purpose in life. Although that work was challenging and shaking the old racial ways of the Navy, the Navy hierarchy showed me appreciation for me doing my part to push the Navy toward a new more inclusive, fair and just direction.

Our current commander in chief, President Trump, is not operating with that perspective toward NFL players who kneel. Our current president and others seem to think that I served in the U.S. Navy to honor the flag and a song. Don't be ridiculous. I served our country to defend the U.S. Constitution against all enemies foreign and domestic. Without the U.S. Constitution, both the national anthem and the flag are meaningless.

Not the flag, but our constitution grants us our rights as U.S. citizens. One of those is "… the right of the people peaceably to assemble, and to petition the government for a redress of grievances," a right that must include protest by not standing during the national anthem.

There are people who now say they want to thank me for my service. Some of the same people criticize Colin Kaepernick's peaceful protest. Really, to thank me and the other women and men who serve and have served our country, read, learn, and then support the U.S. Constitution.

I am a proud U.S. Navy veteran, even though I served during a time (1972-1976) when many whites in the Navy did not want black sailors like me (or my older and younger brothers) to be able to advance in rank. I did my service, nonetheless, in the belief that America will one day live up to the (real) American dream of freedom and equality for all its citizens.

While in the Navy, I worked against the existing racial discrimination of the Navy in a lot of ways. I trained and worked as a racial awareness group discussion leader. Known for that, when I walked the base at Naval Air Station Cecil Field, Fla., I saluted officers, saluted the flag, and I also raised my arm and fist in the black power salute to other African American sailors. Patriotism and protest are not in competition with each other.

Colin Kaepernick not standing for the national anthem does not offend me. In fact, Kaepernick's symbolic protest reminds me of what I served to protect in America.

Patriotism comes in many forms, including protesting injustices that still occur in our great nation. Our U.S. Constitution does not specify the form that peaceful protests must take; that would be un-American. But in the First Amendment, our U.S. Constitution does guarantee us the right to peaceful protest however we see fit. In the "…land of the free, home of the brave," giving in to us-versus-them competitive thinking when we see peaceful protests is putting on psychological blinders to that fundamental part of our American identity.

Look, we veterans are not all the same. We veterans did not all have the same motivations and experiences while we served. I would not dishonor the service of other veterans by trying to speak for all of us.

Speaking for myself, I did not put my life at risk on aircraft carriers (USS *Intrepid*, USS *Independence*) for a piece of cloth. Between my 20th and 24th birthdays, I was far away from home in the roaring (sometimes stormy) Atlantic Ocean and Mediterranean Sea, walking through hangar decks, going up and down on ship-side elevators, surrounded by weapons of mass destruction, with F-8, A-4, S2A war aviation landing over my head.

I was out there being a jealous guardian. I was out there doing my part to ensure that our constitution lives on to ground our American lives; to provide citizen rights to all of us, no matter our sex, race, creed, color, mental health condition, sexual orientation, education level, bodily condition, political affiliation, socioeconomic status, gender identity or age. I was out there to help ensure that any American citizen can raise their voice in peaceful protest, "… to petition the government for a redress of grievances" however the citizen sees fit – kneeling during the national anthem, speaking at a city council meeting, raising a fist to the sounds of our national anthem, or running for political office.

I am saddened that our current commander in chief does not understand that.

#VeteransForKaepernick

"We think we've come so far. The torture of heretics, the burning of witches, it's all ancient history. Then, before you can blink an eye, it suddenly threatens to start all over again… waiting for the right climate in which to flourish, spreading fear in the name of righteousness. Vigilance, that is the price we have to continually pay."

Captain Jean-Luc Picard, Star Trek: The Next Generation

The Drumhead Episode, Stardate: 44769.2

Original Airdate: 29 Apr, 1991

"May I say to you as you continue your protest, you will confront moments of difficulty. But let us realize that no great and lasting gain comes in history without suffering and sacrifice.

Let nobody stop you; you are doing something that will ultimately save the soul of America."

Martin Luther King Jr.

"A Creative Protest"

Speech given on February 16, 1960.

Durham, NC

39: American Bigotry: Now It's Personal

Seeing intergroup disrespect today, no one can blame it on the law.

No time in American history is untouched by our nation's struggle with racial bigotry. But this time, it's personal.

"That's just how it is." "That's just the way things work." "It's just the way things are."

In the past, during the time I was growing up in the Jim Crow South of legal racial segregation, white Americans could be consoled by the fact that bigotry was supported by laws. Even well-meaning whites could and did say, "...What can I do? It's not up to me. It's just the way things are."

No one should try to deny the role of the law. Indeed, about that social reality, editorial writer for the *Fayetteville Observer* Gene Smith pointed out that:

> "The culprit was the law. The Klan didn't make it all but impossible for 20th century blacks to vote in Mississippi or bar nonwhites from public universities. The law did that."[1]

After the revolution that was the modern Civil Rights Movement, after the elimination of the immoral, unjust laws of racial discrimination through the court system, no one can now point to laws of racial bigotry and say, "It's just the way things are." Today, when a

Charlottesville happens, when the KKK, neo-Nazis gather in public to rally for white supremacy, it's personal because no one can blame the situation. Whether a person participates or simply observes such a rally, it is clear that what is at work is personal intergroup hate. No one can blame the laws of the land.

Without the support of law, interpersonal-intergroup conflict does to individuals what any interpersonal conflict does to people: it pushes us to confront the personal questions raised by the conflict.[2] Who am I and who do I want to be? Without the support of law, seeing racial bigotry pushes individuals to ask "Who am I in this moment of American history? Where do I stand? What are my values? What do I believe?"

"Race prejudice as a sense of group position." I remember being startled when, years ago, I read the sociological paper with that title. Writing in 1958, with me reading it around 1977, Professor Herbert Blumer[3] made these important points:

> ...race prejudice exists basically in a *sense of group position rather than in a set of feelings* which members of one racial group have toward the members of another racial group.

> To characterize another racial group is, by opposition, to define one's own group. This is equivalent to placing the two groups in relation to each other, or defining their positions vis-a-vis each other. It is the sense of social position emerging from this *collective process of characterization* which provides the basis of race prejudice.

In America, the intergroup relation between blacks and whites was built through a collective process that began with the enslavement of African peoples, then evolved into the (actual and implied) Jim Crow laws of racial segregation, all of which rested on the claim that whites were superior and blacks inferior. That set up the group prejudice that began to live on its own in the feelings children developed about their group membership.

Yet somehow, we teach 21st century American children in a way that leaves them believing that was a long time ago, in a galaxy far, far away. So young people make uninformed mistakes that explode with a crash in their lives. A few colleges and universities have called on me to help their students, as did Yavapai College in Prescott, AZ.

October 4-5, 2017, I gave a series of talks at Yavapai College (Prescott, AZ) as part of their school intervention against on-campus intergroup hostilities. Their "Respect Starts Here" campaign,[4] I thought, was a really good model for colleges and universities dealing with neo-diversity anxieties on their campuses. It was really a campaign: "...work in an organized and active way toward a particular goal, typically a political or social one. See crusade," the dictionary entry reads.

What I saw at Yavapai College was a "respect campaign" that touched and involved all the constituents of the college. That campaign had these elements:

A broad theme—Respect Begins Here

Respect posters strategically placed across the campus.

Kindness rocks painted by students of Geography and their professors; strategically placed all over campus.

Convocation speakers who told their own stories to highlight the need for respect at Yavapai.

Chalk for change (on various walkways on campus)

Short videos of students interviewed about their life stories posted to the Yavapai College YouTube channel.

A core event featuring an outside speaker—me. To galvanize the respect idea by introducing ideas about what it takes today to interact with people with respect. Students invited and given extra credit for attendance.

Speaker also does an address for faculty, the larger community and meets with college administrators.

To keep all these elements working together, Yavapai had a team with a lead person, Dr. Mark Shelley. Hosted by Mark, from the time I arrived on the Yavapai campus they really worked me. My contribution to the campaign was a series of talks to students, three on one day, and the next day a talk to faculty, and then finally a talk to the wider community through a life-long learning program. It was invigorating and felt worthwhile.

While at Yavapai College, I was surprised by joy. After one of the three talks (for students) I gave on neo-diversity on the first day (10/5/2017), I had an unexpected, shocking encounter. An elderly white woman slowly walked up to me. She took my hand, squeezed, and pulled herself close to me. Her daughter introduced this lady to me to tell me this elderly woman was a holocaust survivor. As I bent down to greet her, she held on to me, looking me in the eyes, telling me, "…you and I are alike."

Esther Basch, a survivor of the holocaust said to me, "…you and I are alike." She said "…as you talked, I was feeling what you feel. It's like what I lived through… so much separation… so much separation…"

I was speechless.

At 16 years old, Ms. Esther Basch was in a Nazi concentration camp because she is a Jew. "You and I are alike," she said is how she felt about my words about my living through some of the years of America's Jim Crow legal racial segregation.

"You and I have seen so much separation… so much separation," she said.

"Thank you for teaching," she said.

Esther put her arms around me and seemed not to want to let me go. I did not want to let her go; such a warm, loving spirit.

Esther held onto me as if I were her long-lost grandson. People smiled as they watched us. Unexpectedly, I had met and had a brief, warm, loving interaction with a holocaust survivor. Life is, indeed, a big town.

To my surprise and further joy, Esther came back the next day to listen to me again.

"I love you," she said to me at our second encounter.

I kissed her on the cheek as I tried not to cry. I was not completely successful in that effort.

####

In my talks, I had used my experience of growing up in the Jim Crow South to flash frame social change in America: "I grew up in

the Jim Crow segregated-by-law American South, and now today we live with neo-diversity, this time where our racial and other group contacts are not controlled and restricted by law."

A few weeks later, Dr. Mark Shelley let me know the impact I had during my visit to Yavapai College by sending me quotes from student reflections on my presentation. One student wrote:

> I also agree with Nacoste that racism is not ancient history. I know that when I was young, I used to think that racism was so long ago that people living during that time were now dead. This presentation made me realize how recent this all was (Nacoste still looks young).

Although I am not yet dead, and that is flattering, it makes the more important and broader point that young people have been mis-educated about the history of racial struggle in America; a terrible mis-education that leaves too many believing it was all "…so long ago that people living during that time were now dead." Not even the Nazi war crimes of attempted genocide of Jewish people, the Holocaust, was that long ago. For that, supported by "the greatest generation" Jim Crow legal segregation was still going strong in America during and after the defeat of Hitler and his "Final Solution," which is why we must ask, what happens to individual psychology while we are still in the midst of changes in our nation's sense of group positions?

What happens to an individual's social psychology in the face of the failure and collapse of the institutional and organizational support for their race-superior sense of group position? What happens, psychologically, when the removal of obvious forms of structural racism, sexism, or heterosexism means that what used to be taken for granted can't be?

I am asking you to think about what happens psychologically when black and Latinx people, now less hindered by the law, show high achievement in all kinds of domains (not just sports)? What happens, psychologically, when standards of woman beauty broaden to more realistically include women of color (Miss USA), hijab-wearing Muslim women (cover of Vogue), curvy women TV weather reporters, First Lady Michelle Obama?[5]

Really, the question I am asking you to ponder is this: What happens when the race-superior sense of group position is shown to have been built on a house of cards? Well, the answer is intergroup anxiety.

Immoral and unconstitutional, laws of racial segregation, Jim Crow, did something very social-psychological. Those laws set up the context for racial stereotypes to live in people as if true. No interaction meant no opportunity for anything to contradict the false categories that hold up racial stereotypes. Imagine living that way and then suddenly having to deal with real information that made it clear that your beliefs about a group were false; stereotypes that had nothing to do with real people.

In his science fiction novel *The Moons of Barsk*, Lawrence M. Schoen sets up this situation for a character to explore. Trying to explain the problem to his friend Rina, Pizlo talks about an encounter he had with someone who had never encountered someone of Rina and Pizlo's species:

> "I told him my name, and asked him for his. He told me his… so I said 'Hullo, Ciochon. My name is Pizlo.' And he scowled at me."
>
> "Why would he do that?"
>
> "That's what I asked him. And he said if he called me by name, then I'd stop being [just one of our species]."
>
> "That's dumb, too," said Rina. "What else could you be?"
>
> "No, you see, he didn't mean it like that. Like before, when I asked you what you knew about [his species].

Everything you said was true, but none of it really told you anything about Ciochon, about his life and his family, about his hobbies and his favorite foods, or his hopes and plans. It was like that. He said that if he called me by name that I'd become a real person to him, that he couldn't see me as a monster anymore."

"What's wrong with that?"

"It bothered him," [Pizlo said]. "He said that when you live in a [segregated world of a] space station you spend a lot of time in your own head, thinking about the same stuff over and over. And that if he came to see that the one [alien of our species] he'd actually met wasn't a monster, then what did that say about all the other [supposed] monsters? Because he'd roll it all around in his head and eventually have to accept that an entire [group] was a lot of people to be wrong about. And not just that, but it called into doubt other things that he knew to be absolutely true, taught to him by the same teachers and leaders who explained about us being monsters. It's like talking to me, admitting I was real, would end up breaking everything he knew. [Ciochon] started rocking and sniffling. I mean he was thinking real hard, but it was making him pretty upset."[6]

In America's past, the fundamental intergroup relation was about black-white interactions, and that relation was negative with everything designed to show and to keep blacks as inferior. Truth told, though, the negative intergroup relation of black-white interactions in America was built with false categories.

For those who have wondered why it has been so hard for too many white Americans to leave behind (get over) the group prejudices that had been supported by Jim Crow legal segregation, the truth is we have not directly addressed the social psychology of the leftover sense of race-superior group position. With vigor, we knocked down the house of cards. But people are still trying to hold on to the image of that house and the major adjoining rooms in that house.

Adjoining rooms where, at one time, the sense of male superiority to women lived in comfort without challenge. Another where the sense of superiority of heterosexuals lounged at ease in simple relief, and yet another adjoining room in which the sense of superiority of Christianity prayed in contentment, and too an adjoining room where the sense of superiority of having an unhindered body stretched out in safety and walked with boldness up the stairs with no hand holds.

Then, because of a powerful quake that revealed the faulty construction, America declared the house of legal racial segregation unlivable. Part of the house had to be demolished. When that deconstruction work began, workers found so much shoddy design it meant that taking down one part meant other load bearing walls were now unsupportable.

After taking down Jim Crow laws of discrimination, after starting to rebuild with a Civil Rights Act and Voting Rights Act blueprint, it became clear that, of course, women must have equal rights in this new open-air building (Title IX). What made that clear was the neo-diversity of the workers. Brown workers, gay workers, women workers, Muslim workers, American Indian workers, Transgender workers. That neo-diversity of people as workers was not buying into living in separate rooms let alone separate neighborhoods, schools, hospitals, movie theaters, and public bathrooms. That neo-diversity of workers was also and certainly not going to accept even having to live with separate shopping.

Faulty construction was found in those old, superior-group-position buildings and those who had been living in them were now in need of healing. Yes, healing and recovery from living in those constructions that had been fuming with invisible, poisonous gases attached to the shabby construction materials. Now torn down, those who had been taught to rely on that poorly built construction were left exposed, bereft and anxious, because now the intergroup relation is vague.

There are no more monsters. Or worse, as the poet Jack Gilbert has said, we are all monsters. Now "…Safe and helpless, the monster must fashion his own blessing or doom."[7]

A negative intergroup relation activates a superior-group position of prejudice and ethnocentrism. A vague intergroup relation activates individual uncertainty and interaction anxiety – "…Oh no, what are the rules for social interaction with '…one of them?'"

With a vague intergroup situation that does not give us a structural excuse for our intergroup behavior or the intergroup behavior of others, what we just did (or said), the way we have seen others interacting, exaggerates individual self-concern. That self-concern about how this "…makes me look" is intensified and sets off cognitive shortcut strategies of self-defense. Oversimplified ways of thinking take over and combine with sudden heightened emotions, causing what a person says to come out as yell of self-defense:

A. "It was just a joke!" a white student at UNC-Charlotte who had been called out for putting up a "Colored" sign over a water-fountain in a residence hall.[8]

B. "What I said was in poor taste and erroneous," Raymond Moore, CEO Indian Hills Tennis Club apologizing for earlier saying, "If I was a lady player, I'd go down every night on my knees and thank God that Roger Federer and Rafael Nadal were born, because they have carried this sport. They really have."[9]

C. "Jews will not replace us" chant white supremacists

at a KKK rally on a college campus.[10]

Without Jim Crow laws, without a social structure of legalized discrimination to point to, these kinds of statements are made and rooted in the panic of self-concern. Wait, what happened? Am I now going to be embarrassed in my daily social interactions with women, blacks, American-Muslims, American-Mexicans? Am I going to be the subject of criticism? How are people in "my" group evaluating me? How are people in those other groups evaluating me?

All that self-concern is moving through the social psychology of a person because there are no more shields from personal scrutiny. Gone are laws of discrimination that provided an easy out. "…I mean what can I do? It's just the way things are." Now, to defend themselves from scrutiny, individuals are turning in circles, twisting themselves in knots, saying "…the problem is political correctness." Worse, caught in the 65 mph whirlwind of a floorless roller coaster of intergroup emotions, the individual blurts out a defense: "There's been no racial oppression for 100 years…"[11] Worse still, the FOX TV commentator Tucker Carlson boldly declares that all the talk of America's white supremacy problem is "… a hoax. It's just a conspiracy theory used to divide the country and keep a hold on power."[12]

These psychologically panicked responses are what happens to an individual's social psychology in the face of the failure and collapse of the institutional and organizational support for their race-superior sense of group position. Avoidance and denial is the social psychology of what we are seeing moving across our nation. When bigotry pops out, that reality leaves only self-incrimination, which for too many is too painful to face. The reason is simple: there is no institutional backup for personal prejudice and bigotry. No one can say, "…well that's just the way things are."

Nope.

Now, you see, it's personal.

40: An American Eclipse

I don't teach in the summers. Sometimes I write. Summer 2017, I was a lazy bum. I spent the summer reading… for fun. Novels, literary fiction, young adult fiction, with one or two nonfiction books. One of the nonfiction books was David Baron's *American Eclipse*, which really hit me because, in an interesting social context, the story told showed how tethered we are to multiple intergroup histories.

Neo-diversity, you see, is not an ahistorical idea. I could not have come to the idea of describing our current social psychological environment as neo-diverse without understanding the intergroup history of America.

Each intergroup historical period has had its own level of social psychological darkness. Foreboding and dark ways in which people were socialized to think of each other as only members of groups – us versus them. Summer 2017, as we were coming to an actual eclipse I was reminded of the intergroup histories of our nation and the dark social psychological remnants of each period.

> *No part of our history is untouched by the one-time American enslavement of African peoples.*

That thought flashed into my mind as I began to read *American Eclipse*.[1] I picked up *American Eclipse* from my summer book stack to break away (for a little while) from my summer reading of fiction. A nonfiction book, *American Eclipse* is about early American astronomers and their attempt to observe and measure the total eclipse of the sun in 1898. Within two pages of reading, in setting the context for the lives of astronomers at that time, the author talks about the civil war ending and that end motivating scientists to get to work. That's when I had that first flash thought:

> *Nothing in the psychology of American enterprise is uninfluenced by the one-time enslavement of African peoples.*

To see, observe and measure the effects of the eclipse of 1898 meant heading to the then still somewhat untamed American West. At that place and time, people yet remembered George Armstrong Custer's attempt to eradicate Indians; people still talked about "Indian savages."

No part of our history is untouched by the unfair, genocidal treatment of American Indians.

Yep, that flashed through my mind as I read. I went on, learning the history of American astronomy, enjoying the writing, enjoying the well-written story that includes the inventor Thomas Edison, among other inventors and scientists interested in the eclipse. Those scientists included a name I didn't know because, well, because this person was a "woman scientist," Maria Mitchell. Another flash:

> *Nothing in the psychology of the American enterprise is uninfluenced by the too-long resistance to acknowledging the powerful intellect of women.*

Let me just say this: If you are at all interested in early American scientific endeavors of astronomy (and a bit about early meteorology), *American Eclipse* is a fun, five-star read. In it you get real glimpses into the actual lives and motivations of a bunch of eclipse obsessed scientists, their technological challenges and human adventures leading up to their chance to see and measure the 1898 total eclipse that could be observed from America. You see, this book *American Eclipse* is not about any of my flashes; not the enslavement of Africans, not the stealing of land and life from American Indians, not demeaning views of women. It's just that those are part of the intergroup context of America even in a book about early American astronomy.

In Baron's well-researched book, *American Eclipse*, there are statements people made in 1898 that are the same cringe-worthy statements some people make today about blacks, American Indians, and women. That is why it is more than fair to say that nothing in the psychology of our 21st century is uninfluenced by our histories of intergroup bigotries. Yet, know this too:

> *Nothing in our American psychology has been so profound, and important, as those marginalized and discounted peoples pushing through, and defeating, America's too-many intergroup bigotries.*

That is why in 21st century America we arrive at a neo-diverse social environment – this time and circumstance where people from many different groups are free to walk around and be engaged in the American promise of "…the pursuit of happiness."[2]

But given our intergroup histories and our associated long psychological struggle with multiple, intergroup bigotries, today there are Americans who find it a hardship to have to encounter and interact with people from so many different groups by way of race, yes, but also sexual orientation, religion, bodily condition, sex-of-person, mental health condition, gender identity, age, and on and on. Indeed, recent survey research is clear in showing that lots of Americans are experiencing interpersonal anxiety about this neo-diversity.[3] My knowledge of that research has been the reason that in my activist teaching and writing I have been calling out to Americans to say:

"Welcome to the future. The future is not coming. It's here and now."

I have been making this proclamation loudly, because not understanding that is causing a lot of confusion in America. All of the intergroup tensions we are witnessing in America today are because for too long in this country, to organize our daily social interactions, we have relied on false categories: race, sex-of-person, religion, and sexual orientation. We have relied too much on those false categories for getting through our daily walk through life.

Oh, don't misunderstand me. There are ways in which these are real characteristics of persons. Look at any photo of me and you will see that I am, indeed, a big, giant, dark-skinned black man. Yet that information becomes a false category when people try to use that information, that category, to make judgments to guide the way they interact with me. For too long in America we have relied on false categories that make us-versus-them distinctions. We have used us-versus-them ways of thinking about people to do what? To keep 'them' in their place? To try to keep the world simple? Now, today, in the future we are living in, we are seeing that those categories don't work. Those categories are false.

It is false, you see, to believe that women aren't smart enough to be engineers, physicists and mathematicians. It is false, you see, to believe that all Muslims are terrorists. It is false, you see, to believe that gay, lesbian, bi-sexual, and transgender people have no place at North Carolina State University where I am a professor, and where we have created and staffed our Gay, Lesbian, Bi-sexual, Transgender Student Center.

In the future we are already living those false categories don't work. Resistance to accepting that social reality is ripping through our whole nation making too many Americans anxious, tense and sometimes angry. A white nationalist rally in Charlottesville is only one recent example of that irrational, dangerous anger. Just witness all the irrational calls to the police because a black person is… eating lunch, having a picnic in a park, walking into the neighborhood swimming pool…

Why does the truth do this to people? Well, since as children too many people were taught to rely on false categories of us versus them, false categories that now don't work, people struggle. People wrestle mightily with the question, "Who are among the 'we' and who are among the 'they?'"[4] Our too-long history of relying on false categories is now tearing at the soul of America.

"We hold these truths to be self-evident, that all men are created equal, that they are endowed with certain inalienable rights, among these are life, liberty and the pursuit of happiness." That is the soul of America. We soil and wound that soul when we try to rely on false categories. With today's neo-diversity we must find ways to stop ourselves from using our historical reliance on false, cognitive, intergroup categories. We must work out this struggle because no matter what, neo-diversity is the social psychological reality we are all living in and must find productive ways to manage in our interpersonal lives. Our neo-diversity future is not coming, it is here and now.

41: Our Light Against Bigotry

America has a mission statement. Using that mission statement to stand up to bigotry is how we will save the soul of America.

As always, toward the end of the semester in my "Interdependence and Race" course, I teach my students the social psychology of what it takes to stand up to bigotry. All through the course I have been teaching my students the differences between important intergroup concepts: prejudice is not bigotry is not racism. All through the semester I have been teaching my students to understand the power to damage social interactions carried by interpersonal-intergroup anxiety. All through the semester I have been building to my standing-up-to-bigotry lectures.

To get my students ready for those lectures, for that new understanding, from Interdependence theory proper[1] I have developed, and introduce to my students my levels-of-interdependence hypothesis:

"Whenever a social (non-verbal, verbal or symbolic) cue in social interaction creates or magnifies interpersonal anxiety, the interaction between two people will shift from a casual, easy-flow level of interaction to an intense, identity level of interaction."

Less formally, the hypothesis describes what can cause an interaction to go from a "…Hey, how's it going?" casual kind of interaction to a "…What did you just say to me!?" intense interaction moment. With that hypothesis, over a number of lectures I teach my students how to analyze how this happens by giving them a tool, a model, for seeing the stages of social interaction.[2]

Remember, every actual, imagined or implied (by observation), social interaction goes through five stages:

Stage I – each person assesses the situation: where, why, when, who? Where am I going? Why or for what purpose am I going there? When am I supposed to be there? Who else will be there?

Stage II – each person assesses possible outcomes for self: how will I be treated? Will I have a good time?

Stage III – each person tries to find a cognitive, shortcut way of understanding what might be going to happen (It's a party versus It's a funeral) or what is happening in the moment. We do this to avoid or to solve an actual or potential interaction problem.

Stage IV – each person experiences large or small identity concerns that can heighten emotion: am I being myself? How am I coming across? What am I saying?

Stage V – each person engages in interpersonal behavior: What is said or done. We attempt to interact safely, in a way that is appropriate to the situation or interaction moment.

Teaching the concepts and the model, I am giving my students interaction-scene-investigation tools they can use to analyze and understand social interaction. Learning how to use those tools, my students begin to see why interactions between people from different demographic groups can activate neo-diversity anxiety[3] and cause real problems in everyday social interaction. Not only that, but giving them real-world examples to analyze, my students also learn how to analyze in what stage of an interaction that interaction anxiety took over in a variety of neo-diverse social interactions gone bad.

Having learned how to use these conceptual tools, my students are then ready to understand how and why anti-group slurs have a dangerous and damaging power in social interaction. In the most intense lecture of the class, I analyze the power of a whole host of anti-group slurs: racial (ni****), sex-of-person (bit**), ethnic (greaseba**), bodily condition (cri*), mental health condition (reta**), religious (sand-nig***).

Then I ask my students the most important question of the semester:

"What are you prepared to do?"

In that classroom moment, I am *not* challenging my students to become politicians or even to become political. I am *not* challenging my students to take on the task of building social movements, to participate in a protest, or even to just vote. No, none of that.

I am challenging my students to consider this question:

> "What are you prepared to do in your everyday social
> interactions when someone you are interacting with
> refers to people as a stereotype, uses hate language
> against interracial marriage or hate language against
> marriage equality for gay, lesbian and transgender
> people, or speaks of women in a demeaning way, or
> uses any racial slur?"

That's the challenge I call out to these students who have enrolled themselves in my "Interdependence and Race" course. I ask, "…is it bigotry on your part, to be silent when your interaction partner uses anti-group slurs? Is your silence, is your silent tolerance for intolerance, bigotry?"

I ask and then I go silent.

Slowly I move my head left to right, back to left, letting my students see my eyes scan the room. Silent, I let everyone in the room feel me looking at each and every one of my students.

In that moment, no student dare disturbs the sound of my silence.

Then I answer for them, and the answer is "Yes." Showing tolerance for intolerance is your bigotry by your silent agreement. Now my students' eyes are on wide on me, pleading with me:

"But what am I supposed to do?"

I can see that question on their wide-eyed faces. I can feel that question in the quiet of their squirming in their seats.

I will not, I do not, of course, leave them squirming. Just when I can feel they can't take the tension much longer, I begin talking to introduce a research-based strategy for standing up to bigotry during a social interaction.[4]

To set that up, I remind my students of the five stages of social interaction. I do that to show them what hearing an anti-group slur does to the social interaction itself: it introduces uncertainty about how to proceed – "Wait, what?" (Stage II). It is in Stage II where people begin to go silent with worry, how will other people evaluate and treat me if I say something.

That worry drives people to try to identify a short-cut way of thinking that will let them avoid the interaction problem created by the anti-group slur – "I'm sure that was just a joke." Now with both the worry (Stage II), the possible strategy for avoidance (Stage III), a person's emotional concerns (Stage IV) about "who am I" to speak up goes hot and heats up the worry, the chosen strategy. All that pushes into the actual behavior (Stage V) of keeping quiet, not speaking up against bigotry.

Now, with their learning of how the model works in real social interaction, my students see the root causes of their own silence in the face of another person's language bigotry. Not that they actually agree with the bigotry, not that they are bigots, but that the social force of interpersonal anxiety has taken over outside of their awareness. For my students, from that understanding emerges the most important thing they get from learning to use the stages of the model: how to accept and then control their own interaction anxiety in the moment. You see, knowing what is happening allows for anyone to take control of the interaction moment for themselves.

With that grounding, I can then walk my students through the research-based strategy[4] for standing up to bigotry. Turns out each of us has the power to influence our social interactions.

When the person you are interacting with uses negative racial, gender, or ethnic language, do not tolerate it. But, don't call that person names. Instead of name-calling, speak for yourself.

Don't try to tell that person they are wrong. Don't try to tell that person it's just not a good idea to talk that way. Instead, let that person know your standards for continuing to interact with you. Just quietly, but firmly, express your personal standard for the interaction. Speak into that moment, and speak for yourself. Simply say, "I am very uncomfortable with that kind of language. I find it offensive. It hurts me." Speaking in the "I" is critical to avoid shaming the person. But speaking "…it hurts me" hits the person in Stage IV (identity): who am I to think this person would accept that way of talking.

A very sophisticated set of experiments shows that this strategy has powerful effects on the perpetrator of the language bigotry. Confronted in this quiet but firm way, the person who has expressed the bigotry now experiences negative self-evaluations (Stage IV identity-emotions). Confronted in this quiet but firm way, the person experiences a hot mix of anger at myself, annoyance with myself, regret, disgust with myself.

With all that heating up in the person, yes, that person will also feel anger at being confronted and be annoyed with you. No surprise, that that mix of hot emotions (Stage IV) motivates the person to lash out (Stage V) at the person who has quietly challenged their bigotry.

Of late, with genuine concern a student will ask, "…But what if the other person asks you why do you even care?" That question is, of course, the other person lashing out by pointing to your demographic group membership to say, "…look you're not even one of them… you're not transgender, you're not Jewish, you're not white…" Lashing out, that person is implying that all you can ever care about, all you can ever be is a representative of your own demographic group.

How does one answer that insulting attempt to trap you in a group-identity stereotype? How? With America's mission statement, that's how.

When my students ask me about people trying to use that strategy to push one of my students to be quiet, to push my students to tolerate intolerance, I say this: Tell that person, "I care because I am a true American who believes in America's mission statement that 'We hold these truths to be self-evident, that all men are created equal…'"

If you believe in the founding principles of America, when anyone who tries it with you, that's what you tell them, that's the torch you hold up. Now lit up, that torch will shine a light into the interaction moment. That will reduce other people's use of anti-group sentiments to try to make their point. That light will scatter the roaches of intolerance.

Trusting in and using the light of America's mission statement is how we can influence our social interactions away from the casual acceptance of intolerance in our interactions with other people. Trusting in and using America's mission statement is how we will save the soul of America.

That is what Dr. Martin Luther King Jr. was getting at when he said, "The greatest tragedy of this age will not be the vitriolic words and deeds of the children of darkness, but the appalling silence of the children of light."

Truth told, America cannot afford for us to be silent in the face of bigotry. Being silent would violate America's mission statement. Now you know that you do not have to be silent. Now you have an interpersonal strategy. We all can use the interpersonal strategy I teach my students as a light to scatter the roaches of intolerance with America's true brightness. Same as the Kingdom of Wakanda, as individuals we must step out of the shadows and light the way forward. We've come too far to go dark now.

42: Humanity Forever

I am at ground zero. I am witness to an explosion that is not one of destruction but, instead, is an explosion of rainbows of life. Teaching at a university, teaching what I teach, I am at ground zero. Surrounded by young people who are trying to navigate life in 21st century, neo-diverse America, I am in a constant state of learning.

I teach about social interaction, social life and social change. That is why no matter my preference, young people are constantly in my space, listening, learning, asking, and not leaving me alone to be an old man.

Nope. Not happening.

"Dr. Nacoste... so what about...how should I think about... you just made me think of... here's a video I thought you might find interesting... have you see this article... what do you think about what happened in..."

Won't... leave... me... alone...

I am in a constant state of teaching, advising, listening, and learning.

Sometimes that gets to be very personal. I have a new son, a son who is transgender. Jay, a former student who was Katie, who graduated years ago, contacted me to tell me of their transition. Then they came to visit me. Right there – did you catch my use of pronouns? "Their," "they," rather than "his" or "her."

I have learned. I have had to learn because "back in my day," no one talked about preferred pronouns. When I was growing up, there was no respectful language that could be used to refer to transgender persons. There was no respectful language trans-people could use about themselves, and none that non-trans people could use to refer to trans-people. Yet now, for many today, the word "transgender" is a generally understood term of reference.[1] Even with that, there is more to the future we are already living in than language.

The Spring 2018 semester had just started. Right at that beginning, over the weekend before there had been any class meetings, I received two emails from two different transgender students. Each young person was letting me know they were in gender identity transition. Each was alerting me to the pronouns they would like me to use to refer to them in class. Yes, two transgender students felt it OK and reasonable to reveal themselves to me so that I could be respectful when we were in interaction with each other. How could this be?

Well, again I say, turns out nothing in our American psychology has been so profound, challenging, and important as discounted peoples pushing through, and defeating, America's too-many intergroup bigotries. That fight against bigotry continues on many, and newer, fronts every day.

The successes of those fights to defeat intergroup bigotry in America has led our nation (and most college and university campuses) to a new interpersonal situation: neo-diversity. Neo-diversity is this now-future in which each of us has some occasion to encounter and interact with, on equal footing, a person or persons who are not like us on some group dimension that turns an interpersonal interaction into an interpersonal-intergroup interaction. Neo-diversity is the future we are already living on the campus of NCSU where I teach, and in America writ large.

Neo-diversity is a wrinkle in time[2] in the space-time fabric of America. For the fact that we are already living in the future, neo-diversity social change is hard on our individual psychology. You see, human psychology is designed to comprehend most things in a straight line, keep it simple fashion. Yet neo-diversity social change has been occurring in multiple and multidimensional ways simultaneously. Taking the fabric of America and folding, wrinkling many social dimensions into each other so that each change touches and connects to all the others – that is neo-diversity. No doubt, that is a challenge to our cognitive-economic system,[3] which pushes us to process information by keeping it simple.

Still, we should not panic. We cannot afford to panic. We must be and we are stronger than that as Americans. The question is not how do we go backward to when we did not have to concern ourselves with respecting people not like us. Right now, in fact, one of the pressing questions is why are so many of us so easily panicked?

Documenting Light[4] is a novel about the developing romance between a self-described "…nonbinary, feminine, trans-person" and a self-described "…regular old trans dude." In their novel, E. E. Ottman observes that the intergroup histories we are taught are incomplete by intention; incomplete on purpose. They write:

> What gets taught at anything lower than a three-hundred-level college course is very political. You were never taught queer history because there are people with a vested interest in you not learning queer history. But the same can be said for race history—of all sorts—and most gender history too, not to mention disability history. We don't learn it, not because historians don't study it but because the people who make the decision about what goes into history textbooks aren't fans.

Look, in this wrinkle in time I too, a highly educated and black man, have also had to learn how to interact in this new interpersonal world of neo-diversity. To continue to live the good life that America provides to so many of us, we must learn how to interact with people "not like me" with respect. We must stand against bigotry. As Mrs. Which puts it in *A Wrinkle in Time*, "There will no longer be so many pleasant things to look at if responsible people do not do something about the unpleasant ones."

In the case of the students who emailed me at this beginning of that Spring 2018 semester, I responded telling both how much I appreciated their communication to me. I thanked both of these young people. I asked both to introduce themselves to me discreetly on the first day of class so that I could make sure to be able to identify them by sight and use the appropriate pronouns in our interactions.

To alert our students to this social change dynamic on our campus, I wrote and published and essay in our student newspaper about these students and their contacting me. I ended my essay[5] by saying:

> I know each is very vulnerable right now. Sadly, I know too that because of the challenge of this wrinkle in time, each will encounter disrespect from some. But not in my classrooms. Hear me loud and clear when I say, trust that I will protect each in every way I can inside and outside of my classrooms on our campus.
>
> #TransgenderAlly

Many of our politicians are too far removed from the ground zero of neo-diversity, and so have no idea what is happening. Many have no idea of the positive and powerful changes to social interaction that are coming, that are already being lived. Some are aware but unfortunately are spending their energies pushing back in a futile attempt to stop the humane growth of our democracy.

I have the privilege to live and work at that ground zero of neo-diversity that is a university like NCSU. I am stronger for it. I am a better human being for it. Yes, young people can sometimes get on my nerves and refuse to let me sit in a rocking chair to be an old man.

Nonetheless, I am proud to have young people push and prod me to pay attention to the beautiful exploding rainbows of 21st century life.

Emails are how requests usually come to me at the start. Speaking to the (local) Model-United-Nations, though, started with a conversation. A brown-skinned, dark-haired female of East-Indian descent was sitting across from me in my office. A week before, Sumana had come to my office to ask to set up an appointment. Now she was at that appointment, making her request.

"Model U.N.? Tell me more," I said.

Sumana explained enough for me to say, "Sure, I'll be your keynote speaker." It helped that we were talking about this in November and the conference was a few months away and would happen on a Friday, the one day of the week I do not teach. After our conversation, later that day I got an email from Sumana that read:

> Hello Dr. Nacoste, I spoke with you earlier today about speaking at a middle school Model UN conference that I organize with my friend and co-director Elise Ashkin-Baker. Thank you so much for agreeing to speak at our conference. I really appreciate your interest and, as a student in your class, admire your work.
>
> I realize that I failed to really describe the structure of the conference. The organization is run by myself and Elise (who is a student at UNC-Chapel Hill). We were given the organization by our Model UN teacher and mentor, who had to move out of the state. The organization was created because there were no existing middle school MUN conferences in North Carolina and our mentor wanted to create one that would be accessible to all students in NC. The conference is run by a staff of volunteer high school students who Elise and I meet with and train throughout the

year. The actual conference is similar to most Model UN conferences, in that students break off into committees, that mimic those in the actual UN (Human Rights Council, World Health Organization, etc.), after Opening Ceremonies. During committee, students debate and work together to form resolutions revolving around topics relating to the overarching theme of the conference. This year's theme is the rise of extremism.

This conference will be our sixth conference and we are expecting around 150 students. I have attached a link to our website below. Please, let me know if you have any questions about the conference or if you would like to meet prior to further discuss the conference.

And so it came to pass on March 3, 2018, at the campus of the University of North Carolina Chapel Hill, I was the keynote speaker at the annual meeting of the Triangle Model United Nations. As it is stated on the Triangle Model UN website, "Our mission is to create a Model United Nation's conference for middle school students in North Carolina and beyond that is professional, high quality, and allows for and embraces the diversity of delegates from different backgrounds, preparation levels and experiences."[6]

As keynote speaker, I took it as my job to deliver an opening message that would connect to the meeting theme of examining ways to fight "...the rise of nationalism and extremism... and move toward unified development." That my audience was middle school students gave me pause. How could I talk about the rise of extremism in a way that would excite and engage the thinking of these middle school Model UN delegates?

I had just seen the movie, "Black Panther." Wow! Given the way the movie had especially captured the imagination of young people, I decided to present myself as a proxy delegate sent by King T'Challa, the Black Panther. Declaring myself the delegate from the Kingdom of Wakanda, I presented the Wakandan anti-bigotry proposal to the gathering of the Triangle Model UN. Here, then, is my keynote speech offering that proposal:

"Good morning.

> To the Secretary General of this United Nations, and to the distinguished representatives, delegates and ambassadors of the nations represented here today, I bring you greetings from the Kingdom of Wakanda and King T'Challa, the Black Panther.

> Wakanda Forever!"

There was an audible reaction from my audience; gasps and giggles.

> As you know, Wakanda is the newest member of your, now our, United Nations. As the delegate representing Wakanda for King T'Challa, the Black Panther, I thank you for this opportunity to present our proposal for dealing with, slowing down and ending the rise of extremism around the world.

> What is our proposal? We of Wakanda believe that to deal with, slow and eventually stop the rise of global extremism, the United Nations must create a program to train interpersonal leaders.

> We take the rise of extremism in America as the example for a place to start. Although you may think we Wakandans are too new to the world community to make any suggestions, we know America's racial

history because we have watched how those stolen from Africa have been treated.

Our proposal for the training of interpersonal leaders is grounded in the vision of America's late and great Reverend Dr. Martin Luther King Jr. To quote Dr. King's 1968 prophecy,

"We've got some difficult days ahead." And now, today, we live in those difficult days.

Charlottesville, VA, July 2017. White nationalist march through the campus of the University of V.A. chanting, "You will not replace us." Who are the 'you' that those white males fear will replace them? Some were heard to say Jews… but it could be any group of so-called "others": Muslims, gay and lesbian individuals, Hispanics, women, African Americans, immigrants.

That rally was no isolated incident of extremism. February 21, 2018, from the Southern Poverty Law Center, news services across America and the world gave this report on the rise of extremism in this country. To quote the report: "The number of U.S. hate groups rose again in 2017."[7]

How did America and the global community get to this point? The answer is both simple and complex: rapid social change.

Rapid social change has created a new kind of diversity environment: a social environment of neo-diversity.[8] Rapid social change has created a neo-diverse interpersonal environment where people from many different groups have to encounter and interact with other people from other groups whether they want to or not.

America is one of the best examples of that, since America has gone from a past society of racial segregation by law to today's society where all people can walk into and out of any social environment, no matter their race. In today's America, that freedom of movement includes people of different religions, sexual orientations, mental health conditions, ethnicities, gender identities, or bodily conditions.

In the old racially segregated America, black people could not go to places and freely interact with white people. In that segregated world, people did not have to think about who they were interacting with by race. People did not have to be concerned about how they talked about people of another race because no one of another race would hear it or could do anything about it. Everybody in the situation was a "we."

With the old racial laws gone, with the new social environment of neo-diversity a mix of people are all in the same room, and for too many Americans that causes anxiety. An anxiety that is captured in the question, "Who are among the 'we' and who are among the 'they?'"[9]

That intergroup anxiety is dangerous because that anxiety can activate prejudice and bigotry in individuals that can come out in startling ways. In Charlottesville, VA, the chant by the white supremacists was, "You will not replace us."

To truly understand that chant, you must understand that prejudice is not bigotry is not racism. Prejudice is a set of anti-group feelings that reside inside a person's psychology. Bigotry, though, is an individual's outward, behavioral display of a prejudice against a group of people (e.g., that anti-group chant). Racism would be a system of laws that made the outward display of prejudice legal; laws that would support people acting on the meaning of that chant (job discrimination, for example).

That chant in Charlottesville was a neo-diversity, anxiety-driven bigotry about who is in charge; who has power. That's the neo-diversity anxiety of "who are among the 'we' and who are among the 'they?'" That is a bigotry that says that only whites are human and worthy of being in power.

What can the UN do about that? Yes, one should rightly ask, what can a program to train interpersonal leaders do about the rise of that kind of prejudice and bigotry?

All extremism starts small.

All extremism starts with individual prejudice but grows strongest when that prejudice is expressed in behavior that goes unchallenged. When bigotry goes unchallenged, when we let people we are interacting with use the language that demeans other groups of people, that bigotry starts to get stronger and stronger.

True, sometimes it takes a while for a person's individual prejudice to show itself. Sometimes the prejudice felt by people we know is quiet. Understand, though, that that hibernating bigotry[10] is just waiting for the right stimulus to wake it up.

When that hibernating bigotry roars awake, too often in America the behavior goes unchallenged. People say, "They're not serious, they're just joking…" "It's just a joke," people claim.

That is exactly what the so-called friends of Dylann Roof said about the way he talked about black people. His friends said that they took the hateful things he said about black people, that "Black people are ruining America" to be "…just a joke."

Yes, they said it was just a joke and were stunned when he walked into an African American church in Charleston, SC, and shot and killed nine African Americans who were doing a bible study. His bigotry that his friends called a joke went unchallenged, but it was not just a joke, and so it grew stronger and stronger with daily (unchallenged) repetition until he felt he had to kill some black people.[11]

That is why it is important to understand that no, it's not just a joke when we hear another person's bigotry. There are no innocent anti-group jokes[12] because those groups are made up of real human beings.

That is why in moments when hibernating bigotry roars awake, we need individuals who will speak up against that kind of expressed thinking. We need interpersonal leaders.

We must and can train individuals to stand up against bigotry when it comes up in their social interactions with another person. We must and can train individuals to take a public stance against bigotry that comes up during their everyday social interactions. What would that training be like? Your American social psychologists have studied and shown that there is something we can teach people to say in the face of anybody expressing anti-group feelings. This interpersonal strategy is simple.

When someone makes a statement of bigotry, the best way to challenge that bigotry is for someone to say, "I'm sorry, I find that kind of language offensive, it hurts me."

Research[13] shows that this strategy works to stop bigotry from getting stronger. That is why we must train interpersonal leaders, people who know how to stand up to bigotry in their own social interactions with other people.

In his first and still only speech to this UN, King T'Challa, the Black Panther of Wakanda, said:

Wakanda will no longer watch from the shadows. We cannot. We must not.

We [of Wakanda] will work to be an example of how we as brothers and sisters on this earth should treat each other. Now, more than ever, the illusions of division threaten our very existence. We all know the truth: more connects us than separates us. But in times of crisis, the wise build bridges, while the foolish build barriers. We must find a way to look after one another as if we were one single tribe.[14]

What King T'Challa was saying, and all of Wakanda is saying through me today, is that we must deal with each other as if we are all of the same tribe, no worry about who are the 'we' and who are among the 'they.' No us versus them. We must treat each other with respect for the humanity that we are all members of. No us versus them.

Humanity Forever!

How do we create that world where we all respect each other no matter our tribes, no matter our background group memberships? Again, we must train people to stand against bigotry by using this interpersonal strategy:

"I'm sorry, I find that kind of language offensive, it hurts me."

As the representative of Wakanda, to you the UN, I thank you for listening to the Wakandan proposal to you for action, to create training programs to develop interpersonal leaders who will speak up against bigotry in all its forms.

We need, humanity needs, interpersonal leaders who will speak up against bigotry against women, bigotry against the disabled, bigotry against any race, bigotry against religion, bigotry against homosexuals, transgender or the gender fluid. We need, humanity needs, interpersonal leaders who will stand up against bigotry in all its forms.

To slow and stop the rise of global nationalism and extremism, our world needs interpersonal leaders who are trained in how to speak up against bigotry in the small interpersonal moments where extremism starts. That is what the Nobel Peace Prize winner, your Dr. Martin Luther King Jr., was telling the world when he said,

"The greatest tragedy of this age will not be the vitriolic words and deeds of the children of darkness. But the appalling silence of the children of light."

You delegates of the United Nations are the representatives of the "Children of Light."

Thank you for your time and attention.

Humanity Forever!

Having now heard from Wakanda, the delegates broke into small groups to work on United Nations stuff. After the enthusiastic applause, a few handshakes and thanks, I made my way to my car and drove back to Raleigh. I hoped that I had delivered an important message in an entertaining way. But this was one of those speaking engagements that was a moment in time with no follow-up interactions. I spoke and then I was gone.

I was pleased then to receive, a couple of days after, an email from Sumana. She wrote to say:

We received many positive comments regarding your talk from both teachers and students. Several of the teachers told us they thought your talk was a perfect fit for the theme of the conference and said they thoroughly enjoyed it. I also overheard many students discussing your Black Panther reference, which I think they really appreciated.

43: Teaching About Neo-Diversity Matters

Everywhere… 2017 Miss America, a black woman, is surprised she says, "…by the racism I have encountered."

Everywhere… sports, NBA star Lebron James' home is spray painted with a racial slur.

Everywhere…city, county government administrators. Flint Michigan county commissioner blames the city water crisis on "n****** who don't pay their bills."

Everywhere…nooses, swastikas, KKK rallies… around the nation, not just in the Deep South.

What is the stimulus for all these forms of intergroup tension? Simply put, it's rapid social change. In the conceptual language I have developed, it's all about neo-diversity.

Summer 2006, at Oxford University England, I was one of the scholars participating in the Oxford Round Table on "Global Security Challenges in the 21st Century." It was in my paper presentation for that set of discussions that I introduced the concept of neo-diversity. I used my new concept of neo-diversity to begin to analyze the way rapid social change was causing more and more people from many different groups to be in contact and non-voluntary interaction with each other. I argued that the social psychology of that neo-diversity was activating old (and creating some new) intergroup tensions and interaction anxieties in everyday life; intergroup tensions and interaction anxieties that could become volatile.

That presentation became my and the first paper published on neo-diversity.[1] In 2009, in my second paper about the concept, I used the neo-diversity idea to debunk the claim that because we elected Senator Barack Obama to the presidency that we were a post-racial nation.[2]

Back in 2006, I had also begun to envision, then design and began to teach, my college course "Interpersonal Relationships and Race." As you are now well aware, in that course I teach the social psychology of neo-diversity to help young people understand and productively adapt to the multi-group context of their lives. In 2006, I first taught the course as a special topics course with an enrollment of 20 students. In 2012, I did the administrative work to get my course made a part of the standing curriculum of the Department of Psychology with the title "Interdependence and Race."

Students had been more and more drawn to my course, so much so that I had gone from teaching it once an academic year to teaching it every semester with an average enrollment of 60 students. Fall 2018, I was stunned to see the enrollment was 80 students.

Why so much demand? Turns out my course fits the time we live in and that young people are thrust into unprepared. In America we are no longer talking about "the Negro problem," no longer just "race-relations," no longer just "desegregation and integration." We have struggled with and wobbled part way through those intergroup phases into today's neo-diversity – that interpersonal situation in which we all have to encounter and sometimes interact with people from different groups. Most receive little or no help from family, so at North Carolina State University, a good many find their way to my class to ask and explore their questions.

Fall 2018, those 80 students came with the most sophisticated set of questions I have encountered at the beginning of the semester. First day of class, syllabus day, I asked them to go home and think about what topics they hoped we would get to talk about in a course called "Interdependence and Race." At the second class meeting, I said, "Okay, I asked you to think about something for me, so let's hear your thoughts. What kinds of topics do you hope we get to talk about in this course?" Hands went up:

- If intergroup tension is created in a social interaction, how do you cope with it?

- How do interdependence and race affect art and music?

- How does race intersect with things like gender, religion, disabilities, and sexual orientation, etc.?

- How can we fix it (all the tension that is going on)?

- What causes a person to rely on stereotypes?

- How can you spot someone's reliance on stereotypes?

- The intersections between these topics with modern politics.

- How to resolve interpersonal intergroup tension in a *new* dyad.

- How interdependence and race has been reflected over time and in education (through school systems, etc.).

- How to react to someone's reliance on stereotypes during an interaction.

- Multiracial identity.

- The historical aspects, where did stereotypes come from?

- How intersectionality affects leadership style.

- How stereotypes and race influence law enforcement.

- How to respond as a bystander when you see someone else behaving in ways that are relying on a stereotype.

- How to deal with a moment where a person is trying to figure out interpersonal intergroup tension, by viewing it from a group's perspective.

- Who can define race? (Can you choose your race?)

- How stereotypes were used in the past versus in modern day, and how they may change in the future.

- Stereotype threat and code switching.

- How stereotypes affect romantic relationships.

Yikes! Fall 2018, these young people came with sophisticated questions about neo-diversity matters in America. Well, they came to the right place because I teach my course in an exciting but blunt way. With no sugar coating, I teach to describe and analyze for students the modern day struggles we have with intergroup tension caused by our nation's neo-diversity.

To be clear, then, President Trump is not the cause of all the current intergroup tensions in America. People's willingness to embrace or overlook presidential candidate Trump's anti-group rhetoric is just part of the evidence of the hibernating bigotry that we have been ignoring by tolerating other people's and our own language bigotry. We have wobbled through the other intergroup phases, dragging with us and trying to ignore hibernating bigotry: prejudiced feelings that only show up in outward behavior when the right stimulus shakes it awake. We have been too quick to give camouflaged hibernating bigotry a pass as "…just a joke." Now we are seeing the consequences of that wobbly effort everywhere.

With all that is going on, how are my former students doing? Has going through my course on neo-diversity helped at all, and if so how?

June 2017, I got this email:

Hello Dr. Nacoste, I hope your summer is treating you well. Today, a truly disturbing event occurred at my sister's high school that I wanted to share with you for your PSY 411 course.

This morning, a banner was displayed on Wakefield High School's building saying, "Bring Tripp Back #smartlunch". This refers to the previous principal Tripp Crayton who during his time as principal allowed the school to have smart lunch, an hour-long lunch for students. However, the new principal has taken away smart lunch with the hopes of promoting students to stay on campus during lunch and take advantage of teacher help. Now, this was not the issue.

Alongside the banner, the same students hung a black doll by the neck with rope as if it were lynched. These students threatened the current principal who is black. I am completely horrified and disgusted that something like this has happened. Supposedly, students had done this as their senior prank; however, this was definitely not a prank. It was an act of hatred.

Dr. Nacoste, your work is incredibly important and exactly what every individual in our nation needs. I cannot express enough how much I appreciate the lifelong lessons you have taught in your course. In these moments of hatred, your lessons and the work you are doing is the light that shines through.

This story did, in fact, make the local newspaper[3] and the TV news. But I was curious about one thing, so I followed up with this student. I asked my question this way. I said:

I appreciate your kind words about my teaching. Even so, I have a question. If you can answer this, tell me... in the face of seeing this kind of event, how does my teaching help you? I'd just like your thoughts, if you don't mind.

Being summer, it took a little while, but a week or so later, my former student replied. She said:

> For me, your course truly opened my eyes. I was aware of hate acts occurring across the nation- I would witness them myself, experience the hate, or see it on the news. But I viewed this all with such a tunnel vision. I saw these hate acts as isolated events and foolishly thought that only racists or extremists committed these acts. And as a result, though these events would upset me, I did not take them as seriously and view them as being detrimental to our society. Your class changed me to having more of a funnel view. Becoming aware of why bigotry still exists really altered my perspective. Besides helping me in my own life, understanding hibernating bigotry in a neo-diverse America has reinforced why events like these should be taken very seriously. They are not random. They do not affect a small percent of us. And like you have taught me, we are all guilty.

Going on, my former student commented on how going through my course also helped her to see how the lack of such education was influencing her friends. She wrote:

> It was interesting for me to see my friends' reactions to the hate crime at Wakefield High School. They were stunned like me; but, only because they did not think that things like this happen anymore. In fact, they did not see it as being an issue. Instead, they blamed the event on kids being immature or it being 'a bad joke.'

From there, my student wrote:

> Hearing their thoughts, I could not help but be
> appalled, because this was NOT immaturity over a
> change of school policy or disagreement with a prin-
> cipal- this was a hate crime against a whole commu-
> nity. In fact, using your course material I was able to
> explain to my friends why I could not see things the
> way they did as well as why I felt that they should
> take it more seriously. Because, to me, when you have
> the "…it's just a joke" mentality, nothing will change
> and hate crimes will only multiply.

It appears then that my teaching about neo-diversity does what I
hope it will do. After leaving the course and going on with life, what
they learned in my course gives my students a framework through
which to process and understand what is going on around them in life.
Teaching about neo-diversity also gives young people strategies for
managing their social interactions and managing their own behavior
in intergroup situations. That is also why I continue to not only teach,
but also to write for national audiences.

Indeed, my book *Taking on Diversity*[4] has already been used in
courses as a tool for socializing students away from neo-diversity anxiety to appropriate respect for other student citizens. May 2017, Dr.
Mark Shelley of Yavapai College wrote to let me know he had used
my book in his "Race and Ethnic Relations" course. He sent along
student reactions.

One of his students, a self-identified white female in her late 20s
wrote:

> I am now aware that hibernating bigotry simply
> waits with great patience, and strikes when awak-
> ened by an appropriate stimulus. I observed this type
> of bigotry in my father this week as he was telling
> me about his hometown in California, which had a

serious landslide shut down a major highway. After I stated that it will take several days to clear the roads, his immediate response was, "Yeah, because all of California's money is going to those freakin' sanctuary cities." This bigoted statement was a result of the prejudice against Mexicans he bears, which usually hides, just waiting to escape. It was clearly not shared by my Mother, who gave him quite a dirty look after his comment. My newly attained awareness regarding hibernating bigotry highlights the complex nature of prejudice.

We have been setting young people up by saying or letting others get away with saying, "It's just a joke." With that false idea as their guide, too many young people are fooled into thinking that, "If it's just a joke then everyone will understand that we were just joking when we posted those memes about women and black people."

Apparently, that's what 10 young people admitted to Harvard University thought. For them, it was just joking around to use racial and gender slurs in an online "private" chat group attached to the Harvard University admissions online network. Sure, it was just a joke until… Harvard learned what was going on and took back the admissions of 10 of those students.[5]

Teaching young people the truth of neo-diversity matters in consequential ways. None of my students think "…It's all just a big joke."

44: Heralding Neo-Diversity

I have become a herald.

Yavapai College- Prescott, AZ (October 2017)

University of Georgia- Athens, GA (April 2018)

Shippensburg University- Shippensburg, PA (October 2018)

University of Nebraska-Lincoln, Lincoln, NA (March 2019)

Appalachian College Association, Emory & Henry College, Emory, VA (June 2019)

Called, I have been traveling to colleges and universities proclaiming the age and dynamics of neo-diversity. Finding out about my idea of and my work to herald the coming of neo-diversity and the challenges that neo-diversity presents, calls comes to me. Why?

Public colleges and universities, through immoral laws (and sometimes law-like customs), used to be segregated by race, and so, did not admit black people or Latinx people. Some also segregated by sex-of-person – no women allowed. With segregation-by-law eliminated, that means students walk onto college and university campuses that are struggling to right that history of discrimination, to increase their diversity. In that changing social environment, using the word "inclusion," colleges and universities also struggle to figure out ways to help students from different groups interact with each other with respect.

Toward that end, most colleges and universities make some, at least general and vague, statements about being a diverse and inclusive place. Lately, some of those institutions are realizing what those messages are up against. Those messages are bumping into a mix of intergroup ignorance and arrogance walking the campus, especially among new students.

Young people are coming out of a world where other people, adults, pretty much controlled everything for them. Before coming to college, their activities and friends were mostly controlled by parents, including the frequency of their interactions with people "…not like us"; people from other groups. At college, those social controls are gone. One of my students who admitted struggling mightily with being on our neo-diverse campus wrote:

> "When I asked my parents a few weeks ago why I was never heavily exposed to other races as a child, they called that lack of exposure protection, but I now call it ignorance."

Unaware of their own limited intergroup experiences, young people walk onto a neo-diverse campus unprepared. Carrying in their social psychology a mix of intergroup ignorance and intergroup arrogance they hear messages of diversity and inclusion from the college or university that they do not fully understand.

Intergroup ignorance – "Hey, why are you so angry? What did I say? Oh… I didn't know 'spic' was a racial slur."[1] Intergroup arrogance brought from home: "I can talk to anybody anyway I want to… I can say what I want about them… My parents say they should not be here anyway." When that intergroup ignorance and intergroup arrogance comes out in interpersonal behavior, when that bigotry goes public, things happen:

A Gay, Lesbian, Bisexual Transgender Campus Center is defaced.

Racial graffiti is painted on a campus walkway.

A group chat filled with words of anti-Muslim sentiments of hate and demeaning views of women goes public.

Somebody at that college or university has seen a video of one of my lectures on neo-diversity. Somebody there has read my newest book, and… I get an email:

"Helping us at Yavapai"

"Request for possible assistance-Shippensburg"

October 21, 2018, I travelled to Shippensburg University to do that neo-diversity thing that I do. That thing is simple: to help faculty, students, and staff see that we are no longer dealing just with race relations. To quote the poet Sterling Brown, if you are on the train thinking only about race-relations, then you need to know that, "… this is the wrong line we been riding.."[2]

Asking me about the state of race relations in America is asking the wrong question. It turns out the intergroup issues burning the fabric of America are not just related to race or gender or religion or sexual orientation or mental health condition or gender identity or bodily condition or…

Heating up the intergroup social environment of America is people from all of those categories, all at the same time, demanding respect. That is the fire of our neo-diversity – that new interpersonal situation in which none of us can avoid having to encounter and sometimes interact with people not like us on some dimension. Whenever and wherever those neo-diversity interactions happen, members of all groups expect and demand respect. With their intergroup-ignorance and intergroup arrogance, many young people are jolted, shocked and burned by that fire when they come to a neo-diverse college or university with all the different kinds of people and all the messages of diversity and inclusion respect.

Just before I travelled to Shippensburg University, I asked the question I always ask, "…Has anything related to neo-diversity happened recently?" "Yes" was the answer. On October 1, 2018, someone had defaced the office door used by Students Advocating For Equality (SAFE), a Shippensburg student LGBT group, with sexual orientation slurs.[3] Now I had some sense of the neo-diversity tensions on that campus. Now I had a concrete, college-relevant example to talk about with students, on which to give them a new perspective.

At Shippensburg I got a unique opportunity. Yes, in the early evening of October 22, 2018, I would be doing a campus-wide lecture on neo-diversity to help launch the university's new climate survey. What about the rest of the day leading up to that event? For that time, at professors' requests, I spoke and interacted with four small classes of students, all of whom were in their first year, first semester of college. With a room of 15 to 25 students at a time, these were up close and personal interactions.

In each classroom, I got the students thinking and talking about their past life situations in which they experienced interaction-anxiety—a nervousness about interacting with someone. In various ways, they talked about how that anxiety made them "…act goofy."

Then I pointed out that neo-diversity anxiety works the same way. Neo-diversity anxiety is a feeling of being nervous about interacting with a person not like you on some group dimension. Could be a Muslim, a woman, a person who uses a wheel chair, a black person, a person who supports the LGBT community and so in your head "…must be gay," or a person who has proudly made it clear to you that they are gay, lesbian, or transgender. Sometimes, we agreed, that neo-diversity anxiety makes people act goofy.

How? That anxiety can create a psychological push "…in you" to interact using a stereotype to guide how you interact with that person. Sometimes, I pointed out, it goes beyond just acting goofy.

Sometimes that anxiety can also push people into bigotry – behavioral expression of anti-group feelings that come out as verbally expressed stereotypes, verbally (or written) expression of group slurs, attempts to avoid interacting with 'them.' Connecting that to coming to a neo-diverse campus and experiencing neo-diversity anxiety about interacting with someone "…not like you," I asked the students in these small groups, "…What skills do you need in those moments to have a respectful interaction with a fellow student?"

Here's one tip I said: "Never try to interact with a person as representative of a group. Why? Because it is insulting to that person. You must understand," I said, "that people know the stereotypes of their group,[4] so when you try to interact with an individual as a representative of the group they happen to be a member of, you use a stereotype and they see what you are doing."

With that said, I asked, "What other social skills do you need to cope with neo-diversity?" We talked. To keep the points of that conversation on all of our minds, I did something I have not done in years. I picked up a piece of chalk, yes chalk, and wrote the students' thoughts on the "black board."

To tether us to the 21st century, at the end of my first classroom session one of my hosts took a digital photo of what I wrote on the board. In that first session we had concluded that these are some of the social skills people need to cope with their neo-diversity anxiety and interact well, interact with respect on Shippensburg's neo-diverse campus:

1. *Never try to interact with a person as a representative of a group.* The students agreed with me that this was the most basic starting point.

2. *Go slow.* When I let them know that my approach to all that is going on is interpersonal, I informed them that one of the discoveries from social psychology is that in social interaction, (a) self-disclosures should come slowly as if peeling and onion, and (b) self-disclosures should be asked for slowly.[5] That adds up to the "…go slow" rule for coping with neo-diversity anxiety. The students liked that.

3. *Live with the anxiety.* Too often, we talked about, we try to get past our anxiety and that's when we "…make it worse." We blurt out an inappropriate question, like "…What are you?" Instead, it's better to acknowledge to yourself you are feeling anxious and then remind yourself to follow rule 2: *go slow* and live with the anxiety for a while.

4. *Agree to disagree.* Meeting new people means encountering people with different approaches to living life in the social world; for

example, different political beliefs. Other people have their own social histories and experiences. From their experiences, those "other people" have already come to some of their opinions, just as you have. Agree to disagree without being competitive, without feeling threatened, without attacking the other person. In other words, expect to encounter disagreements; expect to be surprised.

5. *Learning conversations.* Since on campus, and in life, you will be meeting a mix of new people, make your conversations, learning conversations. How? (A) Avoid relying on stereotypes. (B) Go slow; interact with the intent to learn what the other person is willing to tell you. (C) Live in the moment, live with the anxiety. (D) Agree to disagree; no one is going to change anybody in the moment, so learn how people think without trying to change how they think or what they think.

Not always in the same order, but each small class of students talked about each of these as part of their social interaction skillset they had to work on to participate in the university's effort to build a truly inclusive (i.e., respectful) social climate. Later in my general lecture on neo-diversity, I went over much of this in a different, a bit more formal, way. To round out my time at Shippensburg University, I said in the big lecture:

> You have the opportunity to develop your social skills and learn how to have respectful interactions with people not like you. That will make you ready to be a productive citizen in neo-diverse America that will continue be neo-diverse.
>
> Your university is trying to make sure that each of you has that opportunity. The university also has an obligation to check-in on the neo-diversity climate. That is why a climate survey is done. I am honored to be here to herald the launch of Shippensburg University's first climate survey."

Understand this: building an inclusive community takes work. The university must do its part by inviting (admitting) a neo-diversity of people to the table of the learning it offers. And too, the university must monitor how things are going at the table. No organization can be truly inclusive if the organization does not check in on the social interaction climate for its neo-diverse clientele. That includes the U.S. Pentagon that has climate surveys done for all of the armed forces.

I know this because, in the past, the Pentagon has called on me to help analyze some of those survey responses at the (Department of) Defense Equal Opportunity Management Institute (at Patrick Air Force Base).[6] We need to know, Shippensburg needs to know "…what are the conversations like among those they have invited to the learning table." "Is anybody being left out?" "Is anybody being spoken to with the language of stereotypes and group slurs?"

At Shippensburg, at the end of each small group session, one or more of the students asked in one or more ways, "Will we get through the difficult and heated days of intergroup anxiety America is experiencing today?" Some of these young people are worried, some scared by what they are witnessing happen in America. In answer to their concerned query, I told those young people what I truly believe:

We are not a nation of bigots. Yes, we will get through this heated time. How? By developing healthy and respectful ways of interacting with people "…not like us." "We are not done," I told them.

"Our true American spirit will prevail by us doing the work of learning to incorporate neo-diversity into the mindset of America, the foundation for which is already established. 'We hold these truths to be self-evident, that all men are created equal…'"

That is why I travel to wherever I am called. That is what I herald when I get wherever that call takes me. That's how I ended up in Appalachia.

45: Neo-Diversity in Appalachia?

Since 2006 I have been saying, lecturing, writing essays and books to herald that America is in the midst of a struggle with its neo-diversity. Everywhere in America, all across America people are trying to understand and manage neo-diversity – this new interpersonal situation in which we all have to encounter and sometimes interact with people who do not look like, sound like, worship like or love like "us." There has been no better confirmation of that for me than my being invited and hired to be the lead instructor for the Appalachian College Association 2019 Summer Teaching and Leadership Institute, June 3-7.

When I got the first email, I had never heard of the Appalachian College Association. I found out that "The Appalachian College Association is a non-profit consortium of thirty-five private four-year liberal arts institutions located in the central Appalachian Mountains in Kentucky, North Carolina, Tennessee, Virginia, and West Virginia".[1]

Why did the Association want me to lead the institute? In their first email to me, after describing the theme for the summer teaching and learning institute as "Diversity and Engaged Pedagogy," they said:

> With your recent book *Taking on Diversity*, as well as *Making Gumbo in the University*, and basically the way [we] see your life's work - teaching us through social psychology how to relate to one another more meaningfully, you are the perfect person for this role.

"Diversity and Engaged Pedagogy": pedagogy is, of course, teaching. The Association's full description of their 2019 Summer Teaching and Leadership Institute said:

> The changing landscape of higher education has many of us thinking and re-thinking about what it means to be an effective educator with an increasingly diverse student body. The diversity we encounter in our classrooms ranges from identity-based diversities such as race, ethnicity, gender, sexuality, class, and the various intersections of identity positions, to diversity more broadly defined such as learning styles, college preparedness, and neurodiversity. Engaged pedagogy is a powerful tool we can harness to address the diverse needs of our students as we create spaces that "transform boundaries into freedom."
>
> In Track One of the 2019 TLI, ACA instructors will not only learn about various diversities and the effects on learning, but also, receive hands-on training in engaged pedagogical techniques designed to build creative and collaborative learning environments that foster community, integrity, and critical thinking.

Having learned about the content of my book *Taking on Diversity* and learning of my reputation as a classroom professor, the organizers were especially interested in my work on neo-diversity in the classroom and on college campuses. As the description of their motivation indicates, those small (900 to 1,200 student) campuses were beginning to realize that in every classroom there are people with different visible and invisible group identities. They realized that their teaching was less effective when they did not take into account the neo-diversity mix in their classrooms. My job was to lay out strategies for their teaching in a neo-diverse classroom.

I spent a week at Emory & Henry College (Emory, VA) leading college professors through teaching workshops and workshops on facilitating difficult conversations. What questions did the college professors who teach in Appalachia come with? The first exercise I put them through was to get them to reveal those questions. At the table where they had just eaten dinner, the participants wrote out their responses to this query, "What do you hope we will get to talk about at a conference with the theme Diversity and Engaged Pedagogies?"

Later, with the pieces of paper in hand, I put those questions into thematic categories.

Theme I: Defining diversity

Participants hoped to talk about:

- Diversity extends beyond racial and ethnic differences; let's talk about all.

- Understanding the meaning of diversity; definition appears to vary in different contexts

- Inclusivity; treating people with respect

Theme II: Setting up the classroom tone/environment to encourage dialogue

Participants hoped to talk about:

- How to ensure a safe but challenging classroom space open for discussion

- In my classroom, I hope to be able to offer something all my students would like; a type of education and shared belonging in said endeavor

- How to start the conversation and also how to continue to talk about such important topics, with sensitivity and courage.

- Ways to get students to be less fearful of conversations on issues of diversity (e.g., race, class, gender, sexuality) and to question their own fears.

Theme III: Generating conversation

Participants hoped to talk about:

- Managing resistance to inclusion among conservative students and including those students too in the discussion of inclusion

- How to bring diverse situations and discussions into classrooms typically lacking diversity

- Effective strategies for my department to address the diversity/inclusion of our students

- How to encourage students that it's okay to not know about diversity on campus but to admit they don't know or understand

Theme IV: Engaging specific populations of students

Participants hoped to talk about:

- I would like to honor the student needs in an inclusive way toward groups/individuals different from my own. What is the best way to learn about those needs in a respectful way?

- How to make our classrooms safe spaces for those with diverse mental health issues

- Transgender in the classroom/preferred gender pronouns in the classroom/how to work with neo-gender populations.

- Being able to tie all different cultures and ethnic backgrounds to classroom activities

- Teaching a class to both strongly prepared and 1ˢᵗ generation Appalachian students.

There were other questions, yet those four themes seemed to me to capture the major teaching concerns the participants came with to the Appalachian College Association Summer 2019 Teaching and Learning Institute. Even a cursory reading of those themes showed why I had been called to be the lead instructor. Without being able to give it the formal name, all these questions and concerns were about neo-diversity in the classroom of these Appalachian colleges.

As for me, as always, I went in hot.

I did a lot of work during that week. I oriented my co-instructors to the concept of neo-diversity. I thought it important to change their language about "diversity" to "neo-diversity." To do that, before everyone else arrived I led a discussion/orientation of my co-instructors during which we talked through my Psychology Today blog essay "Gays, Lesbians, Transgender... Oh my!"[2] Here the point was to move my co-instructors away from thinking about diversity as categories of people to the interpersonal situation of interacting with people "...not like me." Since each co-instructor would be conducting their own workshops, for continuity with my focus I wanted their thinking and ways of talking to be centered on the interpersonal dynamics that neo-diversity can activate.

From that first meeting with my co-instructors, that evening I gave my keynote address on "Teaching College in the Age of Neo-Diversity." After that as planned, on three different afternoons I did my workshop "You Want to Talk About What? Facilitating Sensitive Conversations." One session I did was completely unplanned. It was the result of my keynote address. In that address, I talked about the fact that I created my "Interdependence and Race" course for which I developed the concept of neo-diversity. Interest in the content and construction of that course was high. Asked if I would be willing to do a session of "How to create a diversity course," I did.

Participants' responses to my teaching leadership for the teaching institute were positive and powerful. I know this because on the last morning I led a discussion that my students who have taken my social psychology classes would recognize. After breakfast, I said to the gathering:

> "We have been on a road less travelled. Now there is a light ahead. Gaze upon it, think on it and then write down what you see in that light. After this week of discussion of neo-diversity in the college classroom, what do you see in that light? What one-new-thought are you taking with you about neo-diversity and engaged teaching in the college classroom? Take a moment and write down that new thought."

After they did so, I asked for volunteers who would like to share. Here are some of the shared new thoughts:

> "On a road less traveled, where we sometimes feel alone and we'll have to labor through these issues alone, as a teacher and someone with agency, we are allies and we have allies."

> "Our school doesn't have a diversity or inclusion statement. That's a new goal for us."

> "Making my office more accessible and inclusive, overtly - really posting diversity statements and inclusion statements."

> "Diversity is not often overt. It takes a while to emerge. The more we understand diversity, the more we get to know ourselves, because of how we respond to it."

> "The importance of getting students the tools to talk about neo-diversity topics. We need to set those tools up so they feel comfortable when the topics come up."

"Language is important. The words we use have power and meaning. We have to be vigilant. I'm going to make mistakes. It's going to be ok."

"Diversity is not just about welcoming a group of 'they' into 'us' but also recognizing that our own uniqueness desperately wants to be welcomed."

"Multiple oppressions can be manifesting in our students (and us) all at once. We're all struggling with all the things. Family, financial, academic, mental health, etc."

"Never treat an individual as a representative of a group. Look for people to surprise us."

"Our students have a job to get. Students are going to need these (social interaction) skills."

"I need to do self-work before entering into sensitive settings. I'm not giving enough attention to my own emotional preparation."

"I came here with preconceptions of how people would respond to this Teaching and Learning Institute. The experience this week has given me more of a sense of cultural respect. Humility - how much we have to learn about the people of this region."

As if planned, the last professor to speak had this to say as her one-new-thought. She said:

"I think I am the outlier here. I think that most of you are more liberal than me. But never did I feel disrespected or excluded this week as we talked about diversity issues. That let me know we can do this. For me, my one new thought is, diversity is Christ-centered. Remember, it was women he appeared to first, after his resurrection. I think I see how we can write a diversity statement that will be well received by Christian institutions. We start with, Christ is our chief diversity officer."

I almost leapt out of the room. Not because I am Christian, but because this woman's experience validated how and why I approach diversity as neo-diversity. Not as a matter of group categories, not as a matter of calling people out, but as a matter of pointing out that our new *interpersonal situation* (of neo-diversity) means that no matter what, we are all here sharing the same social spaces. That means that to be productive we have to learn to interact with each other with respect in those spaces.

I had a good time with this group of college professors who teach in Appalachia. Humbled, I was, by their openness and reactions to learning about neo-diversity. That last session, where participants revealed the impact of my time and work with them, really hit me. I came in thinking that this would be an "interesting" experience in Appalachia. Halfway through the week, and certainly by the end, I was truly excited. I began to realize that with a group of college professors from 15 or so different Appalachian colleges, these professors learning about and engagement with the neo-diversity idea would now be rippling out into the whole of the Appalachian College Association campuses.

46: Seize the Time

Hear, hear!

Three cheers to those who marched to save the soul of America.

But do understand that our tolerance for intolerance is how we have let a social pneumonia infect the soul of our great democracy. Of late we have acted surprised by our fellow Americans acceptance of, or ability to ignore, the bigotry of a major political candidate. I must say, though, there is something fake about that surprise. Fake because all along the way to this moment, so many of us have tolerated the filthy conditions of bigotry we heard, saw, and smelled being expressed toward many groups every day in our social neighborhoods of life and work..

Now we are acting surprised, even though we heard the language of bigotry come from people we interacted with in our everyday lives. Passive, tolerant of intolerance in our social interactions, we let the cold wet air and festering conditions of bigotry rest on the chest of America as "…just a joke." Now, today, we are living with the walking pneumonia of our past tolerance for intolerance. Our tolerance for intolerance is why today we are hearing a sickening breath rattle in the breathing of our once strong-breathing democracy.

Yet, we are in danger of continuing to add to the problem of tolerance for intolerance by speaking ill of those who are new to the struggle. Yes, some people are only now beginning to understand what has been going on and what is at stake for all of us. That is nothing new.

Not all who proclaim themselves to be 'woke' get that. I am disheartened when I see "us versus them" rise up among those who say they care about social Justice. Not "us versus them" between people who seek a just society for all versus those who are fighting to keep themselves in power. No, not just that…

"Us versus them" among people who say they want a just society but can't put up with people who don't think about the issues exactly the way they do.

"Women's marches without intersectionality is just white supremacy."

"Marched last year, but not marching today because I realized these people are marching against 45 (Trump), not against systematic racism, etc."

Trolling others is not social justice work. Throwing shade at others is not the work of "…the woke." If we keep demeaning the motives of people of goodwill who are trying to march for, work for justice in some way, our fight for justice will always be futile. If we keep rejecting the idea of working with people who are learning to try to work for justice, our fight for justice will flounder. If we reject the idea of working with people because they are not woke in the way you would like, there is no hope of achieving real social justice. If for you to march for justice, everybody has to see everything from your perspective, you are not woke.

To work for justice always means working with people you do not always agree with on focus, strategy, priorities, or vision. Even Martin Luther King, Jr. had to be brought into a full understanding that the issues of oppression were more than racial. That happened through his interactions and civil conversations with others who were working on racial/social justice, but with different strategies and focus.

Even if they are trying, no one can see past their limited perspective without direct contact and (civil) confrontation with a different perspective. When you think someone is making a mistake of vision, talk to the person, not at the person. Don't berate people.

Disagree, use your voice to raise issues, but do not withdraw your participation. In the 1960s my father, a janitor and a bus driver, was also a grassroots politician in Jim Crow South. Mr. O-geese worked with all kinds of people who had a mix of motivations, some with limited and mostly self-interested vision, but he worked with those people to push the justice agenda.

Yes, he was frustrated by those people sometimes; I heard him tell my mother so. But he went on using the small doorway into their frame of reference to get things done. My father, Mr. O-geese, worked in solidarity and effort with those folks, using his fierce, strong yet respectful voice, making his case and teaching that sometimes helped people see that their vision was too narrow, sometimes not.

My father's efforts included being the one to keep people moving and working in the direction of true racial/social justice, even if at the time those people were making mistakes of vision while still agitating for some kind of justice. That's what it takes. Yes, it can be irritating, frustrating and slow going. To live woke, that is something you must understand and accept.

####

In 1968, I participated in my first bit of social justice work. When I was 17, I walked neighborhoods doing door-to-door voter registration of black people (some of whom didn't care). Since then, I have been working on matters of social justice, including during the time I was in the U.S. Navy (1972-1976) (sometimes for people who weren't 'woke'). So I could look around at whole generations of people, members of many different groups, some of whom have been 'woke' for only a decade but now feel righteous, and say to you all, "…where've you been? What took you so long?"

I don't do that because I know that no one is in the social world in the same way, in the same situation. Today we have a situation that wakes us all up. In this time, all that matters is that people, all kinds of people, are woke and trying to find their own way, from where they live, to work in the struggle. Let's accept people as they start from where they are, not from where you think they should be already. Let's not put up us-versus-them barriers between ourselves and people who are newly trying to get involved.

As an original member of the Black Panther Party for Self-Defense, Bobby Seale said, "…seize the time." Echoing Mr. Seale, I say:

Seize the time

no one is late.

Welcome all who are coming to realize

what is at stake.

Seize the time.

Offer your hand in faith

to any who now want to stand up

to fight the hate.

Seize the time!

Seize… the… time!

In that spirit, we now are witnessing a moment of clarification. In that spirit, thousands upon thousands (of women, children, gays and lesbians, males, Jews, Christians, transgender persons, Muslims, cisgender persons) marched to begin anew the work to save the soul of America. Bringing a balm of warmth and ointment, we are now beginning to do the work to heal the patient called America.

I was in tears as I watched and listened to speeches given at the "March for our Lives" daylong event. What got me was the combination of youth, passion and eloquence calling out for change. What got me, too, was the call for a recognition of the need for respect for America's neo-diversity. One of the speakers said, "… they will try to divide us, but it does not matter your age, your skin color, your sexual orientation, the amount of money you make, gun violence is killing all of us." Many speakers were talking about creating a neo-diversity fusion movement, a movement that is inclusive of race, religion, mental health condition, ethnicity, bodily condition, and gender identity working with each other with respect toward the goal of ending gun violence.

David Hogg said it this way:

> Today is the beginning of spring, and tomorrow is the beginning of democracy. Now is the time to come together, not as Democrats, not as Republicans, but as Americans. Americans of the same flesh and blood, that care about one thing and one thing only, and that's the future of this country and the children that are going to lead it.

> Now, they will try to separate us in demographics. They will try to separate us by religion, race, congressional district, and class. They will fail. We will come together. We will get rid of these public servants that only serve the gun lobby, and we will save lives. You are those heroes.

Hear, hear! Three cheers to the marchers and the supporters (old and new). Now onward to organize old and new voters, to develop new fierce focus, to develop and activate new activist strategies, to be the new hope for healing the soul of America.

#womensmarch; #2017Newbeginnings

####

Yet we must not underestimate the power of neo-diversity anxiety. Even with, likely because of the continuing marches and election change, an old version of neo-diversity anxiety was just rattled. That anxiety had been resting in a tension system in America that we must be vigilant to watch over and manage. When the hurting soul of America cried out "…thoughts and prayers are not enough," an old anxiety called out to America. Startled out of its slumber, that old anxiety yelled "…send her back."[1]

Summer 2019, President Trump told "the Squad" to "go back" to the countries they came from. To these four recently elected congresswomen, President Trump had a strong reaction to their criticisms of his policies. Although each of these elected officials are non-white, each is an American citizen, but President Trump said about them, "Why don't they go back and help fix the totally broken and crime infested places from which they came. Then come back and show us how it is done."[2]

That old anxiety, now expressed again, seemed to have consequences. Not just at President Trump's North Carolina rally where some of his supporters chanted "…send her back." Some are connecting it to the mass shootings over one week that came soon after President Trump's July 14th statements.

> Gilroy, CA Garlic Festival—July 28, 2019—three shot down and killed.

> El Paso, TX Walmart, August 3, 2019—22 shot down and killed.

> Dayton, Ohio downtown—August 4, 2019—nine shot down and killed.

One news story carried the title, "A community targeted: This time it wasn't a viral video or a racist tweet. It was something far more terrifying." In that story, the director of the Southern Border Communities Coalition made the claim that, "Rhetoric… has emboldened [white supremacists] to act out in ways that are extraordinarily violent and hurtful to our communities."[3]

Social scientists have been tracking the rise of hate groups and hate crimes in that context. Another news story notes:

...after a terrorist shooting by a Muslim couple that killed 14 people in San Bernardo, CA, in 2015, [President] Trump made a campaign trill plea for a "total and complete shutdown of Muslims entering the United States." Over the next 10 days, reported hate crimes against Muslims and Arabs nationwide spiked 23%.

We see a correlation around the time of statements of political leaders and fluctuations in hate crimes,' said Brian Levin, director of the Center for the Study of Hate and Extremism at California State University-San Bernardino. "Could there be other intervening causes," he asked. "Yes. But it's certainly a significant correlation that can't be ignored."[4]

What has shaken the old "love it or leave it" anxiety awake? Is President Trump solely responsible? Not by a long shot. That old anxiety has been slumbering, hibernating for quite some time in America. What has awakened it? Neo-diversity – America's new interpersonal situation where we all have to encounter and sometimes interact with people who do not look like, sound like, worship like, love like 'us.'[5]

Neo-diversity anxiety is what made attractive that powerful voice declaring "... I think they hate America. If they don't like it, they should go back where they came from." Unfocused, free-floating intergroup anxiety[6] is why that voice rings true to those who are already struggling with the neo-diversity anxiety question, "...Who are among the 'we' and who are among the 'they?'"[7]

This "...who can be an American" identity anxiety is complex. It is not just political. Resistance to hearing the truth about America's violent history of race is also part of the social psychology of that anxiety. "You can't preach that," ministers say when it comes to what truths they can challenge their congregations to learn about, and process the meaning of, for their everyday walk through life. As a professor, as a scholar, I don't have that problem.

In my "Interdependence and Race" course,[8] I can talk about my own experiences as a black person growing up in the Jim Crow South of legal racial segregation. Yet, although I mention my place and experience in that racial history, I do not rely on my personal narrative to lay out the truth of that American history. I use scholarly resources.

For race in the America military, I use Naval historian John Darrell Sherwood's *Black Sailor, White Navy*, a history of the 350 major racial incidents in the Navy from 1970-1975.[9] I like using that book because Dr. Sherwood uses Department of Defense documents to detail and analyze every incident. I also like it because the book covers the race riot I lived through on the USS *Intrepid* (CVS 11) during the time I served onboard that aircraft carrier (see Chapter 10).

For a broad, detailed history of the racial laws of discrimination, institutionally supported violence against black people and eventual change in America, I use Duke University historian Dr. Tim Tyson's *Blood Done Sign My Name*.[10] I like that scholarly resource because not only is it a documented history (including FBI files), Dr. Tyson interviews black and white people of North Carolina who describe their personal experiences during the time of Jim Crow.

Hard to believe then that someone not at my university, someone not a scholar, was so filled with anxiety about my teaching they tried to convince my students that I exaggerated the truth of the racial history of America. For my "Interdependence and Race" course, in 2010 I wrote a book specifically for the course: *What Rough Beast: Interpersonal Relationships and Race*. In my book I review most of the major social psychology theories and experiments on intergroup tension to give my students a social scientific understanding of modern intergroup relations.[11] I require that 320-page book for the course, and have students buy it as a course packet from which I make no money.

For the past 10 years I have had it printed and bound by a close by, off-campus vendor who sells the book as a course packet (at a low cost of about $28 or so). Spring 2019, we had a problem.

The first week of class, as I sat in my office there came an unexpected knock at my door. I opened the door to find one of my students, a white female, quite visibly upset. She came to tell me that while attempting to buy the course book, at the counter the white male waiting on her made some negative comments about me as a black man. That was only the beginning. She told me a disturbing story. I had her write up the incident.

She wrote:

> A bit to my concern [this man] followed me out of the store. As we walked out of the store, he continued to explain to me that he is a recent graduate of NC State. I asked him if he had ever taken a psychology class with Dr. Nacoste. He replied that he never had, but "had a professor a lot like him."
>
> I believe that I had a confused look on my face because I did not understand what he meant by "a professor a lot like him." To offer me more explanation he continued by saying, "I believe that blacks that have lived through the '60s and '70s fabricate their stories to make a point."
>
> I was so taken aback by this statement that I had no idea what to say. The only thing I knew to say was to stand up for Dr. Nacoste's honor. I said, "Dr. Nacoste is a very well-respected professor at NC State and I do not think he would lie about anything."
>
> This was a sad rebuttal for such an accusation but it was all I could think of in the moment. The man mumbled a response that I don't remember.

At this point, I was very uncomfortable and wanted to remove myself from the situation. I politely said goodbye and wished him a good day. I walked to my car and sat there for a moment in shock of this interaction. All I could think was, *What in the world just happened?*

I had to work her through her emotions. Then after that unexpected meeting with this student, that afternoon at our next class meeting, I asked for any student who felt they had an awkward/disturbing interaction while buying the course packet to see me. Six white female students stayed after to report a similar interaction.

Right then, other students asked me if they should still go to that vendor, and at first I said, "…yeah… just buy the book." That night I changed my mind thinking about the hijab-wearing Muslim women who would have to go to that vendor. The same evening I emailed my class and told those who had not yet bought the book to "stay away from [that vendor]." I asked students to email me if they still needed a copy of the book so I could get a count and buy the books myself. They did and I did as promised. That is how I handled that neo-diversity bigotry problem for my students in the immediate. I also decided that I would no longer do business with that vendor. I let my students know that as well.

Not just at political rallies is free-floating neo-diversity anxiety having the effect of people wanting to deny America's intergroup problems of mistreatment of people of color. Reveal the truth and those who can't handle the truth lash out in anxiety driven panic:

"America, love it or leave it." "Race relations were never that bad, he's exaggerating."

These are classic examples of hibernating bigotry – a bigotry that sleeps until the right stimulus comes along to wake it up.[12] Anxiety about having to face the truth because that truth tarnishes the shiny "America the beautiful" identity, and that stirs the hibernating bigotry awake.

Back in 2013, my students said I "had to" do a TED talk about neo-diversity. Pushed by my pushy students, I did a 19-minute TEDxNCSU talk with the title "Speaking Up For Neo-diverse America."[13] My TEDxNCSU talk came to mind because of the recent version of statements saying to other Americans "… if they don't like it here, go back where you came from…"

I started my TEDx talk singing "America the Beautiful." That was my way of getting the listeners to begin to pay attention to what I had to say about "….love it or leave it" bigotry. Singing done, I pointed out how it was that too many Americans have bought the sales pitch of "America the beautiful" and so do not want to hear about the injustices we have done and do.

After viewing my TEDxNCSU talk, one student decided to take my "Interdependence and Race" course. For one of his reflections on Dr. Tyson's *Blood Done Sign My Name*, this white male wrote:

> It's hard to believe that this racial murder and all the other racial stuff was taking place just 40 years ago. About this time in our history we are taught about everything BUT the intense racial war.
>
> They show people images of Blacks like Bill Russell to desensitize us about the hardships Blacks faced during that time. It really blows my mind that while Henry Marrow was beat to death and his killers acquitted in Oxford, we have Bill Russell over here winning championships in Boston. How does that work out? It hurts me to admit it, but I believe that our country's attempts to change history will ultimately work. So many people are not taught this stuff that the "sales pitch" is what will endure over time.

I do not agree that the sales pitch will be the American legacy. Yet I do admit that many have let the sales pitch influence them to buy an unrealistic, shiny image of America. August 8, 2019, a news story caught my eye: "Some white people don't want to hear about slavery at plantations built by slaves."[14] A white couple visited a plantation and were appalled that during part of the tour, the tour guide talked about the mistreatment of the enslaved Africans. In their review of their experience, one white couple said they were "…extremely disappointed. We felt we were being lectured and bashed." Another wrote, "…tour was all about how hard it was for the slaves…" One commentator on cultural affairs said this about that, "For as much as some of us may wish otherwise, the 'peculiar institution' [of slavery] is no artifact of the dead past. It shaped today. It is shaping tomorrow. And we cannot fix that until we face that."[15]

Facing our very real intergroup histories does not make America a lemon. Today, in these times, I do not regret and in fact am proud to have served my country in the U.S. Navy among some sailors who did not want me to serve because of the color of my skin. I served anyway. Even then, though, I worked to point out that the sales pitch has not been factual about America's racial road history. Yet now when someone points out our past real and our ongoing dirty, clogged and smoky American engine problems of intergroup injustice, those who have bought the sales pitch say "America… love it or leave it." That is the social psychology of "…love it or leave it" sentiment.

Tried during the civil rights movement, yelled at black and white people who protested racial injustices, it didn't work then. It won't work now. Why? Because that anxiety has no ground to stand on. As the saying goes, "…the truth will out."

To serve our country in the U.S. Navy, I had to take the required oath to protect our constitution against all enemies, foreign *and domestic*. No matter what anyone says, no matter what a president of the U.S. claims, prejudice and bigotry are domestic enemies of our nation's constitution; domestic enemies of the soul of America. To truly live woke, we must all live out our obligation to fight against tendencies of prejudice and bigotry in ourselves (there are no innocent), in the behavior of those in our social circles (there are no innocent anti-group jokes) and in the behavior of those we elect to public office. Fighting, struggling with and defeating those tendencies is what will eventually make America the "...home of the brave."

No, there has been no apocalypse. ...No, we are not going to hell in a hand basket.

Yes, we've got some difficult days ahead. In these (and the always coming) difficult days, in that struggle, each of us has something, small or large, that we can do. That is why there is still hope.

We shall overcome.

We can continue to move toward that more perfect union.

We can save the soul of America.

Every day take a breath. Be close to those you love. Gather your strength to continue the struggle. In your social interactions, talk to every person with respect as an individual, not with disrespect as a representative of a group.

Live woke.

#Neo-diversity

Afterword I

"Where do we go from here?"
Martin Luther King Jr. (1963)

End of the semester, May 2016, student reflection on my "Interdependence and Race" course.

Student A (cisgender white male):

When I was old enough to recognize the implicit views I had towards blacks, I felt very guilty. Guilt is always a paralytic emotion and it led to me becoming avoidant—afraid of situations that might make those implicit biases arise and force me to see myself in an un-preferred light. As a student in your class Dr. Nacoste, I now realize it is only because of the *mere exposure effect* happening at NC State that I have been able to overthrow the ideas that were given to me as a child.

The *mere exposure effect* is the fact that "…repeated exposure to a stimulus leads to liking for or comfort with that stimulus." It is because of this social psychological fact that I have overcome implicit biases instilled in me as a child. It is because of the diversity at NC State and putting myself in new, scary situations with people different from me that I have learned.

Your class has taught me that my upbringing, society, the media, music, and much more have left me with more implicit stereotypes than I am aware of. Now I know that the most effective way to overcome these is to step outside my comfort zone, expose myself to new people, to exist in a seemingly anxious space, slow down (don't panic), and work through it. I've found how much I appreciate, enjoy and learn from these diverse spaces.

My personal strategy for truly overcoming these biases is to "merely expose" myself to those different than me by building meaningful cross-racial, cross-religious, cross-sexual orientation type relationships. I won't run from the anxious spaces—I'll work hard to expose myself to new ones.

Your class taught me that fear and anxiety are the root of so many of our interaction problems in America. More importantly, however, your class taught me that humility is among the best teachers there are. It takes humility to put yourself in new situations and be honest that you know that you actually know nothing about this given individual. It turns out, that's exactly where learning begins.

Afterword II

"Where do we go from here?"
Martin Luther King Jr. (1963)

End of the semester, May 2018, student reflection on my "Interdependence and Race" course.

Student A (cisgender African (naturalized American citizen) female):

The most important new thought that I learned in this class is "there are no innocent." This means that no one, nor one group such as race, gender, sexuality etc. is innocent, because we all have our faults even if one is in a minority group or oppressed. I'll be very honest, before taking your class Dr. Nacoste, I had a huge mindset shift. I went from what I like to call my "African bubble of ignorance" to what I like to call "a state of extreme wokeness." I knew nothing really about African-American culture or the struggles that we sometime face so I thought everything was circumstantial. Then I took *Psychology and the African-American Experience* and learned about the systematic and systemic side of racism, racial profiling and so many topics were discussed and so many current events were brought up. Then I came to your class Dr. Nacoste. And on the first day I remember "there are no innocent" standing out to me and my reaction was "oh man, I don't agree" so many ideas and examples came into my mind and I was really hoping that we'd have open floor discussions so I could bring up all of my "great points."

Now at the end of your class, I wholeheartedly agree, there are no innocent. *I thought that I was completely woke* and my method of thinking was correct. I thought "I'm a minority, I can never do any wrong" which is so untrue. I never thought I'd have to, but I check myself now. It was so interesting too because coming off of that extreme woke state, I found myself talking recklessly and saying all kinds of things, but never when I was around races different from mine. Then I found myself in an interracial relationship and sometimes things would slip out that I had no idea how bad they sounded until I say them. For example, I used to have a habit of saying "…that person looks very Republican," which looking back on it, what does that even mean? One day I went to the shooting range with my white boyfriend and I said that a lady at the NRA booth "…looked very NRA." My boyfriend was not pleased and he calmly educated me.

The "there are no innocent" concept is so true. It has changed the way I interact with everyone and the way I approach situations. I've realized that I was definitely not innocent in the way I spoke and behaved in many situations. This concept has helped me so, so, much and I now educate friends and family.

Acknowledgements

I have never met Trevor Noah. I have never talked with Trevor Noah. I do not know Trevor Noah. Yet, I thank Mr. Trevor Noah.

On Facebook, I happened to come across a Daily Show "…behind the scenes." Mr. Noah was doing a bit about being "woke." With funny examples, he said some people can be "…too woke." I was at a loss. From my old man, civil rights protest generation standpoint, this idea of being "woke" was a curiosity. "Too woke?" With that, I went on alert to this younger generation's idea of being "woke." My thanks to Mr. Noah for his bit of social commentary that made me pay attention.

Mx. Kinesha Harris and Mx. Anna Taylor were my beta readers. These two were not just readers. In the very early stages of my developing this book, while they were still students at NC State, we met to talk about their reactions to (preliminary) chapters. To Kinesha and Anna, you have my most important thanks and deepest gratitude for your help in shaping this book.

For copy-editing I turned to Mr. Gideon Brookins. This is the second of my books for which Gideon has been my copy-editor. I have known Gideon since he was a boy, and have enjoyed watching the man, and the professional he has become. Thanks Gideon for making this book a better one.

My thanks also to the staff at Psychology Today for giving me blogging space. It was through that platform that I began to work out the elements of some of these essays for consumption by non-scholars. It is important to say to that Psychology Today is not responsible for any errors that appear in those early versions of my essays, nor any that appear in these heavily revised essays. Any errors are mine and mine alone.

Finally, my thanks to all of my students who have taken to ground the lessons of neo-diversity I teach. Thanks to those who are now teachers who speak up for the respect and dignity of all in the neo-diversity mix of their classrooms.

Thanks to all those who are now physician assistants, nurses, doctors and health care administrators, who speak with respect to the neo-diversity mix of people they work to heal.

Thanks to those former students of mine who are social workers, school counselors, college advisors, who speak to and speak up for the respect and dignity of all who make up the ne-diversity mix of their clients.

Thanks to those in our military who have taken your interaction skills into your units to defend and protect American interest here and abroad.

It has been my privilege and honor to learn from and teach you all. Thank you.

Live woke.

About the Author

Rupert Nacoste is a black-Creole native of the Louisiana bayou country and a Navy veteran. During his time in service (1972-1976), to deal with its serious racial problems, the U. S. Navy trained him (and others) to be a facilitator of racial dialogues among sailors. From that 1974 point onward, adding academic degrees, Dr. Nacoste has worked as a scholar-activist of interpersonal and intergroup relationships. On the faculty of North Carolina State University since 1988, he is the winner of the 2013 UNC Board of Governor's Teaching Excellence award because he uses a captivating oratory style to engage people to see their own role in moments of tension in social interaction.

References

Chapter 1:

1. Sherwood, J.D. (2007). *Black sailor, white navy: Racial unrest in the fleet during the Vietnam War Era*. New York: New York University Press. (http://nyupress.org/books/9780814740361/)

2. DeYoung, Sarah (2018). Some comments on your visit to UGA. Email correspondence (April 26).

3. Blow, C. (2016, July 12). "Questions that bare our souls," Opinion page, News & Observer (Raleigh, NC).

4. Powell, C. (2009, July 5). What makes America great. Parade: The Sunday Newspaper Magazine. p. 4 (emphasis added)

5. Appadurai, A. (2006). Fear of small numbers: An essay on the geography of anger, (Durham, NC: Duke University Press)

6. Dr. Seuss (1961). The Sneetches and other stories (p. 13). New York: Random House

7. Ibid; p. 21

Chapter 2:

1. Diamond, J. (2015). Rudy Giuliani: Obama doesn't love America. CNN, February 20 (https://www.cnn.com/2015/02/19/politics/rudy-giuliani-obama-america-love/index.html)

2. See the survey report here: http://www.mintpressnews.com/meet-the-new-american-center/170707/

Chapter 3:

1. Everett, P. (2005). Wounded. Saint Paul, Minnesota: Graywolf Press.

2. Kaufman, David (2009, June 6). Introducing America's First Black, Female Rabbi. Time Magazine (http://content.time.com/time/nation/article/0,8599,1903245,00.html)

Chapter 4:

1. Racism Insurance: https://www.youtube.com/watch?v=xeukZ6RcUd8.

Chapter 5:

1. Worland, Justin (2015). Ben Carson Says a Muslim Shouldn't Be President, Time, September 20 (http://time.com/4041624/ben-carson-muslim-president/)

Chapter 6:

1. Feynman, Richard P. (1998). *The meaning of it all: Thoughts of a citizen-scientist.* Reading, Massachusetts: Perseus Books.

2. Nacoste, R.W. (2012). *Howl of the Wolf: North Carolina State University Students Call Out For Social Change.* Raleigh, NC: Lulu.com

3. Mansfield, F. (2014, October 21). "Watermelon-gate: NAACP weighs in on Academic Magnet Controversy," *Moultrie News, e-Edition* (http://www.moultrienews.com/archives/watermelon-gate-naacp-weighs-in-on-academic-magnet-controversy/article_68d9266e-255c-58fc-a984-bf284d0ad206.html)

4. Pi, S. (2015, January 30). Respect for the Real American Dream: Dr. Rupert Nacoste speaks at Academic Magnet High School, *The Talon (The student news site of Academic Magnet High School)* (https://amhsnewspaper.com/4021/news/respect-for-the-real-american-dream-dr-rupert-nacoste-speaks-at-amhs/)

Chapter 7:

1. Kaufman, Scott (2016, August 4) *Salon.com* (http://www.salon.com/2016/08/04/when_i_grew_up_those_things_werent_called_racist_clint_eastwood_on_why_hes_voting_for_donald_trump/)

2. Kingkade, Tyler (2015). Oklahoma Frat Boys Caught Singing 'There Will Never Be A N***** In SAE'. HuffPost, March 8 (https://www.huffingtonpost.com/2015/03/08/frat-racist-sae-oklahoma_n_6828212.html)

3. President David Boren releases full statement on Sigma Alpha Epsilon incident, OUDaily, March 9, 2015 (http://www.oudaily.com/news/president-david-boren-releases-full-statement-on-sigma-alpha-epsilon/article_02b02ee2-c667-11e4-903d-4fdd71bf61d2.html)

Chapter 8:

1. Sherwood, J.D. (2007). *Black sailor, white navy: Racial unrest in the fleet during the Vietnam War Era.* New York: New York University Press. (http://nyupress.org/books/9780814740361/)

2. Pearson, Michael (2015) A timeline of the University of Missouri protests, as Top officials resign, CNN, November 10 (https://www.cnn.com/2015/11/09/us/missouri-protest-timeline/index.html)

Chapter 9:

1. Lewin, K. (1935). *A dynamic theory of personality.* New York: McGraw-Hill.; Ross, L. & Nisbett, R.E. (1991). *The person and the situation: Perspectives of social psychology.* New York: McGraw-Hill Publishing Co.

2. Alabama Police Chief apologies to Freedom Rider Congressman, *USA Today* (http://usnews.nbcnews.com/_news/2013/03/03/17167907-alabama-police-chief-apologizes-to-freedom-rider-congressman?lite)

3. Kelley, H.H., Holmes, J. G, Kerr, N. L., Reis, H. T., Rusbult, C. E. & Van Lange,

P.A.M. (2003). Atlas of interpersonal situations, Cambridge, UK: Cambridge University Press.

Chapter 10:

1. Mott, J. (2013). The Returned, Toronto, Canada: Harlequin MIRA.
2. America is nervous about 'diversity." *NBCNews.com* (2013) (http://nbcpolitics.nbcnews.com/ news/2013/10/15/20961149-very-anxious-is-america-scared-of-diversity?lite)

Chapter 11:

1. Thibaut, J.W. & Kelley, H.H. (1959). The social psychology of groups. New York: John Wiley
2. Zane, J. Peder (2016), Laws can't come from discomfort, *News & Observer* (http://www.newsobserver.com/opinion/opn-columns-blogs/j-peder-zane/article70101502.html).
3. Levy, B. (2016, July 13). "The HB2-hate crime connection." *News & Observer* (p. 13A, Opinion Page).
4. Blythe, Anne (2016, August 2). Federal judge has lots of questions about HB2. News & Observer, pp. 1 and 9A.
5. "State Senator Buck Newton says we must keep NC 'straight.' (http://www.huffingtonpost.com/entry/buck-newton-north-carolina_us_571f82c4e4b01a5ebde34e2c)

Chapter 12:

1. America is nervous about 'diversity." *NBCNews.com* (2013) (http://nbcpolitics.nbcnews.com/_news/2013/10/15/20961149-very-anxious-is-america-scared-of-diversity?lite)
2. Freeman, D. & Freeman, J. (2008). Paranoia: The Twenty-First Century Fear (p. 23). Great Clarendon Street, Oxford: Oxford University Press.
3. Newport, F. (2011) Americans Greatly Overestimate Percent Gay, Lesbian in U.S. (http://www.gallup.com/poll/147824/adults-estimate-americans-gay-lesbian.aspx)

Chapter 13:

1. Associated Press (2016) "Dylann Roof's confession shown to jury at Charleston church shooting trial." CBS News, December 9 (https://www.cbsnews.com/news/dylann-roof-confession-fbi-jury-charleston-church-shooting-trial/)

Chapter 14:

1. McCrummen, S. & Izadi, E. (2015). Confederate flag comes down on South Carolina's statehouse grounds. Washington Post, July 10 (https://www.washingtonpost.com/news/post-nation/wp/2015/07/10/watch-live-as-the-confederate-flag-comes-down-in-south-carolina/?utm_term=.32f026c5cea7)

Chapter 15:

1. Khokhryakova, O. (2016, July 18). "Blade runner takes dream to Paralympic trials." *News & Observer*, p. 1B.
2. Kelley, H.H. (1979). Personal relationships: Their structures and processes. Hillsdale, NJ: Lawrence Erlbaum Associates, Inc.

Chapter 16:

1. Button, L. (2015, September 30). "Bookstores Host Community Conversations on Race, Diversity. *American Booksellers Association* (http://www.bookweb.org/news/bookstores-host-community-conversations-race-diversity)

Chapter 17:

1. Laurenceau, J-P., Barrett, L.F. & Pietromonaco, P.R. (1998). Intimacy as an interpersonal process: The importance of self-disclosure, partner disclosure, and perceived partner responsiveness in interpersonal exchanges. Journal of Personality and Social Psychology, 74, 1238-1251.
2. Nacoste, R.W. (2015, "Hibernating bigotry," pp. 163-175). Taking on Diversity: How we can move from anxiety to respect. Amherst, NY: Prometheus Books.

Chapter 18:

1. Illusory correlation: The belief that two variables are correlated when in fact they are not. Gilovich, T., Keltner, D., Chen, S. & Nisbett, R. E. (2019). Social Psychology(5th Ed.). New York: W.W. Norton.

Chapter 19:

1. "Tom Hanks' son defends using the N-word," *MSN.com* (http://www.msn.com/en-us/music/news/tom-hanks%e2%80%99-son-chet-defends-...)

Chapter 20: N/A

Chapter 21:

1. Judith Martin, Nicholas Martin and Jacobina Martin (2016), "Miss Manners: Name-calling is not the same thing as debate", Washington Post (February 7) (https://www.washingtonpost.com/lifestyle/style/miss-manners-name-calling-is-not-the-same-thing-as-debate/2016/02/05/c4aadbce-c11f-11e5-bcda-62a36b394160_story.html)
2. Minimal group paradigm; Gilovich, T., Keltner, D., Chen, S. & Nisbett, R. E. (2016). Social Psychology, 4th Edition. New York: W.W. Norton & Company, Inc.
3. Capobianco, L. (2015). Breaking the barriers set by ethnic, racial slurs. The Southington Observer, July 24.
4. Durango, J. Frat suspended over 'freshman daughter drop off' signs, USA Today (2015, August 24) (http://college.usatoday.com/2015/08/24/banners-targeting-freshmen-women-near-old-dominion-spark-outrage/).

Chapter 22:

1. Theory of mind: the ability to recognize that other people have beliefs and desires. Gilovich, T., Keltner, D., Chen, S. & Nisbett, R. E. (2019). Social Psychology (5th Ed.). New York: W.W. Norton.

Chapter 23:

1. American Psychological Association Awards for Distinguished Scientific Contributions, 1983; John W. Thibaut. Citation reads in part: "For his sustained contributions to our

understanding of the processes and structures of social interdependence… A profound thinker and a comprehensive scholar, he has inspired students and colleagues by his intellectual enthusiasm and his wisdom concerning the fabric of social life." American Psychologist (March, 1984), 39, pp. 262-265.

2. Lewin, K., Dembo, T., Festinger, L., & Sears, P.S. (1944). Levels of aspiration. In J. McV. Hunt (Ed.), Personality and behavior disorders. New York: Ronald (pp. 333-378).

3. Thibaut, J.W. & Kelley, H.H. (1954, p 169). The social psychology of groups. New York: John Wiley.

4. Ibid., p. 175

5. Kelley, H.H. & Thibaut, J.W. (1978). Interpersonal relations: A theory of interdependence. New York: Wiley.

6. Fallon, K. (Ed.) (1970, p. 1) No man is an island: Selected from the writings of John Donne. Los Angeles, CA: Stanyan Books.

Chapter 24:

1. Regan, R. (2007). *Comedy Central, Brian Regan: Standing Up* (DVD). Hollywood, CA: Paramount Pictures (Comedy Partners). Transcription by Rupert W. Nacoste, Ph.D.

2. Shaver, P. (1977). Principles of social psychology. Psychology Press (1ˢᵗ Ed.).

3. Devine, P.G. & Elliot, A. J. (1995). Are racial stereotypes really fading? The Princeton Trilogy Revisited. *Personality and Social Psychology Bulletin*, 21, 1139-1150.

4. Ibid; p. 1146.

5. Guinote, A. & Fiske, S. T. (2003). Being in the outgroup territory increases stereotypic perceptions of outgroups: Situational sources of category activation. Group Processes & Intergroup Relations, 6, 323-331.

Chapter 25:

1. Bradley, Joh Ed. Restoration (2003). New York: Doubleday

2. Trayvon Martin Timeline of events, *ABC News* (http://abcnews.go.com/blogs/head-lines/2012/03/trayvon-martin-case-timeline-of-events/)

3. Dr. Seuss (1961). *The Sneetches and other stories* (p. 13). New York: Random House

4. Schaller, M., Park, J.H., & Mueller, A. (2003). Fear of the dark: Interactive effects of beliefs about danger and ambient darkness on ethnic stereotypes. Personality and Social Psychology Bulletin, 29, 637-649.

Chapter 26:

1. "Gates call: Witness unsure she sees crime. (2009, July 29). *The Associate Press* (MSNBC. com)

2. Ibid.

3. Wilson, M. & Moore, S. (2009, July 25). Cop's don't get paid to be abused. *New York Times* (http://www.msnbc.msn.com/id/32136369/ns/us_news-the_new_york_times/)

4. Robinson, E. (2009, July 29). Powers of two. *News and Observer* (p. 9A).

5. Freeman, D. & Freeman, J. (2008). Paranoia: The Twenty-First Century Fear (p. 90).

Great Clarendon Street, Oxford: Oxford University Press.

6.   Schaefer, K. (2015, June 17). A conversation with Rupert Nacoste, *Technician* (North Carolina State University student newspaper).

Chapter 27:

1.   Papenfuss, M. (2018). College apologizes to Native American Brothers detained after joining campus tour. Huffington Post (May 5) (https://www.huffington-post.com/entry/native-american-brothers-detained-on-colorado-college-tour_us_5aed1450e4b041fd2d26d559)

2.   Simpson, G. E. & Yinger, J. M. (1953). Racial and cultural minorities: An analysis of Prejudice and Discrimination (4th Ed.). New York: Harper & Row.

3.   Nacoste, R. W. (2015). Taking on diversity: How we can move from anxiety to respect (Amherst, NY: Prometheus Books)

4.   Tyson, T. (2004). Blood Done Sign My Name (New York: Broadway Books).

5.   Moe, J.L., Nacoste, R.W., & Insko, C.A. (1981). Belief versus race as determinants of discrimination: A study of adolescents in 1966 and 1979. Journal of Personality and Social Psychology, 41, 1031-1050.

6.   Mendelson, E. (Ed.). W. H. Auden Collected Poems. New York: Vintage International, Vintage Books, 1991 (p. 251).

7.   Dokoupil, T. (2013). 'Very anxious': Is America scared of diversity?, NBC News (October 15); http://nbcpolitics.nbcnews.com/_news/2013/10/15/20961149-very-anxious-is-america-scared-of-diversity?lite

8.   Marcin, T. (2018). "NEARLY 20 PERCENT OF AMERICANS THINK INTERRACIAL MARRIAGE IS 'MORALLY WRONG,' POLL FINDS," Newsweek (March 14); http://www.newsweek.com/20-percent-america-thinks-interracial-marriage-morally-wrong-poll-finds-845608

Chapter 28:

1.   Moe, J.L., Nacoste, R.W., & Insko, C.A. (1981). Belief versus race as determinants of discrimination: A study of adolescents in 1966 and 1979. Journal of Personality and Social Psychology, 41, 1031-1050.

2.   Smith, Gene (2013, June 11). Medgar Evers: Lost in a search for the American Dream, Fayetteville Observer

3.   'Very anxious': Is America scared of diversity? By Tony Dokoupil, Senior Staff Writer, NBC News (10/15/2013) (http://nbcpolitics.nbcnews.com/_news/2013/10/15/20961149-very-anxious-is-america-scared-of-diversity?lite)

4.   Interracial couple denied marriage license; La. justice of the peace cites concerns about any children couple might have. Associated Press, Oct. 15, 2009 (http://www.msnbc.msn.com/id/33332436/ns/us_news-race_and_ethnicity/)

Chapter 29:

1.   "Cheerios commercial causes racist backlash," *Huffington Post* (2013, October 31):

(http://www.huffingtonpost.com/2013/05/31/cheerios-commercial-racist-back-lash_n_3363507.html)

2. "1ˢᵗ Miss America of Indian descent slammed as Arab," *New York Daily News* (2016), (http://www.nydailynews.com/news/national/1st-america-indian-descent-slammed-arab-article-1.1457133)

3. Stewart, D. (2012) "Racist Hunger Games Fans Are Very Disappointed," March 26 (http://jezebel.com/5896408/racist-hunger-games-fans-dont-care-how-much-money-the-movie-made)

4. Bonilla-Silva, E. & Embrick, D.G. (2007). "Every Place Has a Ghetto…": The significance of whites' social and residential segregation. *Symbolic Interaction*, 30, 323-345.

5. McClelland, K. & Linnander, E. (2006). The role of contact and information in racial attitude change among white college students. *Sociological Inquiry*, 76, 81-115

6. Pettigrew, T. F. (1997). Generalized intergroup contact effects on prejudice. *Personality and Social Psychology Bulletin*, 23, 173-185.

7. Allport, G. (1954). *The nature of prejudice.*

8. See Pettigrew (1997) above.

9. Quillan, L. & Campbell, M. E. (2003). Beyond black and white: The present and future of multiracial friendship segregation. *American Sociological Review*, 68, 540-566.

Chapter 30:

1. Nacoste, R. W. (2017). Sometimes bigotry is just bigotry. Psychology Today (https://www.psychologytoday.com/us/blog/quiet-revolution/201703/sometimes-bigotry-is-just-bigotry)

Chapter 31: N/A

Chapter 32:

1. Sherwood, J. D. (2007). Black Sailor, White Navy: Racial unrest in the fleet during the Vietnam War era. New York: New York University Press.

2. Moe, J.L., Nacoste, R.W., & Insko, C.A. (1981). Belief versus race as determinants of discrimination: A study of adolescents in 1966 and 1979. Journal of Personality and Social Psychology, 41, 1031-1050.

3. Nacoste, R. W (2915). Taking on diversity: How we can move from anxiety to respect. Amherst, NY: Prometheus Books.

4. Gilovich, T., Keltner, D. Chen, S. & Nisbett, R. E. (2016, 4ᵗʰ Ed., p. 411). Social Psychology. New York: W.W. Norton & Company.

Chapter 33:

1. McCarthy, C. (2006). *The Road* (p. 74). New York: Vintage International (A division of Random House).

2. Wu, J. (2011, March 13). Wake-up call for racial diversity on campus: Students initiate the campaign 'Wake Up! It's Serious' to promote awareness of racial intolerance. *Technician*.

3. Take 5 with Ann McCracken (One-By-One). *The Sanford Herald* (p. 1, and 6A). Saturday, June 25, 2011.

4. Altman, I. & Taylor, D. (1973/1983). *Social penetration: The development of interpersonal relationships.* New York: Irvington Publishers, Inc.; Laurenceau, J-P., Barrett, L.F. & Pietromonaco, P.R. (1998). Intimacy as an interpersonal process: The importance of self-disclosure, partner disclosure, and perceived partner responsiveness in interpersonal exchanges. *Journal of Personality and Social Psychology,* 74, 1238-1251.

5. Czopp, A. M., Monteith, M.J. & Mark, A. Y. (2006). Standing up for change: Reducing bias through interpersonal confrontation. *Journal of Personality and Social Psychology,* 90, 784-803.

Chapter 34:

1. See Whitehead, B. D. (2003). *Why there are no good men left: The romantic plight of the new single woman.* (New York: Broadway Books)

Chapter 35:

1. Mischel, W. (1979). On the interface of cognition and personality: Beyond the person-situation debate. *American Psychologist,* 34, 740-754.

2. Brooks, D. (2007). "The End of Integration." Op-Ed, New York Times (https://www.nytimes.com/2007/07/06/opinion/06brooks.html)

3. For a systematic study of this sheltering idea see, Bishop, B. (2008). The Big Sort: Why the clustering of like-minded America is tearing us apart. Boston: Houghton Mifflin Company.

4. Barton Swaim, "The revolt against political correctness has backfired," *News & Observer,* November 4, 2016, p. 11A.

Chapter 36:

1. Douglas, A. & Chason, R. (2017, January 22). NC women at Washington march say country's problems go beyond Trump. *News & Observer* (pp. 1-2A)

Chapter 37:

1. Wilson, M. & Moore, S. (2009, July 25). Cop's don't get paid to be abused. *New York Times* (http://www.msnbc.msn.com/id/32136369/ns/us_news-the_new_york_times/)

2. Sanburn, J. (2014, November). All the ways Darren Wilson described being afraid of Michael Brown. *Time* (http://time.com/3605346/darren-wilson-michael-brown-demon/)

3. Fundamental attribution error: "The failure to recognize the importance of situational influences on behavior, and the corresponding tendency to overemphasize the importance of dispositions on behavior." Gilovich, T., Keltner, D., Chen, S. & Nisbett, R. E. (2016). Social Psychology, 4ᵗʰ Edition. New York: W.W. Norton & Company, Inc.

4. Bontemps, A.

5. "Daddy liked his conversation the way he liked his gumbo," is the first line of my memoir of my life of work on diversity issues, especially my two-years as NCSU's first Vice

Provost for Diversity and African American Affairs. To tell my story, I had to include stories of my black-Creole upbringing, much of it through stories about my father, Mr. O-geese. *"Making Gumbo in the University"* (2010; Austin, TX: Plain View Press) is my memoir.

6. Neaves, L. (2017) Students display solidarity through United not Divided rally. The Technician, February 21 (http://www.technicianonline.com/news/article_b9341b36-f7f9-11e6-b1c4-fb8e44d39f4c.html)

7. March for our Lives Founders (2018, October). Glimmer of Hope: How Tragedy Sparked a Movement. New York: Razorbill/Penguin Random House.

Chapter 38:

1. Smith, Gene (2013, June 11). Medgar Evers: Lost in a search for the American Dream, Fayetteville Observer

2. Rusbult, C. E., Verette, J., Whitney, G. A., Slovik, L. F., & Lipkus, I. (1991). Accommodation processes in close relationships: Theory and preliminary research evidence. Journal of Personality and Social Psychology, 60, 53–78.

3. Blumer, H. (1958) Race Prejudice as a Sense of Group Position, Pacific Sociological Review, Vol. 1, No. 1 (Spring, 1958), pp. 3-7

4. McCormack, J. (2017, September 22). North Carolina Professor Nacoste Speaks on Diversity at Yavapai College-Featured, Prescott eNews (http://www.prescottenews.com/index.php/education/yavapai-college/item/30708-north-carolina-professor-nacoste-speaks-on-diversity-at-yavapai-college)

5. Wiener-Bronner, D. (2016, June 06). A black woman was crowned Miss USA, and the reactions got pretty racist, Splinter Magazine; Durosomo, D. (2017, June 01). Halima Aden Becomes the First Model to Wear Hijab on the Cover of Vogue, okayafrica.com; Lake, E. (2017, November 6). Facebook post body-shaming news reporter Demetria Obilor for wearing a figure-hugging dress on air gets the internet in a frenzy, The Sun (Online and Fox News); Simpson, I. (2016, December 27). West Virginia official who called Michelle Obama 'ape in heels' fired, Reuters (https://www.reuters.com/article/us-west-virginia-firstlady/west-virginia-official-who-called-michelle-obama-ape-in-heels-fired-idUSKBN14G1HH)

6. Schoen, Lawrence M. (2018). The Moons of Barsk. New York: A Tom Doherty Associates (TOR) Book

7. Gilbert, Jack (2012). Collected Poems of Jack Gilbert. New York: Alfred A. Knopf

8. Helms, A.D. (2017, September 29) "Student: 'Colored' water found sign was a joke: It wasn't funny. Charlotte Observer (http://www.newsobserver.com/news/local/article176199026.html)

9. Scott, N. (2016, March 21). Indian Wells needs to fire CEO Raymond Moore over his sexist remarks, USATODAY.com

10. Gabbatt, A. (2017, August 16). 'Jews will not replace us': Vice film lays bare horror of neo-Nazis in America. The Guardian (https://www.theguardian.com/us-news/2017/

aug/16/charlottesville-neo-nazis-vice-news-hbo)

11. Delk, J. (2017, October 11). Mike Ditka apologizes for saying there's been no racial oppression in past century. The Hill (http://thehill.com/blogs/blog-briefing-room/354930-ditka-apologizes-for-saying-theres-been-no-racial-oppression-in-past)

12. Stelter, B. (2019). "Tucker Carlson wrongly tells his viewers the country's white supremacy problem 'is a hoax'," CNN Business (Wednesday, August 7) (https://www.cnn.com/2019/08/07/media/tucker-carlson-white-supremacy-reliable-sources/index.html)

Chapter 39:

1. Baron, D. (2017) American Eclipse: A nation's epic race to catch the shadow of the moon and win the glory of the world. New York: Liveright.

2. Nacoste, R. W. (2015). Taking on Diversity: How we can move from anxiety to respect (Amherst, NY: Prometheus Books).

3. Dokoupil, T. (2013, October 15). 'Very anxious': Is America scared of diversity? NBC News (http://nbcpolitics.nbcnews.com/_news/2013/10/15/20961149-very-anxious-is-america-scared-of-diversity?lite)

4. Appadurai, A. (2006). Fear of small numbers: An essay on the geography of anger. Durham, NC: Duke University Press.

Chapter 40:

1. Kelley, H.H. & Thibaut, J.W. (1978). Interpersonal relationships: A theory of interdependence. New York (Wiley); Kelley, H.H. (1979). Personal Relationships: Their structures and processes. (Hillsdale, NJ: Lawrence Erlbaum Associates, Publishers).

2. Nacoste, R.W. (2006). What Rough Beast: Intergroup Tensions in the Age of Neo-Diversity. Forum on Public Policy, 2 (#3), 556-569.

3. Nacoste, R. W. (2009). Post-Racial?: Something Even More Bizarre and Inexplicable. Making Connections: Interdisciplinary Approaches to Cultural Diversity, 11, 1-10.

4. Czopp, A. M., Monteith, M.J. & Mark, A. Y. (2006). Standing up for a change: reducing bias through interpersonal confrontation. Journal of Personality and Social Psychology, 90 (#5), 784-803.

Chapter 41:

1. "Gender Revolution," National Geographic (2017, January) (Special Issue, whole).

2. L'Engle, Madeleine (1962). A Wrinkle in Time, New York: Farrar, Straus and Giroux

3. Mischel, W. (1979). On the interface of cognition and personality: Beyond the person-situation debate. American Psychologist, 34, 740-754.

4. Ottman, E.E. (2016). Documenting light. Green Bay, WI: Brain Mill Press. You will find my review of this novel here: https://oied.ncsu.edu/home/2016/11/10/transgender-in-the-light-of-our-humanity-book-review/

5. Nacoste, R. W. (2018). Preferred pronouns? Technician (January 9) (http://www.technicianonline.com/opinion/columns/article_8facb5fc-f5a5-11e7-bcab-c7c2e160553a.html)

6. Triangle Model United Nations, Inc.: http://www.trianglemun.org/

7. Simpson, I. (2018). Number of U.S. hate groups jumps 20 percent since 2014: Watchdog. Reuters (February 21) (https://www.msn.com/en-us/news/us/number-of-us-hate-groups-jumps-20-percent-since-2014-watchdog/ar-BBJpZuP)

8. Nacoste, R. W. (2009). Post-Racial?: Something Even More Bizarre and Inexplicable. Making Connections: Interdisciplinary Approaches to Cultural Diversity, 11, 1-10.

9. Appadurai, A. (2006). Fear of small numbers: An essay on the geography of anger, (Durham, NC: Duke University Press)

10. Nacoste, R.W. (2015). Taking on diversity: How we can move from anxiety to respect (Amherst, NY: Prometheus Books).

11. Nacoste, R.W. (2015). After Charleston, what now? Stop tolerating intolerance. News & Observer OP-ED (June 22) (http://www.newsobserver.com/opinion/op-ed/article25185835.html)

12. Nacoste, R. W. (2015). Sometimes a joke is not just a joke, Psychology Today Blog-A Quiet Revolution (September 22) (https://www.psychologytoday.com/blog/quiet-revolution/201509/sometimes-joke-is-not-just-joke)

13. Czopp, A.M., Monteith, M.J. & Mark, A.Y. (2006). Standing up for a change: Reducing bias through interpersonal confrontation. Journal of Personality and Social Psychology, 90, 784-803.

14. Coogler, R. & Cole, J.R. Black Panther, directed by Ryan Coogler, Walt Disney Studios Motion Pictures, 2018.

Chapter 42:

1. Nacoste, R.W. (2006). What Rough Beast: Intergroup Tensions in the Age of Neo-Diversity. Forum on Public Policy, 2 (#3), 556-569.

2. Nacoste, R. W. (2009). Post-Racial?: Something Even More Bizarre and Inexplicable. Making Connections: Interdisciplinary Approaches to Cultural Diversity, 11, 1-10.

3. Hui, T. Keung (May 30). Teddy bear hung from noose at Wake Count high school building. News & Observer (2017): http://www.newsobserver.com/news/local/education/article153354789.html

4. Nacoste, R. W. (2015). Taking on Diversity: How we can move from anxiety to respect (Amherst, NY: Prometheus Books).

5. Schmidt, S. (June 5). Harvard withdraws 10 acceptances for 'offensive' memes in private group chat. Washington Post (2017): https://www.washingtonpost.com/news/morning-mix/wp/2017/06/05/harvard-withdraws-10-acceptances-for-offensive-memes-in-private-chat/?utm_term=.95eb7d354341.

Chapter 43:

1. Nacoste, R. W. (2012). Howl of the Wolf: North Carolina State University Students Call Out for Social Change (Raleigh, NC, Lulu.com). One student tells the story of being excited about a dinner of beans, ground beef and tacos, and saying to his host, "Oh I love this; at home we call it 'spic' food" not being aware of the result insult of that

term.

2.   The collected works of Sterling Brown (Michael, S. Harper, Editor). Evanston, ILL: Northwestern University Press, 1980.

3.   Laughman, A. (2018). "Shippensburg University supports LGBT community after attack." The Slate, October 9, p. A2; Wise, J. (2018), LGBT students deserve more from administration, The Slate, October 9, p. A3.

4.   Here I am referring to what social psychologist call a meta-stereotype. And there is research on this phenomenon; Vorauer, J. D., Hunter, A. J., Main, K. J. & Roy, S. A. (2000), Meta-stereotype activation: Evidence From Indirect Measures for Specific Evaluative Concerns Experienced by Members of Dominant Groups in Intergroup Interaction, Journal of Personality and Social Psychology, 76, 694-707.

5.   Altman, D. & Taylor, D. Social Penetration: The Development of Interpersonal Relationships. New York: Holt, 1973.

6.   Nacoste, R.W. (2001). See no evil, hear no evil: Senior leaders' social comparisons, and the low salience of racial issues. In M.R. Dansby, J.B. Stewart and S.C. Webb (Eds.), Managing Diversity in the Military: Research Perspectives from the Defense Equal Opportunity Management Institute. New Brunswick, NJ: Transaction Publishers.

Chapter 44:

1.   Appalachian College Association (https://acaweb.org/)

2.   Nacoste, R. W. (2016, June 13), "Gays and Lesbians and Transgender… Oh my!" Psychology Today Blog (https://www.psychologytoday.com/us/blog/quiet-revolution/201606/gays-and-lesbians-and-transgenderedoh-my)

Chapter 45:

1.   Editorial Board (2019, July 18) 'Send her back': A dark reminder of who we are. Charlotte Observer (https://www.charlotteobserver.com/opinion/editorials/article232821229.html)

2.   Rogers, Katie & Fandos, Nicholas (2019, July 14). "Trump Tells Congresswomen to 'Go Back' to the Countries They Came From," The New York Times (July 14) (https://www.nytimes.com/2019/07/14/us/politics/trump-twitter-squad-congress.html)

3.   Chavez, N. & Shoichet, C. E. (2019). A community targeted: This time it wasn't a viral video or a racist tweet. It was something far more terrifying. CNN (Wednesday, August 7); (https://www.cnn.com/2019/08/06/us/el-paso-shooting-latino-immigrant-fears/index.html)

4.   Kunzelman, M. & Galvan, A. (2019, Associated Press). "Hate-crime surges follow heated rhetoric, data show. News & Observer (Thursday, August 8, p. 5A).

5.   Nacoste, R.W. (2006). "What Rough Beast: Intergroup Tensions in the Age of Neo-Diversity," Forum on Public Policy, 2 (#3), 556-569.

6.   Dokoupil, T. (2013, October 15), "'Very anxious': Is America scared of diversity?" Report on a national Esquire-NBC-News survey (http://nbcpolitics.nbcnews.com/_news/2013/10/15/20961149-very-anxious-is-america-scared-of-diversity?lite).

7. Appadurai, A. (2006). <u>Fear of small numbers: An essay on the geography of anger</u>. Durham, NC: Duke University Press

8. North Carolina State Course Catalog description for PSY 411: The Psychology of Interdependence and Race is designed to explore how interpersonal relationships are structured and how two-person interactions within those structures are influenced by race. Drawing on the major social psychological theory of interpersonal relationships - Interdependence Theory - this course will provide students with an understanding of the various structures of interpersonal relationships in order to explore how and why the presence of race (and other diversity categories) influence the ways in which people try to interact with each other within those interpersonal structures.

9. Sherwood, J. D. (2006). <u>Black Sailor, White Navy: Racial unrest in the fleet during the Vietnam War era</u>. New York: New York University Press.

10. Tyson, T. B. (2004). Blood done sign my name. New York: Broadway Books.

11. For example, Kawakami, K., Phills, C. E, Steele, J.R. & Dovidio, J. F. (2007). (Close) Distance Makes the Heart Grow Fonder: Improving Implicit Racial Attitudes and Interracial Interactions Through Approach Behaviors. <u>Journal of Personality and Social Psychology Bulletin</u>, 92: 957-971; Plant, E. A. & Devine, P. (2003). The antecedents and implications of interracial anxiety. <u>Personality and Social Psychology Bulletin</u>, 29: pp. 790-801

12. Nacoste, R. W. (2015). <u>Taking on Diversity: How We Can Move From Anxiety to Respect</u>. Amherst, NY: Prometheus Books

13. Nacoste, R. W. (2013). Speaking up for neo-diverse America. <u>TEDxNCSU</u> (March 23). (YouTube: <u>https://www.youtube.com/watch?v=Y73bRAwJY6I</u>)

14. Brockell, G. (2019). Some white people don't want to hear about slavery at plantations built by slaves. <u>Washington Post</u> (August 8) (<u>https://www.washingtonpost.com/history/2019/08/08/some-white-people-dont-want-hear-about-slavery-plantations-built-by-slaves/</u>)

15. Pitts, L. (2019) Slavery is no artifact of a dead past. <u>News & Observer</u> (August 19, p. 9A).

Apprentice House Press

Loyola University Maryland

Apprentice House is the country's only campus-based, student-staffed book publishing company. Directed by professors and industry professionals, it is a nonprofit activity of the Communication Department at Loyola University Maryland.

Using state-of-the-art technology and an experiential learning model of education, Apprentice House publishes books in untraditional ways. This dual responsibility as publishers and educators creates an unprecedented collaborative environment among faculty and students, while teaching tomorrow's editors, designers, and marketers.

Outside of class, progress on book projects is carried forth by the AH Book Publishing Club, a co-curricular campus organization supported by Loyola University Maryland's Office of Student Activities.

Eclectic and provocative, Apprentice House titles intend to entertain as well as spark dialogue on a variety of topics. Financial contributions to sustain the press's work are welcomed. Contributions are tax deductible to the fullest extent allowed by the IRS.

To learn more about Apprentice House books or to obtain submission guidelines, please visit www.apprenticehouse.com.

Apprentice House
Communication Department
Loyola University Maryland
4501 N. Charles Street
Baltimore, MD 21210
Ph: 410-617-5265
info@apprenticehouse.com
www.apprenticehouse.com